War upon the Land

environmental
history and the
american
south

War upon the Land

Military Strategy and the
Transformation of Southern Landscapes
during the American Civil War

Lisa M. Brady

The University of Georgia Press

Athens and London

Parts of this book previously appeared in different form as "The Wilderness of War: Nature and Strategy in the American Civil War," in *Environmental History* 10, no. 3 (July 2005): 421–47. The article was edited and reprinted under the same title in *Environmental History and the American South: A Reader*, ed. Paul S. Sutter and Christopher J. Manganiello (Athens: University of Georgia Press, 2009), 168–95. Reprinted with permission of Oxford University Press. Chapter 4 appeared previously in slightly different form as "Devouring the Land: Sherman's 1864–1865 Campaigns," in *War and the Environment: Military Destruction in the Modern Age*, ed. Charles E. Closmann (College Station: Texas A&M University Press, 2009), 49–67. Reprinted by permission of the Texas A&M University Press. Copyright © 2009 Charles E. Closmann.

Set in Adobe Garamond Pro by Graphic Composition, Inc., Bogart, Georgia

Printed digitally in the United States of America

Library of Congress Cataloging-in-Publication Data

Brady, Lisa M., 1971–
War upon the land : military strategy and the transformation of southern landscapes during the American Civil War / Lisa M. Brady.
    p. cm. — (Environmental history and the American South)
    Includes bibliographical references and index.
    ISBN-13: 978-0-8203-2985-7 (cloth : alk. paper)
    ISBN-10: 0-8203-2985-1 (cloth : alk. paper)
    ISBN-13: 978-0-8203-4249-8 (pbk. : alk. paper)
    ISBN-10: 0-8203-4249-1 (pbk. : alk. paper)
    1. United States—History—Civil War, 1861–1865—Environmental aspects.
2. Philosophy of nature—United States—History—19th century. 3. Strategy—History—19th century. 4. Confederate States of America—History, Military. 5. United States—History—Civil War, 1861–1865—Campaigns. I. Title.
    E468.9.B694 2012
    973.7'301—dc23   2011037559

British Library Cataloging-in-Publication Data available

For my husband, David, my mother, Sharon,
and in memory of my father, John.

And for Donald Worster, without whose sage advice and
steady support this book would have never been.

Naturam expelles furca, tamen usque recurret, et mala perrumpet furtim fastidia victrix.

You may drive out Nature with a pitchfork, yet she will ever hurry back, and ere you know it, will burst through your foolish contempt in triumph.

Horace, Epistle to Aristius Fuscus

CONTENTS

List of Illustrations   xi

Foreword, by Paul S. Sutter   xiii

Acknowledgments   xvii

INTRODUCTION Nineteenth-Century Ideas of
Nature and Their Role in Civil War Strategy   1

ONE Hostile Territory: Union Operations
along the Lower Mississippi, 1862–1863   24

TWO Broken Country: Union Campaigns
at and around Vicksburg, 1863   49

THREE Ravaged Ground: Sheridan in
the Shenandoah Valley, 1864   72

FOUR Devoured Land: Sherman's Georgia
and Carolina Campaigns, 1864–1865   93

CONCLUSION Making a Desert and Calling It Peace   127

Notes   141

Bibliography   161

Index   179

ILLUSTRATIONS

1. The Lower Mississippi Valley   27
2. Island No. 10   32
3. Vicksburg and environs   37
4. Digging the canal   38
5. Grant's route to Vicksburg   54
6. Waterways between Jackson and Vicksburg   59
7. Siege of Vicksburg   63
8. The Shenandoah Valley   75
9. Sheridan in the Shenandoah Valley   83
10. Sherman's March   94
11. Carolina terrain   110
12. Sherman burning McPhersonville   118
13. Sherman's March as chaos   130

FOREWORD

Several years ago I spent a summer in southern California on a research fellowship. One weekend while my family was away, I decided to go camping in one of the Sierra Nevada's famous national parks, none of which I had ever visited. I chose Sequoia National Park, which was a bit more proximate than Yosemite and, I hoped, would be a bit less crowded. Sequoia National Park is home to some of the largest trees on earth, *Sequoiadendron giganteum* or giant sequoias, and they are among the great natural wonders of the North American continent. These giant trees gained fame in the years after the Civil War, and Congress protected the most impressive groves with national park status in 1890, making Sequoia one of the earliest additions to the then-embryonic national parks system. As an environmental historian, I felt as if I owed these trees a visit. But what struck me upon encountering them was not merely their awesome size and age—how they dwarfed and effaced the history of the young nation that had adopted them as wards—but the curious fact that the largest of these trees are named after Civil War generals. The most famous in the park are the General Grant and General Sherman trees, which memorialize two of the best-known Union generals, and there is also a General Lee tree, which, though less well known, does give the Confederate leadership its own natural monument. I later learned that a Union veteran named James Wolverton, who had served under Sherman during the war, began this tradition of naming trees after Civil War generals in 1879. But more than the origin of this practice, I was curious about its significance. What did it mean, I wondered, to make these trees stand for famous generals in America's great internecine conflict, and what could I learn from them about how the American environmental tradition intersected with the Civil War?

Since that encounter, I have become convinced that the Civil War era was a watershed moment in American environmental history. In 1864, in the midst of the war, Abraham Lincoln protected the Yosemite Valley, initially as a state park, a move that set the stage for national park preservation in the decades to come. Soon thereafter, Frederick Law Olmsted, of New York Central Park fame, applied his design sensibility to the remarkable valley—though his advice for developing Yosemite for the public would ultimately be rejected. The year 1864 also saw the publication of George Perkins Marsh's landmark book on resource conservation, *Man and Nature*, which Lewis Mumford famously called the "fountainhead of the conservation movement." Two years earlier, a northern-dominated Congress had passed the Homestead Act, which not only enshrined the free soil ideology in land law but also precipitated a dynamic of land colonization in the arid West that set the table for American conservation in all of its guises. And then, just two years after the war ended, a young nature lover who had fled to Canada to avoid the fighting set off on an epic journey through the war-scarred American South, a journey that eventually took him to California's Sierras and a career as the chief celebrant of that state's wild mountain scenery. Like so many Americans in the immediate post–Civil War years, John Muir found the American West to be healing—a redemptive region, to borrow a phrase from the western historian William Deverell. Given all of this, it's perhaps not surprising that Civil War generals found a place of monumental memorialization among giant trees on the Sierras' remote and wild western slopes.

Although wild nature may have become a balm to heal the wounds of a nation after the Civil War and provided a solemn space in which to remember the giants of that conflict, it served a very different function during the war itself, as Lisa Brady shows in this innovative study. *War upon the Land* is not merely an environmental history of the war; in fact, as Brady makes clear in her provocative introduction, much of what an environmental historian might expect from such a treatment is missing here. Instead, Brady's is a book about how the Civil War engaged with, and forever altered, a suite of nineteenth-century American ideas about nature. Brady's study sprang from a fairly simple realization: in reading literate reactions to the war's destruction, she kept coming across observations about how the conflict had made a "wilderness" of the landscape. More than that, she recognized that making a wilderness of the landscape became a centerpiece of Union strategy. At the very moment when a few pioneering thinkers were beginning to give wilderness a positive gloss, it functioned in the context of war not only as a synonym for waste and desolation but also as a weaponized imaginary. *War upon the Land* thus examines the place of wilderness in the history of the Civil War, and as importantly, the place of the Civil War in the history of wilderness. It suggests that we cannot understand the Civil War as a watershed period in American environmental thought without paying careful attention to the war itself.

Brady begins with a basic but important point: not only did the Civil War enact a cruel toll on the bodies of those who fought it—a toll that has been at the center of much of the most important recent Civil War historiography— but it also ravaged the landscapes through which it traveled. The notion of a landscape "scarred by war" has become a commonplace today, but Brady insists we understand the freshness and power of that metaphor in the context of the Civil War, which introduced Americans to a new kind of punctuated environmental destruction. That they made sense of this destruction by using the term "wilderness" was telling, for it suggested their fear that the war was undoing the work of agricultural "improvement"—the harnessing of the productive energies of nature in a true human-environmental partnership—that had become the expanding nation's operative environmental ideal. To undo the work of agricultural improvement, however tenuous it may have been in fact, was to challenge Americans' notions of themselves as civilized. And to the extent that the Civil War was fought in the South, that region felt the bulk of this psychic challenge. As the armies in the conflict transformed the natural world in battle, and in sustaining themselves, the Union leadership came to understand the power of turning the productive portions of the South into a wilderness, literally and figuratively. One important contribution of *War upon the Land*, then, is its evocative explication of how the material damage of war, both incidental and intentional, worked on the minds of those who fought in and observed the conflict.

Another important contribution of *War upon the Land* is its emphasis on military engineering and the mindset of environmental control that came with it. For even as the war wreaked havoc on the landscape of improvement, a group of military engineers pioneered new techniques for controlling the natural world that they hoped would help them win the war. Indeed, Brady suggests that this desire to control the nature of battle—a desire premised on turning the environmental contingencies of warfare into tactical advantages—was one the Civil War's most important environmental dimensions. By focusing on engineers' efforts to control unruly landscapes and environmental forces, Brady makes clear how much those forces mattered to the conduct of war. There is an important irony here: in their very efforts to eliminate what Brady calls the agency of nature, military engineers help us to see that agency in clear and specific ways. But the irony goes one step further, for in many ways that very engineering culture, as it spilled into the post–Civil War world of industry and commerce, encouraged the effacement of nature's role in the conflict, and in human history more broadly. Indeed, as the power of military engineering and technologies increased during the century following the Civil War, Americans increasingly assumed that rather than improving nature, they could win a war against it and master it in the process. The war, then, was a transitional moment when the ideal of improvement began a slow fade to be replaced by an ideal of engineering mastery. And it was in that context that protecting rather than transforming wilderness seemed increasingly like the civilized thing to do. The Civil War, Lisa Brady insists, was a critical moment in this transition.

Which brings me back to my encounter with those commanding trees. *War upon the Land* suggests a couple of ways of making sense of giant sequoias named after Civil War generals. The first is, simply, that the destruction unleashed by the war—of bodies and of landscapes—created an impulse among some to seek out landscapes of healing, memorialization, and even national reconciliation. National parks were important spaces in which the nation repaired itself after the war, spaces that quietly embodied some of the Civil War's environmental legacies. But one also has to wonder if James Wolverton had a more partisan intent when he named those trees; maybe he was memorializing the power of Union leaders and their strategies to turn the South into a wilderness. Lisa Brady's *War upon the Land* demands that we at least consider that subversive possibility.

Paul S. Sutter

ACKNOWLEDGMENTS

During a graduate colloquium on nineteenth-century American history at the University of Kansas, I asked the professor, Phil Paludan, whether anyone had undertaken a study of the Civil War from an environmental perspective. He said, "No—that's what you will do." I am forever indebted to him for that single sentence and for his subsequent support for the project and confidence in my abilities to complete it with competence, if not grace. The main title, "War upon the Land," was also his idea. I am indescribably disappointed that he did not live to see the book published. I flatter myself that he would have been proud of the result and of his role in its creation.

While the genesis of the project stems from that brief interaction with Dr. Paludan, the bulk of its progress and final completion owe a great deal to many fine colleagues and friends. My dissertation committee members deserve enormous gratitude for their keen insights and generosity of spirit: Karl Brooks, Phil Paludan, Ann Schofield, Norm Slade, Ted Wilson, and Don Worster (more on his inestimable contributions later). Kevin Armitage, Maril Hazlett, and Dale Nims suffered through countless drafts as members of a dissertation reading group and helped me to articulate my ideas and improve my prose. Michele Casavant and Maril Hazlett endeavored to keep me sane through many cups of coffee and many more glasses of wine—many, many thanks. I would also like to thank Jay Antle, Robb Campbell, Kip Curtis, Brian Drake, John Egan, John Grigg, Mark Hersey, Nancy Jackson, Marie Kelleher, Martha Robinson, and Frank Zelko for their camaraderie and support. The same goes out to my friends and colleagues at Boise State University.

I was fortunate to have had opportunities to present my work at various stages to numerous scholarly communities, who helped to refine and solidify my arguments: the Nature and Culture Seminar at the University of Kansas; the annual meeting of the American Society for Environmental History; the American Historical Association annual meeting; the German Historical Institute's conference on War and Environment; and the Houston Area Southern History Seminar at Rice University (special thanks to Jacqueline Glass Campbell and John Boles for their kind invitation and gracious hospitality). I am deeply grateful for generous financial support from the University of Kansas Graduate School, the KU Department of History, the Filson Historical

Society, the Ambrose Saricks Family, P.E.O., the U.S. Military Academy, and Boise State University's Department of History and College of Social Sciences and Public Affairs.

Without the kind and patient assistance offered by the staff members of the Filson Historical Society, the Georgia Historical Society, various research and reading rooms at the Library of Congress, the Mississippi Department of Archives and History, the National Archives and Records Administration, the South Carolina Historical Society, the Kansas Collection at the University of Kansas Spencer Research Library, and the Special Collections and Archives Division at the U.S. Military Academy at West Point this book would not have been possible.

Several scholars and friends deserve special mention for their longtime support for my work. Charles Closmann, Adam Rome, and Mark Wetherington all thought my ideas merited publication—for their support and editorial expertise I am truly thankful. John R. McNeill and William Storey have provided feedback through numerous venues and have graciously agreed to present their excellent work alongside mine at several conferences and meetings. Kevin Marsh and Adam Sowards, my two Idaho compatriots, have encouraged and inspired me, even when progress on the manuscript was delayed by our planning and hosting of the Boise ASEH meeting. Jamie Lewis has offered insightful feedback and continuous encouragement. Bill Tsutsui, a truly great mind and wonderful friend, treated me from the beginning as an equal colleague and has been an ardent supporter of my work. Likewise, Mark Fiege has been a constant partner in the evolution of this book, from its inception through its completion. I cannot thank him enough for his faith in me as a scholar.

It has been a joy to work with all associated with the University of Georgia Press. Andrew Berzanskis saw merit in my project early on. Derek Krissoff has ably shepherded it through many stages and iterations, never once losing his patience or good humor. The reviewers of my manuscript and its revisions helped turn a dissertation into a book—no mean feat indeed. They deserve part of the credit (and none of the blame) for its final form. Paul Sutter is the consummate professional, a fabulous editor, and a keen mind—I am honored to have my book included as part of his Environmental History and the American South series.

I have saved for last those to whom I owe the greatest debt. For most of these individuals, I cannot articulate the ways in which they have contributed to my success or helped me through difficult moments, largely because it would take a book to enumerate them. I will simply name each one and hope they will understand the depth of my love and gratitude: Matt, Kelly, Brenna, and Erynn Brady; Lauren Hughes and Jonathan Loewald; Greg and Martha Hughes; Sara, Curtis, Erik, Jacob, and Jessica Meeker; Susanne Thobe and Gary Kunkel; Alison Walker and Tom Stone; Billy and Don Walker.

My husband, David Walker, endured much, complained little, and loved unconditionally. He will be happiest of all by the publication of this book (though perhaps our cat, Sheba, will vie for that position). My parents, John and Sharon, went above and beyond the call of parental duty when they agreed to go on a Grand Southern Adventure—a driving tour of every place mentioned in this book (plus some)—and they did so with enthusiasm and equanimity, in spite of me. It was our last trip together; my father died in 2004.

Finally, I turn to Donald Worster. He was the one professor to return my call when I was searching for a graduate program. When I visited KU's campus, he braved the worst ice storm in recent memory to meet me for dinner at the Mad Greek. He had faith in me as a student and scholar. He endured many a zany dissertation idea and calmly and respectfully guided me away from them. When I finally approached him with my Civil War idea, he enthusiastically jumped on board. Don is brilliant, patient, demanding, kind, responsive, and generous. For all those things, I thank him.

War upon the Land

Nineteenth-Century Ideas of Nature and Their Role in Civil War Strategy

"EGYPT HAD ITS PLAGUES and its all-consuming swarms of locusts. Beautiful tropical regions are cursed with the deadly upas tree. Delig[h]tful valleys are swept with destructive floods. But the United States are afflicted with a curse worse than all these—treason—secession." For George W. Squire, a lieutenant in the Forty-Fourth Indiana Volunteer Infantry, secession was akin to a natural disaster laying waste to his beloved country. Three and a half years of war had taken its toll on the nation and on Squire, who told his wife he was "getting in an awful fever to leave this wilderness of war."[1]

Though Americans were no strangers to warfare, prior to 1861 they generally had been spared from witnessing its ruinous power. Most martial conflicts involving the United States between the Revolution and the Civil War were either limited in size or geographic scope or fought on other nations' territory. Americans attempting to make sense of the carnage and destruction of the Civil War thus had few firsthand experiences from which to draw reference. Even so, the Civil War would have defied any understanding prior wars might have provided. It was the first modern war and therefore differed dramatically from previous American conflicts in kind and scale.

The loss of human life—over 620,000 soldiers, sailors, and marines, as well as unnumbered civilians—is one indicator of the breadth and depth of the war's destruction. In his excellent book *Awaiting the Heavenly Country*, Mark Schantz presented a compelling argument, based on nineteenth-century ideas about death, for why those numbers reached the levels they did. He suggested that "Americans came to fight the Civil War in the midst of a wider cultural world that sent them messages about death that made it easier to kill and to be killed. They understood that death awaited all who were born and prized the ability to face death with a spirit of calm resignation." They believed in a "heavenly eternity" and the potential to be "cherished forever by posterity" and furthermore that "notions of full citizenship were predicated on the willingness of men to lay down their lives."[2] Thus, for Americans, cultural motivations combined with technological developments, strategic decisions, and unsanitary conditions to make the Civil War the nation's deadliest.

Where Schantz helped explicate the reasons for the war's human toll, Drew Gilpin Faust provided insight into the ways Americans tried to make sense of that cost. In *This Republic of Suffering* Faust artfully explored the processes through which such understanding might be had. She explained, "The impact and meaning of the war's death toll went beyond the sheer numbers who died. Death's significance for the Civil War generation arose as well from its violation of prevailing assumptions about life's proper end—about who should die, when and where, and under what circumstances."[3] Faust also suggested, "The presence and fear of death touched Civil War Americans' most fundamental sense of who they were, for in its threat of termination and transformation, death inevitably inspired self-scrutiny and self-definition."[4] Together, Schantz and Faust illustrated that the Civil War was both a time of adherence to cultural traditions and a point of transformation in Americans' thinking about death.

The same can be said about the war with regard to Americans' understanding of and interactions with nature. The physical destruction of the war called into question some of the most fundamental assumptions Americans had been making about nature and about its role in the nation's economic, political, and cultural development. These assumptions had in part guided the nation into war and shaped the ways in which it was fought. Though critiques of such approaches to nature predated the conflict, after the war they gained momentum and helped shape a new American relationship with the natural world, in which conservation of nature became a vaunted ideal.

Though much of the destruction caused by the Civil War was both unintentional and unavoidable, it nonetheless elicited powerful reactions from those who witnessed it. In camp near Edgefield Junction, Tennessee, Capt. Thaddeus Minshall from Ohio declared, "[W]ar is a terrible thing. In its tread it desolates the fair face of nature—all the works of the husbandman, and tramples out all the divine parts of human nature." Four months later, while camped outside of Murfreesboro, Tennessee, Minshall could "but reflect how nature and man are at war. Nature is struling to give every thing a renewed appearance, but the grim monster, war stalks on in the same unvaried course of desolation and ruin."[5] Theodore Upson, a soldier with the One Hundredth Indiana Volunteers, wrote that after Union forces fired a dozen twenty-pound Parrot guns at a Confederate battery on Kennesaw Mountain, "it looks as though there was nothing left but a big hole in the side of the mountain."[6] After that same intense battle, Union major George Ward Nichols remarked that the mountain bore silent testimony to the ravages of armed conflict, "with its grandeur of 'everlasting hill' intensified by the mute records of human warfare—with its impregnable front furrowed and crowned with the marks of war."[7]

Trees in particular seemed to succumb to war's destruction. One soldier after the battle of Franklin, Tennessee, recalled the fate of "a small grove of about 200 locust trees," most of them "about the size of a common bed-post." He wrote, "These little trees were literally cut to pieces by the bullets. Some of them not as large as a man's body had 50 and 60 bullet marks. A reward of $25 has been offered by Several officers to any person who will find in that grove a Tree or Limb 5 feet long which has not been struck by a bullet."[8] John Tilford, second assistant surgeon for the Seventy-Ninth Indiana Infantry, described a similar scene near Atlanta: "The trees in the wood was riddled to splinters by the leaden hail."[9]

It was not just the natural landscape that suffered the scars of war. Describing a hard-hit area of northern Georgia, the *Natchez Weekly Courier* noted how "the utter loneliness, the want of human life, strikes one with a feeling of desolation." Citing the lack of all signs of human improvements in the region—fences, livestock, working mills—the author wrote, "So startling is the utter silence, that even when the wild bird of the forest carols a note, you look around surprised that amid such loneliness any living being should be happy. This is the result of war, stern desolating war!"[10]

George Ward Nichols noted that "in peaceful times" a visitor to the same part of Georgia would find "[t]he soil, which formerly was devoted to the peaceful labors of the agriculturalist has leaped up, as it were, into frowning parapets, supported and surmounted by logs, and guarded in front by tangled abattis, palisades, and *chevaux de frise*." A military landscape had supplanted the agricultural one, but not entirely. Reversing the role of the agriculturalist from victim to perpetrator, it seemed to Nichols "as if some giant plowshare had passed through the land, marring with gigantic and unsightly furrows the rolling plains, laying waste the fields and gardens, and, passing onto the abodes of men, upturning their very hearths, and razing even towns and cities."[11]

Across the South, and in a few places in the North, both the built and natural landscapes bore the marks of conflict. Scholars of the Civil War have provided ample descriptions of that devastation, but few included extensive analysis of nature's role in that pivotal moment in American history. More than mere victim, nature is an active force in human affairs. This book illuminates nature's agency by examining Union military strategy in several key operations through the lens of environmental history. It analyzes wartime events based on the assumptions that nature actively participates in the development of human history and, more specifically, that ideas of nature—not just its physical presence—are an important factor in military decision making.

By taking this approach, I believe we can take a crucial step toward understanding the Civil War more completely. I have chosen the American Civil War not because other scholars have not done justice to it but rather to illustrate the fundamental importance nature has in shaping human decisions even in cases where other issues seem to take precedence. Any war could serve as the subject of this study (and I hope every war will be analyzed in such a way), but the very nature of the Civil War as the first modern war provides unique insight into a nation in transition culturally, economically, politically, and environmentally.

This book does not examine what some may expect from an environmental study: the short- and long-term effects of the introduction into the soil of millions of lead projectiles, for example, or the air and water pollution associated with massive, mobile armies and the protracted battles in which they were engaged. It does not explore the role of disease in the outcomes of battles, nor does it provide an accounting of all the trees, deer, fish, and other natural resources lost to the maw of war. Also missing from the book are extensive treatments of issues or subjects many have come to expect in any study of the Civil War: African American experiences; the views and policies of the Lincoln and Davis administrations; discussion of the causes of secession; the daily lives of soldiers and civilians. These omissions and elisions are the result of trying to craft a tightly focused study rather than a disregard for their intrinsic value to the war's and the nation's history. Every author must make difficult decisions as to what to include and what to leave for others to discover and interpret.

Perhaps more than other types of studies, those that attempt to build bridges between distinct historiographical traditions—in this case, Civil War, military, and environmental history—present unique challenges. Such studies must balance the needs of readers unfamiliar with concepts and terminology specific to each analytical approach with the desires of those who want to engage only with new ideas and narratives. Civil War historians, especially those who focus on military issues, will likely find much about the descriptions of the operations included here to be all too familiar. On close reading, however, I hope these scholars will see that this is not simply a logistical analysis washed with green but one that offers a new and unique way of conceptualizing the processes and consequences of military actions, especially those based on "living off the land." As for environmental historians, the arguments I make about improvements, wilderness, and nature's agency may not be as nuanced as they might wish, considering the enormous amount of excellent scholarship that has dealt with these complex and fundamental ideas. What I hope I provide them is deeper insight into the grave importance of warfare, not as an isolated aberration in humanity's relationship with the natural world but as a crucible in which a society's notions about and interactions with nature are brought to the fore in elemental, immensely important ways.

Subject and source considerations also present some limitations. My choice to focus on Union operations means that southern voices, regardless of race, class, gender, or military service, are in the minority. Southern middle- and upper-class white men and women left plenty of records, and many of them wrote eloquently on environmental themes in their diaries, letters, and memoirs. Nevertheless, they were not involved in developing the tactics and strategies of the campaigns described here, so their voices generally are limited to their reactions to those operations. African American voices are conspicuously rare. Black Americans, in the North and South, slave and free, were tremendously influential during this period of the nation's history. Indeed, their work across the South created the very landscapes through which the Union armies marched, and many used their intimate knowledge of the southern environment to help the Union gain victory and to assert their own freedom.[12] However, I found few primary sources that could help me elucidate even a small proportion of these individuals' views on the role of nature in the context of the campaigns on which I focused. The majority of my sources are thus written by northern, white, middle-class men. I hope these limitations will not prove insurmountable and that readers will find something useful, new, or perhaps even provocative in the pages that follow.

My primary purpose here is to use the war as a window through which we can better see a critical element in the nation's environmental history: that is, how nineteenth-century Americans perceived their natural environment and their place in it. What I discovered is that notions of improvement, control, and wilderness evolved during the war even as they maintained semblances of continuity with their antebellum predecessors. The war did not upend Americans' relationships with or ideas about nature but instead provided the rationale for broadening and expanding them to include nature protection at the national level. The war that established federal authority over states' rights to determine citizenship and other civil rights also established increased federal power to decide what elements in the natural treasury would become permanent fixtures of the national landscape.

This book is an attempt to elucidate the processes through which such transformations occurred. Two main assumptions form the core of its argument. The first is that nineteenth-century ideas about nature influenced strategic planning. This assumption can be further subdivided into three related ideas: first is the notion that control over nature is possible through proper application of science and technology; second, that agriculture presents a means for improving, or civilizing, nature; and third, a corollary of the first two, that despite these perceived powers controlling nature was a tenuous business, liable to be undermined in a variety of ways. Each of these three factors, sometimes together, sometimes individually, influenced Union policy and strategy in the campaigns examined in the following chapters.

The second core assumption is that nature is a historical agent. In suggesting that nature has agency, I am not arguing that it has any level of consciousness or intent but rather, as Linda Nash so cogently articulated, that it has the power to shape *human* decisions. Nash recommended, "[O]ur narratives should emphasize that human intentions do not emerge in a vacuum, that ideas often cannot be clearly distinguished from actions, that so-called human agency cannot be separated from the environments in which that agency emerges." Furthermore, "It is worth considering how our stories might be different if human beings appeared not as the motor of history but as partners in a conversation with the larger world, both animate and inanimate, about the possibilities of existence."[13]

Just such a conversation took place during the turmoil of the Civil War. Nature—in its multitude of forms—shaped the conduct of those engaged in the war just as the effects of war transformed the physical landscape. The armies of the Civil War had to contend with nature's forces even as they battled each other. Often this human-nature conflict was an undercurrent in the unfolding of the war, pitting men against diseases, exposing them to the extremes of weather, and forcing them to exploit their environs for supplemental rations. As importantly, however, the clash between Civil War armies and the physical environment was an intentional act of war, one that superseded direct attacks against human enemies. This development in American military history is thus also part of the nation's environmental history, though such connections have not been adequately explored.

Military scholars might reasonably argue that they have covered the field well enough. As a matter of course, such scholars have integrated elements of nature into their analyses by investigating the effects of weather, terrain, and disease on operations and troop morale, for example. Historian Earl J. Hess did this exceptionally well in "The Nature of Battle," a chapter in his book *The Union Soldier in Battle*. There Hess examined the ways in which the physical environment and the battle environment combined to create an incomprehensible chaos. He suggested, "On all levels—from the smoke-enshrouded vision of the individual to the confused movements of companies struggling through brush-entangled terrain—the soldier struggled against chaos and strove to create a coherent vision of battle."[14] While the physical environment in which soldiers found themselves was important to Hess's arguments about wartime experiences, it was yet an element to be acted on rather than an active agent in war.

Others, too, have looked to elements of the natural world to elucidate military aspects the Civil War. Geographer Harold Winters's *Battling the Elements: Weather and Terrain in the Conduct of War* is an excellent analysis of the "potent and omnipresent synergy between the environment, or physical geography, and battle."[15] Likewise, in *A Great Civil War* historian Russell F. Weigley frequently acknowledged the importance of environmental factors in the outcome of military operations. He noted that Vicksburg's greatest defense was its rugged, broken terrain and suggested that South Carolina's best protection against Sherman's advancing troops in 1865 was not the Confederate army but "geography and weather."[16] In his monumental study *Ninety-Eight Days*, geographer Warren E. Grabau also focused on the fundamental importance of terrain and geography to the defense and ultimate capture of Vicksburg.[17]

Despite this attention to relevant environmental conditions, such discussions often cast nature in a static role. By challenging this assumption, environmental historians have a unique opportunity to reframe the debate and to demonstrate that, in Linda Nash's words, "[i]t is through practical engagement with the world, not disembodied contemplation, that human beings develop their plans."[18] As humans shape the world around them, as they confront its constraints and limitations, and as their actions create new situations to which they must respond, they are engaging in a continually evolving relationship with the natural environment. Their decisions are predicated not only on preexisting assumptions about nature but also on immediate conditions that they may have had a hand in creating.

The first to make this link in the context of the Civil War was Jack Temple Kirby. In his innovative essay on the National Humanities Center website, published in 2001, he presented what he called a "preliminary [environmental] impact statement." Though the war's destruction of fields, forests, and settlements of various sizes was widespread, many elements of the landscape recovered after the fighting ended. However, Kirby contended, the Civil War was "the beginning of the end of southern rural life as it had been known for at least two centuries." This fundamental change forced southerners to renegotiate the terms by which they worked with nature.[19]

Others, too, have examined the war from an environmental perspective. In his thought-provoking essay "The Great Food Fight," Ted Steinberg suggested that the Civil War was fought over two competing visions of how Americans should organize society and the landscape.[20] Mark Fiege made a similar argument in his excellent study "Gettysburg and the Organic Nature of the American Civil War." According to Fiege, the Gettysburg campaign "exemplified the environmental conditions that motivated and influenced the larger conflict." Fiege contended that the war was a battle over "the fate of the American West." He suggested that the North and the South "had opposing visions of western social development" and that these "competing land ideologies, as they might be called, impelled the two sections into war." He further suggested that "much of the struggle between North and South was over geographic space" and that the "side that dominated and defined space, either in the West or in actual theaters of combat, was the side that would prevail."[21]

More recently, studies relating to disease and soldiers' health have taken an environmental turn. Kathryn Shively Meier has examined the connections between environmental conditions and soldiers' psychological and emotional well-being, a unique and provocative approach to the topic of soldier health.[22] Margaret Humphreys and Andrew McIlwaine Bell have illuminated the connections among human bodies, disease organisms, and the exigencies of war.[23] Where Humphreys focused on the lives and deaths of black soldiers, Bell examined the role of insects and disease in shaping strategy. Merging military, medical, and environmental history, Bell argued that the success of campaigns and the development of strategy by both Union and Confederate leadership often hinged on the lowly mosquito and the diseases for which it served as a vector.

Each of these scholars clearly demonstrated that military and environmental histories are inextricably linked in a variety of ways. They have accomplished what Ellen Stroud urged all environmental historians to do: "[B]ring to light connections, transformations, and expressions of power that otherwise remain obscured."[24] Fiege and Bell did this exceptionally well. Fiege's emphasis on the material realities of waging war clearly exposed the power—military and social—that the physical control of nature offered. Bell beautifully demonstrated that material nature, in the form of mosquitoes and viruses, can tip the balance in military affairs, with significant ramifications. As these and the other pioneering works reveal, environmental history can bring important insight to our understanding of the greatest conflict fought on American soil.

This book builds on that growing historiographical momentum and integrates the theoretical and methodological approaches of both military and environmental history, to the mutual benefit of both. In chapters 1 through 4 I pay close attention to the operational level of the war, demonstrating that a very basic assumption about nature guided the actions of Union forces along the Mississippi River, during the siege of Vicksburg, and in the 1864–65 campaigns in the Shenandoah Valley, Georgia, and the Carolinas. That assumption was that human beings had the power to manipulate nature to suit their own ends. In the case of operations along the Mississippi, Union forces attempted to reengineer nature to gain military advantage. In the other examples the assumed power over nature rested with planters and farmers, and the Union intent was to undermine their control, thus removing a critical source of support for the Confederate cause. What became clear in each case, however, was that nature had a power of its own and that Union forces had to contend with the southern environment as much as they did with Confederate troops.

Additional research into the war's intellectual context and consequences, environmentally speaking, is also required. The remainder of this introduction focuses on such issues and suggests how certain ideas about nature influenced the course of the war. The book's conclusion discusses the language used to describe the war's destruction and the ways wartime experiences shifted Americans' perceptions of unmanaged nature. Wilderness metaphors helped Americans articulate and make sense of the war-torn landscape, even as increasing numbers of Americans began in the nineteenth century to regard wilderness in a positive light. As geographer Anne Whiston Spirn has argued, "Landscape metaphors modify perceptions, prompt ideas and actions, molding landscape, in turn."[25] This was certainly true in the aftermath of the Civil War, when Americans sought to reclaim the nation from the "wilderness of war" by protecting nature and establishing memorial parks. In order to understand this postwar shift in attitudes toward unmanaged nature, it is important to know what ideas shaped Americans' perceptions of the same before the war.

Some of the terminology I use will be familiar to environmental historians but may not be to those new to the field. My use of some common terms may not accord with how other scholars, environmental or not, have used them. Some of them are hotly debated. I do not always use terms in the same way that the individuals in my book used them during their lifetimes. Where they used similar language I make every attempt to remain true to their understanding of those words and to avoid attributing to them an ahistorical sense of ecological or environmental consciousness. I have tried to use terms consistently, though some I use interchangeably. While the following discussion may seem on the surface to be a review of general terminology, it is instead an important piece of my argument. By specifying the way I use certain words, I am hoping both to clarify my assumptions and to avoid confusion over language.

A key term used throughout the book is *agroecosystem*. An agroecological system, or agroecosystem, as defined by historian Donald Worster, is "an ecosystem reorganized for agricultural purposes—a domesticated ecosystem." It restructures "the trophic processes in nature, that is, the processes of food and energy flow in the economy of living organisms. Everywhere such a restructuring involves forcing the productive energies in some ecosystem to serve more exclusively a set of conscious purposes often located outside it—namely, the feeding and prospering of a group of humans."[26] In other words, the process by which humans endeavor to draw sustenance or profit from nature through agriculture and animal husbandry creates new ecological systems. They are neither entirely natural nor completely domesticated. They continue to be governed by ecological (natural) forces but are at the same time managed and manipulated by human (cultural) acts and ideas; they are, thus, hybridized landscapes.

Agroecosystems are what tie many societies across the globe and through time to the land and to nature. Steven Stoll has suggested, "Farming defines a specific landscape, the middle landscape—that place somewhere between wilderness and city where settled societies produce all of their food. Farms are where people engage in aggressive manipulations of plants and animals and also where they learn the limits of what they can take from nature."[27] Thus agroecosystems become a fundamental means by which certain human societies interact with and understand the natural environment. The form and appearance of these systems reflect climatic, geological, hydrological, and cultural differences and reveal as much about the societies that create them as the natural resources that support them. In antebellum America, for example, the agroecological systems of the North and West differed greatly from those across the South, not only due to variations in labor systems but also in terms of types of soils, growing periods, precipitation averages, and crops grown. It is important to note that each region was not in itself homogeneous with regard to agroecological development; there were as many differences within the South as there were between the Confederate and Union states.[28] That said, the slave-based plantation system that dominated southern politics and society also formed the agroecological foundation of the Confederacy and would become a major factor in the Civil War.

Agroecosystems may or may not be as stable as the ecological ones they replace. Sustaining such systems requires labor and, often, capital investment. Successfully maintaining an agroecological system also involves gathering knowledge about and constantly reevaluating changing ecological conditions. Failure to provide or attain any one of these necessities may result in failure of the entire system. Furthermore, in creating an agroecological system, humans—individually and corporately—often become dependent on it. If stripped of the means to maintain that system in the long or short term, they may have to rely on other people or entities for survival or potentially fail as a society. In either case, they have lost their ability to restructure nature to their advantage, and a fundamental relationship to the natural world is broken.

Such was the case for many southern farmers and planters during the Civil

War. Though the break may have been temporary for some, I argue that it was nonetheless a significant reason for the Confederacy's demise. Eliciting that break was a primary objective of Union strategy in the last two years of the war. Though the creators and enforcers of that policy did not describe them in ecological terms, the effects of their actions were no less ecological in scope. The reversion of agricultural fields to grasses, tree saplings, and weeds was evidence of this ecological shift. In targeting southern means of production—that is, in attacking the region's agroecological systems—the Union armies under Grant, Sheridan, and Sherman undermined southerners' power to marshal nature's energies, thus striking an important blow against Confederate war efforts.

Another term that is crucial to my argument is *improvement*. Jack Temple Kirby has suggested, "Virtually all Americans alive when the Civil War began viewed nature with due respect, even fear, but as an enemy to civilization, and they usually saw themselves as agents of God's injunction to civilize."[29] To "civilize" meant to "improve." According to historian Daniel Walker Howe, "'Improvement,' in its early nineteenth-century sense, constituted both an individual and a collective responsibility, involving both the cultivation of personal faculties and the development of national resources." Furthermore, "to improve something was to turn it to good account, to make use of its potential." In both the individual and the collective sense, improvement "had a moral as well as a physical meaning; it constituted an obligation, and an imperative."[30] Environmental scholar Steven Stoll noted that to "improve land brought it into 'better account,' claimed it from wilderness, made it serve the purposes of livelihood."[31] Stoll took the argument further, rightly pointing out that in the early nineteenth century "improvement blended ecology with ideology, practice with politics, nature with the future of the Republic." He reasoned that a society "that had witnessed the joining of lakes and oceans through the Erie Canal and the deforestation of vast regions to build cities and a nation of farms expressed little doubt, irony, or hesitation about the mastery of human hands over the world."[32]

In remaking it to suit their needs and desires, Americans had fundamentally altered their relationships with and perceptions of nature and had in some sense naturalized the tools and processes by which they did so. As David Nye has suggested, by the 1830s "mechanical progress had, paradoxically, become an unalterable part of nature."[33] Nye argued that Americans assimilated this new version of nature into their narratives of improvement and development and into the nation's foundational stories, which often revolved around civilizing the American wilderness. Through this logic, if improvements transformed wilderness into civilization, then the destruction of improvements returned civilization to wilderness. Witnesses to the Civil War's devastating power did, in fact, suggest as much. Though they often used *wilderness* metaphorically, that they employed the concept at all is revealing. I discuss the term in more depth below, so suffice it to say here that wilderness, in its broad nineteenth-century usage, implied a lack of control over nature and thus posed a threat to civilized societies. Without power over nature, other forms of power also came into question.

It is important to note, however, that Americans recognized that their abilities to control nature by "improving" it were not absolute. They were well aware that natural forces continued to be a factor in their daily lives. Nevertheless, efforts to control the physical environment or deny such control to the enemy—through engineering and through destructive acts—became an important part of Union strategy in the last two years of the war. Union operations first took advantage of southern improvements, then targeted them as part of a larger military strategy. Neither of these policies was new to the practice of warfare, but I argue that in the context of the Civil War they took on new meaning. Importantly, they were not implemented for the purposes of military necessity—the Union had plenty of resources to support its armies and the means to get those resources to them—but, in Sherman's words, the operations were a "demonstration to the world" of the Union's mastery and power not only over people but over the landscape. The Union army could turn the improvements southerners had made to their environment to its own advantage and, at the same time, use those same improvements against the rebellion.

Like improvement, concepts of nature, landscape, and wilderness are central to my analysis. These three ideas are some of the most contested terms in environmental historiography; thus I wish to describe clearly the ways in which I use each of them in this book. By *nature* I mean the physical environment and the nonhuman elements—animate and inanimate—that it comprises. Some may argue that humans are part of nature and that the two cannot be easily separated into distinct categories. Indeed, the growing literature on health, disease, and the body suggests that we are foolhardy to assume that nature exists somewhere outside ourselves.[34] Others may suggest that there is little "natural" about nature because humans have long lived within it and manipulated it. Timothy LeCain has taken that argument one step further, positing that "the separation between technological and natural environments can be seen as a powerful but misleading illusion."[35] Each of these perspectives has merit; the blurring of the lines between nature and culture is a persistent part of history and does in fact figure into the arguments proposed in this book. However, unless we are willing to forgo all definitions and categorizations, which I am not, we must draw the lines somewhere. Thus, *nature* herein refers to the nonhuman physical environment in its constituent parts or as a larger whole. Union soldiers and officers had to contend with this environment on a daily basis, thus making it an integral part of the larger Civil War story.

Landscape, too, is "a slippery word," as John Stilgoe so aptly put it. "It means more than scenery painting, a pleasant rural vista, or ornamental planting around a country house. It means shaped land, land modified for permanent human occupation, for dwelling, agriculture, manufacturing, government, worship, and for pleasure. A landscape happens not by chance but by contrivance, by premeditation, by design," Stilgoe suggested. Landscape is what is created out of nature by humans "intent on ordering and shaping space for their own ends." But, Stilgoe acknowledged, "landscapes always display a fragile equilibrium between natural and human force; terrain and vegetation are moulded, not dominated." Landscapes are those places betwixt and between "cityscapes," those areas that Stilgoe attributed entirely to human creation, and "wilderness," which Stilgoe defined as the "chaos from which landscapes are created."[36] Geographer D. W. Meinig has argued that, as both place and idea, landscape belies any "simple binary relationship" between humans and the natural world because it reveals an "intricate intimate intermingling of physical, biological, and cultural features."[37] Like agroecological systems, landscapes are the confluence of ecological and cultural processes and contain natural and social significance. Thus, when the Union army added destruction of the Confederate landscape to its larger military goals and strategy, there were ecological and cultural consequences.

Perhaps the most debated term among environmental historians is *wilderness*. As Michael Lewis has noted, "[W]ilderness is simultaneously a real thing and a human construction."[38] In this book I focus almost exclusively on the latter, largely because when my sources used the term, they typically used it metaphorically. When they invoked *wilderness*, or its synonyms *desert* and *wasteland*, Civil War sources were reflecting on devastated landscapes, areas where positive human influence gave way to human-made disaster.[39]

Perceiving wilderness as a dangerous place, and one in need of reclamation or control, has a long history in America, originating in the colonial period. In its dense forests, expansive swamps, and other unfamiliar ecosystems European colonists saw an environment hostile to their intentions and survival but one also ripe for improvement through the civilizing hand of agriculture. Melanie Perreault has suggested that though the landscapes they encountered had been "significantly transformed by the natives who lived there," the colonists "described a land stuck in stasis, waiting for 'civilized' peoples to come and develop it into its full potential." Whether these newcomers saw the landscape as "a hideous and desolate wilderness," in William Bradford's oft-quoted words, or filled with economic promise, "Christianity, paganism, emerging capitalism, and early natural science all played a role in European efforts to explain (and thereby control) the perceived wilderness around them."[40]

According to Roderick Nash, the colonists "recognized that the control and order their civilization imposed on the natural world was absent" from their new surroundings and that such landscapes "constituted a formidable threat." Thus, such landscapes "acquired significance as a dark and sinister symbol."[41] That symbol—wilderness—placed nature and civilization in opposition, a dichotomy that would influence Americans' perceptions of and interactions with the natural landscape for generations.[42] Though definitions of wilderness evolved as those places previously considered wild changed or disappeared at the hands of settlers and slaves, the early understanding of wilderness as "a terrifying symbol of chaos" would remain potent and relevant.[43] It is this perception of wilderness that is most frequently invoked in the context of the Civil War.

In the antebellum period, as in the colonial era, Americans of all backgrounds had to navigate and negotiate with the natural world in order to survive and prosper. The ways they did so were as diverse as the people themselves. In general, however, a few shared, though at times competing, visions shaped how Americans in the early to mid-nineteenth century responded and related to the natural environment, with particular importance for the Civil War.

One approach was that nature existed for the benefit of human society and that it could be made to reach its potential through the proper application of science. In this view nature needed to be subdued, if not eradicated, and the land improved for both material and symbolic purposes. The intellectual antecedents for this perspective lay in part in the sixteenth century and the development of modern scientific inquiry during what has come to be known as the Scientific Revolution. These developments spurred experimentation and innovation, which generated in-depth knowledge about nature's processes and encouraged efforts to control them.

Carolyn Merchant has argued that the Scientific Revolution brought with it a transformation in the ways humans perceived the nonhuman world, shifting conceptions of nature away from an organic model to a mechanistic one and challenging arguments against the radical reorganization of the natural environment to better suit human desires. Nature was reduced to a set of knowable, universal principles that could be explained through rational, even mathematical, language. The result, Merchant suggested, was that "[t]wo new ideas, those of mechanism and of the domination and mastery of nature, became core concepts of the modern world."[44]

One area where the mechanistic view of nature took a firm hold was in the field of engineering. Though the practical application of engineering principles is ancient, recognition of engineering as a distinct occupation gained acceptance only in the seventeenth and eighteenth centuries. The profession began primarily as a military endeavor, and the formal title *engineer* originated with the Corps des Ingenieurs du Genie Militaire (more commonly, *corps du genie*), established by Sébastien Le Prestre de Vauban in 1675.[45] The *corps du genie*, or corps of engineers, focused on civil works—road construction, bridge building, and digging canals—but was also responsible for any military engineering needs that arose, fortifications in particular. Beginning in the late eighteenth century, civil engineering developed as a distinct profession out of this earlier military tradition.[46]

Historian Raymond Merritt suggested that engineers perceived nature as "a symbol of neutral, inert reality" and that they were "nonromantic manipulators of nature" whose "reputations depended on the utilization of nature, rather than its glorification."[47] He pointed to Thomas Telford, who in 1828 established a set of "guiding principles" for engineering and called its practitioners "assistants to the 'Proprietor of the Universe.'" Tellingly, Telford urged engineers to direct their efforts toward marshaling "the great sources of power in nature for the use and convenience of man."[48] Engineers in the United States often earned their credentials by attending one of several schools dedicated to training them. The first, and for years the preeminent, engineering school was the U.S. Military Academy at West Point, founded in 1802. West Point–trained engineers differed from those trained at other institutions in that they also learned the art of war.

Sylvanus Thayer, superintendent from 1817 to 1833, established the regimented academic and military curriculum that each of the academy's graduates was expected to master.[49] A cadet's performance in math, science, and engineering determined in large part his class standing and therefore delimited the branch of service in which he could choose to be placed.[50] James Morrison noted that "the men who graduated at the top of the class chose to enter the Corps of Engineers, and those just below them the Topographical Engineers or Ordnance."[51] As with everything in the armed services, a strict, if informal, hierarchy indicated which branch was most desirable and most prestigious. John Tidball, a West Point graduate of 1848, explained why the best cadets chose the Corps of Engineers over any other: "We were taught with every breath we drew at West Point the utmost reverence for this [order of merit] scale; it becomes [*sic*] a kind of fixture in our minds that the engineers were a species of gods."[52] The curriculum, the institution, and its graduates linked success in engineering to success in a military career.

Thus when the Civil War erupted, a significant proportion of the officers who led the Union (and Confederate) war effort were also engineers. Though an engineer trained at West Point was much like his civilian counterpart in "viewing the landscape from the perspective of a civil engineer," as Robert Fryman suggested, "only the West Point graduate received the indoctrination in tactics and armament that enabled him to perceive the topography as a potential weapon."[53] This education would have important implications when these men sought solutions to military problems. In peacetime West Point graduates concentrated on building the transportation and communication infrastructure of the nation; in war they often engaged in similar endeavors to support logistical and operational needs.[54] These men were also charged with developing creative approaches to overcoming difficult terrain or poor battlefield positions, efforts that frequently relied on technological fixes and on manipulating the landscape through digging canals, exploding mines, and on at least one occasion, attempting to divert a major watercourse. In so doing they sought to exert power over the natural landscape and thereby over their human enemies as well.

Though such notions of control can be traced in part to the Scientific Revolution and the development of a simplistic, mechanistic view of nature, they are also products of the Enlightenment's more complex understanding of the natural environment. Peter Hanns Reill has suggested that the Enlightenment produced a vision that emphasized nature's vitality and questioned the "idea that a few simple, all-encompassing rules could fully account for nature's operations."[55] Ecological ideas were an important part of this intellectual development, as Donald Worster has shown. Although the term *ecology* postdates the Civil War (it was first used in 1866), its intellectual origins can be traced to the Enlightenment, "when it emerged as a more comprehensive way of looking at the earth's fabric of life: a point of view that sought to describe all of the living organisms of the earth as an interacting whole."[56] By the early nineteenth century, Worster argued, "A static world of fixed, hierarchical relations began to give way to another nature, evolving, contingent, revolutionary, conflicted, catastrophic at times, always in a state of flux."[57]

On the one hand, this ecological view inspired what Worster termed the "arcadian" tradition, which placed humanity within the limits of nature and encouraged their "peaceful coexistence."[58] This perspective influenced the Romantic critiques of the early nineteenth century that questioned the wisdom of sacrificing nature on the twin altars of industry and westward expansion. Through their art, Angela Miller has suggested, painters like Thomas Cole warned Americans in the 1820s and 1830s that "the wilderness that guaranteed America's privileged conversation with God and which was central to America's emerging identity as a republic was under attack by Americans themselves." Furthermore, Cole's "*The Course of Empire* series was an object lesson that graphically revealed the catastrophic results of falling away from nature."[59] Such critiques would have even greater currency in the face of the Civil War's devastation.

On the other hand, viewing nature as an interconnected system also led to the development of what Worster called the "imperial" tradition, which "stripped from nature all spiritual qualities and rigidly distanced it from human feelings," making "the domination of the earth [. . .] one of modern man's most important ends."[60] Worster linked this view in part to the 1749 essay "The Oeconomy of Nature," in which Linnaeus identified a strict hierarchy among nature's organisms, suggested that all of nature was created for human use, and (in Worster's paraphrase) urged man to "vigorously pursue his assigned work of utilizing his fellow species to his own advantage."[61]

Somewhere in between these two extremes lies David Nye's notion of "second creation." Neither entirely mechanistic (imperial) nor fully ecological (arcadian) in its conception, second creation represented the view of a hybrid landscape that melded nature's potential to humanity's desires. According to Nye, "[F]or most Americans of the middle of the nineteenth century, the river was waiting to be dammed; similarly, the prairie was waiting to be farmed, the woodlands to be cut down, and the desert to be irrigated. In this view, Americans used new technologies not to overrun nature but to complete the design latent within it. The second creation, though man-made, was in harmony with the first."[62] Central to this view was the notion of improvement.

One of the most visible and important ways Americans attempted to improve nature was through agriculture. While basic assumptions about agriculture's role in improving the American landscape guided farmers across the nation, specific agricultural practices developed in relation to the environmental conditions individual farmers encountered.[63] Soil chemistry, hydrological systems, and climate all played a role in how agriculture developed in various parts of the nation. In the Northeast and Midwest, the areas that would stay loyal to the Union, nutrient-rich alfisols laid the foundation for the practice of continuous cultivation and would help to support the Union cause. Ultisols, which have limited nutrients, are the most common soil types across much of the region that became the Confederacy, making shifting cultivation the more profitable and prevalent form of agriculture.[64] These soil-based differences have led one scholar to suggest that "[t]he link between secession and state activism was, quite literally, rooted in the land, or at least in how southern planters and farmers used their land."[65]

Differences in agroecological systems also contributed to the development of regional cultural identities, which would play key roles in the coming of the Civil War. While any "generalizations about the over 1,300,000 farms in the North must respect their diversity," small family farms predominated in that region, with grain cultivation and livestock constituting the main agricultural pursuits. The main source of labor was the family itself, supplemented with hired hands during planting and harvesting seasons. "The primary goal of most [northern] farmers was self-sufficiency," Phillip Shaw Paludan has suggested. "The age-old ideal of a self-reliant, independent yeoman remained powerful, among those who actually lived that way and also among those who didn't."[66] By the start of the Civil War, though, most northern farmers were closely connected to markets far from home by way of canals and railroads, and many had begun to mechanize their operations. "The changes in agriculture induced by the transportation revolution and mechanization had consequences beyond increasing productivity," Paludan noted, by helping "to make farming generally profitable." Though the goal of many northerners was to own a farm, by 1860 that possibility had diminished as land prices rose and available acreage decreased (despite constant westward expansion). Consequently, tenancy rates increased, exposing "the declining reality of the yeoman farmer of the American dream."[67]

Nonetheless, the perceived connection between landownership and independence was a powerful motivation, one that translated into support for the Union cause in 1861. The political slogan "free soil, free labor, free men" resonated with aspiring property owners, and farm laborers enlisted in the Union armies in greater proportion than any other northern laboring class.[68] As he went off to war, the northern farmer-soldier carried with him certain ideas about what a proper farm should look like. These ideas would be just as important as the gun and ammunition he carried, especially during those campaigns in which destruction of the southern landscape was an integral part of his military duties.

Most of the farms northern soldiers encountered in the South differed greatly from those they left back home, even though the majority of landholders across the southern United States were yeoman farmers engaged in subsistence production similar to their northern counterparts. Differences in climate, vegetation and soil types, disease regimes, crop choices, and labor systems meant that southern farmers developed a unique relationship with the natural environment that did not draw clear distinctions between nature and culture.[69] Albert Cowdrey suggested that the South developed a laissez-faire attitude toward nature that was "at best an ambiguous friend to the wilderness, and a positive enemy of orderly development."[70] A defining characteristic of southern agriculture was the practice of shifting cultivation. John Majewski and Viken Tchakerian described the process of shifting cultivation as beginning with "the burning of forest growth to release nutrients into the soil. After five or six years, when the nutrients had been exhausted, the old field was abandoned to weeds, shrubs, and eventually trees. In the meantime, new fields would be burned and cropped. After fifteen to twenty years, the planter returned to the original old field and began the process anew."[71]

Because they had to dedicate the newer, more fertile fields to their cash or subsistence crops, not to hay or fodder for their farm animals, southern farmers frequently allowed their livestock to forage for themselves in wooded and other marginal lands. With no need, or desire, to keep livestock confined to barnyards or pastures, southern farmers also had less need for fences. This free-range system, begun early in the region's colonial development, came to symbolize to outsiders the "uncivilized" nature of southern agriculture. Virginia DeJohn Anderson found in her study of the Chesapeake that as early as the seventeenth century European visitors derided the colonists' methods of livestock husbandry and therefore disdained the region's landscape as a whole. The lack of fences, which resulted from the colonists' efforts to minimize labor expenditure, clearly demonstrated that the colonists and their landscape "fell short of the mark" of being civilized. The settlers' seeming lack of control over their hogs, cattle, and even horses led their judges to decide that the people had become as feral as their animals—that is, they had become a wild people inhabiting a wild landscape.[72]

The prevalence of old fields and other "waste" areas (places apparently ruined by past activity and those left uncultivated, for whatever reason) also implied to outsiders a lack of control over nature on the part of southern farmers (or at least a lack of initiative to exert such power).[73] According to Mart Stewart, "80 percent of the region in 1860 was uncultivated." However, these "wild lands [of the South] were always the terrain of an array of purposes and of social and cultural differences—so much so, that they were hardly 'wilderness' at all." Instead, old fields and uncultivated lands like forests, wetlands, and savannahs "were linked to cultivated ones through a complex of uses—some of them also agricultural." Stewart explained, "Small farmers and hill folk ranged cattle on wiregrass savannahs and in canebreaks, and hogs in mast-bearing deciduous woods [. . .]. Hunting and gathering were important components of the subsistence strategies to the more than 80 percent of southerners who did not own slaves—and for some of those who did."[74] Furthermore, these uncultivated, "wild" lands were important places of autonomy and subsistence for slaves, who "acquired knowledge about the physical environment in their neighborhoods and annotated their surroundings with meanings that were both subversive of the totality of white power and positive expressions of an African American environmental ethos."[75]

Though productive for those who lived there, the more fluid understanding in the South of what constituted a useful landscape led many outsiders to condemn southern agricultural practices. As Majewski and Tchakerian noted, from northerners' perspective, "southern agriculture lacked the order and refinement that characterized their neat and carefully maintained farms" back home. "The unsightly nature of southern farms and plantations—the recently burnt fields, the seemingly endless forests of pine, and the shockingly neglected livestock—all accentuated the region's relative lack of development." Its "uncultivated landscape and dispersed population created a ramshackle air about the region"; for "Northerners who believed in the economic and moral superiority of free labor [. . .] the desultory state of southern agriculture and the region's general underdevelopment became a powerful indictment of slavery."[76]

The most famous of these critics was Frederick Law Olmsted. During his tour of the South in the 1850s he noted, "[F]or every mile of road-side upon which I saw any evidence of cotton production, I am sure that I saw a hundred of forest or waste land, with only now and then an acre or two of poor corn half smothered in weeds; for every rich man's house, I am sure that I passed a dozen shabby and half-furnished cottages, and at least a hundred cabins—mere hovels, such as none but a poor farmer would house his cattle in at the North." Furthermore, he wrote, "Coming directly from my farm in New York to Eastern Virginia, I was satisfied, after a few weeks' observation, that the most of the people lived very poorly; that the proportion of men improving their condition was much less than in any northern community; and that the natural resources of the land were strangely unused, or were used with poor economy." His opinion of local whites was that "[t]hey work little, and that little, badly; they earn little, they sell little; they buy little, and they have little—very little—of the common comforts and consolations of civilized life." Olmsted was so unimpressed by the people and their seeming lack of control over the landscape that he concluded, "As a whole, the community makes shift to live, some part tolerably, the most part wretchedly enough, with arrangements such as one might expect to find in a country in stress of war."[77] Olmsted directly linked the substandard existence of the southern people, and the substandard level of improvement of their land, to slavery.

Modern scholars often criticize Olmsted's and other antebellum travelers' accounts as revealing more about their authors' own prejudices than about the actual state of affairs in the South.[78] When local voices are added to the chorus, however, a general disappointment with southern agricultural practices (though not its labor system) is still discernable. According to Joan Cashin,

"In the early nineteenth century, most Virginia writers shared the prevailing Anglo-American sense of the aesthetic, that 'beautiful' land was productive and under cultivation."[79] By allowing the land to erode and generally go to waste, southern farmers were relinquishing not only their power over nature but also their claim to being a civilized society.

Edmund Ruffin was perhaps the most vociferous and prolific of these southern critics. Ruffin—farmer, Virginian, southerner—spent a good part of his life studying soil. He conducted experiments to find ways to improve its fertility and wrote treatises about better farming methods. He urged his fellow planters in Virginia and across the South to reform their agricultural practices, not only for increased personal wealth but for the prosperity and stability of the region. He also argued passionately for building fences, enriching soils with marl and manure, and draining wetlands for the purposes of controlling disease and erosion. In an 1852 address to South Carolina planters the noted agronomist declared, "The great error of southern agriculture is the general practice of exhausting culture." Ruffin admonished his audience that it was in their power to stop the decline in soil fertility and if they failed to do so the southern states would become "barren deserts, in which agricultural labours would be hopeless of reward, and civilized men could not exist."[80] According to Jack Temple Kirby, Ruffin and other like-minded critics hoped to reform southern agricultural practices in order "to Europeanize the South Atlantic landscape, to halt American restlessness, [and] to make their countrymen stay put and be civilized."[81] The irony of Ruffin's life—which he devoted to improving and protecting the southern landscape through agricultural reform—is that his fire-eating politics eventually spelled doom for his beloved southern landscape.

Though southern agricultural practices were as diverse as the landscapes in which they operated, one form dominated the rest—politically, socially, and symbolically. Plantations, according to Mart Stewart, "were the backbone of nineteenth-century southern agriculture and drove the economy of the region."[82] They, like farms of all kinds, "constituted agroecological systems that restructured biological processes for agricultural purposes."[83] But because of their place in southern identity and society, plantations took on greater importance during the Civil War period. Beginning in 1861 plantations' agroecological systems turned toward the "feeding and prospering" of the Confederacy, by and large still through the cultivation and sale of cotton.[84] They became the real and symbolic foundations of the Confederacy's social, economic, and political structures. By 1864 those same systems became the real and symbolic targets of Union operations across the South. That year Union leadership developed a strategy that aimed at destroying the Confederacy by devastating the labor and agricultural systems—the very symbols of southern identity—that enabled its armies to fight.

While the Confederacy's agricultural wealth was a military asset, providing food and forage for its men at arms, it was also a vulnerable resource. According to Russell Weigley, "[A] strike against war resources suggested an indirect means of accomplishing the destruction of the enemy armies. If the enemy were deprived of the economic means to maintain armies, then the armies obviously would collapse."[85] Though the Confederacy's war resources included railroads, telegraph lines, armories, and factories, they also included its agroecological systems. U.S. naval captain David Dixon Porter recognized this and noted in July 1862 that farmers around New Orleans had abandoned cotton for corn. He reported, "The corn crop is now coming in. Any one who will look at these immense crops, planted along the river to the exclusion of cotton and sugar, must understand its destination." Porter then suggested, "Let the exportation of it into Secessia be restricted and you have put an end to the war."[86] Henry Kircher, a Union soldier from Illinois, likewise saw the efficacy of attacking the South's agricultural base. In a letter home from Vicksburg he told his parents, "[W]e can do much more damage to the South, and thereby bring it to the realization that they were asses and fools to attempt to ruin our country, if our army at the present would concentrate mainly on destroying the Southern plantations and means of production as much as possible rather than on pressuring them with powder and lead." Hunger, he believed, was a more powerful incentive for Confederate capitulation than bullets.[87]

Union leadership ultimately came to the same conclusion and in the last two years of the war revived the *chevauchée*, or massive foraging raid. According to Mark Grimsley, "The original *chevauchées* dated back to the Hundred Years' War, and were massive raiding expeditions in which the English systematically pillaged or destroyed everything in their path. [. . .] When conducting these raids, the English army resembled an ambient, marauding city, complete with its own facilities to process what it plundered." Grimsley suggested that while these raids "provided sustenance for the army and gave the soldiers a motive to fight, their chief strategic purpose was frequently political and psychological. They demoralized a hostile peasantry and punished a subjugated one." The *chevauchées* also had as a major goal undermining the power and control of the enemy authority or state.[88]

While the *chevauchée* had proven successful in military operations in earlier eras, in the nineteenth century it ostensibly fell outside the scope of "civilized" war. Any attempt to bring war to civilians would have been, and was in the rare cases when it occurred early in the Civil War, condemned as barbaric and untenable. As the war dragged on, though, and as more traditional forms of warfare proved ineffective at achieving Union war aims, Union leadership faced the difficult decision of expanding the scope of their operations beyond engaging soldiers on the field of battle. In the spring of 1863 Ulysses S. Grant initiated one of the first attacks against the Confederacy's agroecological foundations during his siege of Vicksburg. Such actions would be refined into formal policy by summer 1864, when first David Hunter, then Philip Sheridan, tore through the Shenandoah Valley, and they would be perfected under the leadership of William T. Sherman on his marches through Georgia and the Carolinas in late 1864 and early 1865. By targeting the South's agricultural sector, this new Union strategy undermined the region's most basic relationship to the natural world. It destroyed the Confederacy's agroecological foundations and contributed significantly to ultimate Federal victory.

The Union did not simply replicate the older form of the *chevauchée*, however, but adapted it to prevailing needs and conditions. In reinitiating the *chevauchée*, the Union leadership responded to what they believed was military necessity. "They might have preferred at the outset to win the war with a minimum of damage to civilian property," Grimsley stated, but by the end, such actions promised success where other methods had failed.[89] In conducting such operations, Union forces attacked the Confederacy's resources, its physical and imagined landscapes, and its relationship with nature.

Communities imbue their surroundings—both built and natural—with significance and symbolism tied to their sense of shared identity. Such landscapes are inevitably altered by acts of war, by the violent struggle to protect or possess them.[90] By targeting the artifacts and symbols of southern agriculture, Union forces reduced a once productive, "improved" landscape to a symbolic "wasteland" and helped force the Confederacy's capitulation. The operations led by Grant, Sheridan, and Sherman in the final two years of the war reveal an underlying assumption that humans could exert control over nature and frequently incorporated attempts to reshape the environment in order to gain control over key pieces of territory. Far more than simple acreage, the contested territory frequently contained landscapes that had deep meanings for those involved in the conflict. What follows is a study of what those meanings were and how Grant, Sheridan, and Sherman made war upon the land.

CHAPTER ONE

Hostile Territory

*Union Operations along the Lower
Mississippi, 1862–1863*

IN 1860 THE MISSISSIPPI RIVER still flowed largely according to its own rules. Meandering, altering its course without warning, it littered the landscape with sinewy ridges of rich, black alluvial soil, oxbow lakes, swamps, and bayous. On the eve of the Civil War, humans had yet to build the massive dam and levee systems that would hem in its waters and straighten its path. Minor incursions on its freedom—small earthen levees thrown up by farmers, mostly conforming to the river's own natural levee system—followed its course, pleas more than actual protection against the vagaries of the Father of Waters. When the war came crashing along the river valley less than a year later, two separate Union armies endeavored to force Old Man River to bend to their wishes. They failed, but their attempts left a lingering legacy for American military actions, a legacy predicated on the belief that control over nature was possible.

The assumption that human ingenuity could overcome all of nature's challenges permeated nineteenth-century interactions with the Mississippi.[1] According to historian John Barry, "To control the Mississippi River—not simply to find a modus vivendi with it, but to control it, to dictate to it, to make it conform—is a mighty task. It requires more than confidence; it requires hubris. It was the perfect task for the nineteenth century."[2] In the early decades of that century, the Mississippi's whirling eddies and swift, unpredictable currents menaced boats of all kinds, making trade and communication along its length dangerous. But as the main north-south artery connecting the western reaches of the United States with the eastern seaboard and beyond, the river was also a lifeline for farmers, settlers, and merchants in reach of its powerful flow. Thus, harnessing its potential through technology, engineering, and science was of primary importance to the nation's economic, political, and social development.

The first half of the nineteenth century witnessed a multifront operation to rein in the unruly river. In addition to efforts to maintain and expand the river's natural levees, other, more expansive plans evolved. The invention of the steamboat made upstream travel possible by the second decade of the nineteenth century, but dangerous obstacles threatened to limit passage nonetheless. Snags—trees ripped by the river from its banks and either embedded like spikes in the river's bottom or floating along its surface like battering rams—were omnipresent and sank ships on a regular basis. Capt. Henry Shreve, after whom Shreveport, Louisiana, is named, devised a means to remove the snags and by 1832 cleared the river of most of them.[3] That, however, would remain an ongoing endeavor; new snags constantly entered the stream as the river continued to follow the laws of nature, cutting new channels, scouring out its banks, and overflowing them in times of high water.

Midcentury brought an increased interest in taming the Mississippi, or at least mitigating its power. Historian George Pabis noted that between "1846 and 1861, engineers sought to unravel the mysteries of the Mississippi River. They realized that only a thorough survey of the entire lower Mississippi could provide them with the information required to save Louisiana from flooding."[4] In response, the federal government authorized a survey of the Lower Mississippi Valley in 1850 to determine the best way to control flooding and a means by which the river's sandy, tortuous mouth might be engineered for better shipping access. Charles Ellet Jr., a civil engineer, and Andrew Atkinson Humphreys, a military engineer trained at West Point, independently undertook the survey. They came to differing conclusions, but the primary argument of each was that engineering could bring the Mississippi under control. Before their recommendations could be implemented, however, hostilities erupted, leaving the river free from large-scale intervention for a while longer.[5] Far from shifting attention away from the Mississippi River, the Civil War brought heightened focus to it, and the antebellum attempts at controlling the river through engineering would serve as models for the armies fighting along its banks.

When Tennessee seceded in June 1861, the entire Mississippi south of Cairo, Illinois, lay in Confederate-claimed or contested territory. This was a devastating blow to the Union, strategically and psychologically. Geographer Warren Grabau noted, "To the people living in the Old Northwest [. . .], the river was their lifeline to the outside world, as well as the avenue for much of their internal commerce. It had assumed an almost mystical importance."[6] Evidence from the time bears this out. A general in the U.S. Army from Minnesota, Lucius F. Hubbard, recalled, "When the rebellion blockaded the Mississippi river, Minnesota felt that the vital current in a main artery of her being had ceased to flow. She was restive under her sense of isolation, until the barriers of that blockade were broken down."[7] Union general William T. Sherman wrote in May 1861, "The Mississippi River will be a grand theater of war," and "were it not for the physical geography of the country it might be that People could consent to divide and separate in peace. But the Mississippi is too grand an element to be divided, and all its extent must of necessity be under one government."[8] Later that year Sherman told his brother, Senator John Sherman, "If the Confederates take St. Louis and get Kentucky this winter, you will be far more embarrassed than if Washington had fallen into their possession as whatever nation gets control of the Ohio, Mississipi & Missouri Rivers will control the continent. This they know and for this they will labor."[9] The river was the transportation and communication backbone of the nation, and whoever controlled it determined the course of the war in the west.

With possession of the lower Mississippi in 1861, the Confederacy seemed to have the upper hand. Confederate engineers built fortifications and artillery batteries along the Mississippi's eastern escarpment, taking advantage of the high ground the bluffs provided at places like Columbus, Kentucky; Memphis, Tennessee; Vicksburg, Grand Gulf, and Natchez, Mississippi; and Port Hudson and Baton Rouge, Louisiana.[10] However, as historians William Shea and Terrence Winschel have suggested, "In military terms the river was both an asset and a liability to the nascent Confederacy. The Mississippi's silt-laden waters connected many of the western secessionist states, but its broad surface also served as a natural avenue of invasion."[11]

Winfield Scott, commanding general of the U.S. Army in 1861, hoped to exploit that vulnerability as part of his grand strategy. He argued against a full-scale invasion of the southern states, warning that such action would push a peaceful settlement out of reach by the end of a year. Instead, he believed that blockades and economic restrictions would be the best course of action and would reinvigorate latent Union sentiment in the seceded states. Scott's plan included a naval blockade of all seaports south of Washington to Florida and into the Gulf of Mexico and a two-pronged action on the Mississippi River. A new freshwater flotilla comprising armored steam- and gunboats would move downriver from Cairo, Illinois, while powerful warships would proceed upriver from the Gulf, each destroying Confederate fortifications en route. Through these measures, which the press cynically dubbed the "Anaconda Plan," Scott hoped to crush the rebellion with minimal bloodshed and bring the erring southerners to their senses.[12] The Union leadership, both civilian and military, disagreed about the merits of Scott's plan but concurred on the major point: Federal forces must gain absolute control over the Mississippi River.

Abraham Lincoln called the Mississippi "the backbone of the Rebellion."[13] It was an apt metaphor that guided the efforts of various Union commanders in the western theater who equated breaking the back of the Confederacy with

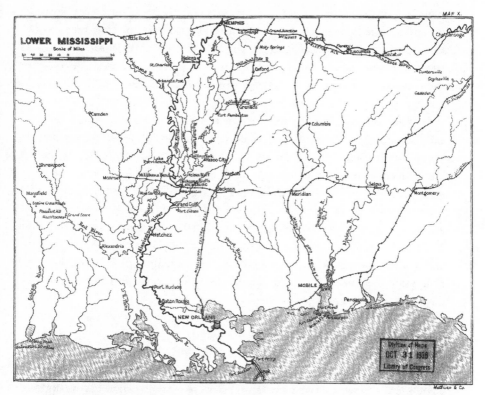

The Lower Mississippi Valley: Map showing the area of Union operations along the Mississippi River, 1861–63. From W. B. Wood, "Civil War in the United States" (1905), Civil War Maps Collection, Geography and Map Division, Library of Congress, g3861sm gcw0102200.

subduing the river itself. Controlling the river came to mean not only having unfettered access to it but literally exerting power over the river's course. Time and again during operations on the Mississippi, Union military leadership turned to engineering and assailed the river as an alternative to attacking their Confederate foes.

Pitting an army against the Mississippi, however, meant engaging every element of the river's hybrid landscape—an environment formed by natural processes but modified by human action. The natural levees, created by the river's yearly floods, were ridges that rose from ten to fifteen feet above the water level and stretched from one hundred yards to several miles beyond the river bank. They provided rich, dry land for the region's cotton cultivation, but they also formed the edges of the area's nearly impassable swamps. The agroecological system developed by white American settlers and their slaves beginning in the mid-eighteenth century was only the most recent in a long succession. The first inhabitants of the area, various Mississippian peoples associated with the Natchez civilization, cultivated its soils and managed its forests, as did later Native American tribes such as the Yazoo, Koroa, Choctaw, and Chickasaw. Spanish, French, and British explorers, trappers, and colonists also had a hand in shaping the landscape.[14]

By 1860 an agricultural system centered on intensive cotton production and maintained by slave labor had transformed the lower Mississippi's natural levees into cropland, replaced forests with cotton, and made rivers and bayous into watery highways, but the boundaries between nature and artifice were not as clearly drawn there as they seemed to be elsewhere in the nation at the time. Agricultural fields abutted dark, mysterious swamps, thick cane breaks encroached on grazing lands, and epidemics of diseases all but eliminated from New England and the Old Northwest frequently threatened southern cities and towns. Such close intermingling of natural elements with the symbols of civilization presented a confusing and unsettling landscape for the Union soldiers sent to conquer it.

The Lower Mississippi Valley's strange environment—its geography, climate, flora and fauna, and unfamiliar agricultural practices, among other aspects—frequently captured the attention of the Federal troops, as their letters and diaries attest. Henry Kircher, from Illinois, wrote to his mother in March 1863, "Now we have been traveling on the various rivers, bayous and narrow passes for 3 weeks, and have gotten to see nothing of either civilization or the world of foe or friend. One can hardly describe how crooked the rivers are here; they consist of nothing but rounded corners. At this time of flood one sees shore seldom or not at all, just here and there a little edge of a plantation sticking out. Otherwise everything is forest, sky and water, and quite often just forest and water above and below."[15]

Others, too, remarked on the watery countryside. In a letter home, Lycurgus Remley of the Twenty-Second Iowa Infantry described his journey down the Mississippi in spring 1863. "The Mississippi is very high at present," he reported, "nearly filling its channels, and in some places overflowing the low bottom land. It looked almost like an inland sea." He concluded, "when the river is not rampant, this must be a fine country, [but] at present, partially submerged, it seems *rather too watery*, to suit my notions."[16] After ten days in camp at Milliken's Bend, Louisiana, Remley derided his surroundings as "this land of cane breaks, alligators, mosquitoes, etc."[17] Lycurgus's brother George noted, "There is something peculiar about the bayous that intersect this state in almost every direction. The water does not seem to be at all particular which way it runs. Some times the bayous were separate and the two parts run in directly opposite ways."[18] Logic did not seem to hold sway in such a landscape.

John Quincy Adams Campbell of the Fifth Iowa also described the scenery as he and his regiment moved down the Mississippi. "The dark forests of cypress that live by both banks may be very inviting to beasts and reptiles, but they have very little attraction for the human eye," Campbell wrote. The cane breaks—dense thickets of river cane or tree grasses that thrived in marginal and disturbed areas across the South—"to a Northerner are a novelty—but one that he soon tires of." Signs of human habitation amid the seeming wilderness "afford[ed] rest here and there to the wearied eye," but the "villages are too few and insignificant to attract attention." For Campbell, more than anything else, it was the Mississippi "in its immensity and *crookedness*" that was "an object of interest."[19] These soldiers' assessments reflected what many northern visitors thought of the southern environment: while it may have had impressive elements, on the whole it was ill managed, wild, and in need of better control.

It was also filled with nuisances and fearsome ailments. Charles Wills from Canton enlisted with the Eighth Illinois Infantry in 1861. In April of that year, while encamped near the Mississippi at Cairo, Illinois, Wills wrote in his diary, "We are more afraid of ague here than of the enemy." In September, near Columbus, Kentucky, he wrote, "We were not troubled any by the enemy but the mosquitoes and fleas gave us the devil." And in March 1862, near Point Pleasant, Missouri, south of New Madrid, "I shake in my boots at the thought of the mosquitoes, flies, etc., we will have to endure."[20]

According to historian Andrew McIlwaine Bell, "most of the New England farm boys and shopkeepers who volunteered to invade the South in 1861 had never been exposed to either yellow fever or malaria. And while their western comrades-in-arms had long been familiar with 'ague,' they too were susceptible to the unique and potentially dangerous strains of the disease that flourished below the Mason-Dixon Line." The "army of mosquitoes" the Union forces fought along the banks of the Mississippi River "was every bit as lethal as the gray-clad army they would face on the battlefield."[21] Two species of mosquito made up that insect battalion. The *Anopheles* mosquito, a vector for malaria, can be found in either salt- or freshwater swampy areas. *Aedes aegypti* is the vector for yellow fever, which "is accordingly an urban disease, for this particular mosquito disdains swamps and lakes."[22] So whether the soldiers were deployed in the backswamps along the Mississippi or in the cities of the Lower Mississippi Valley, they were susceptible to mosquito-borne diseases. The insects' role in transmitting these illnesses was unknown at the time, however, and most soldiers blamed their ill health on the "swamp vapors," decaying organic matter, or bad water they encountered in the lowlands of Mississippi and Louisiana.[23] In any case, the physical environment, unimproved and uncontrolled in the eyes of the invaders, initially was an obstacle to Union success.

For Lt. Col. Edward Bacon from Niles, Michigan, the lower Mississippi's environment was not only contemptible, it verged on dangerous. In his postwar memoirs he complained about the conditions at Camp Williams, near Lake Pontchartrain north of New Orleans, stating, "The dense forest of tall cypress and live oak, their boughs hung with long festoons of Spanish moss, shut out every breeze. The hot sun shines through the stagnant air, which is hazy with swamp vapors." He bemoaned that although his men had been spared the ravages of "the expected yellow fever" while at Camp Williams, diarrhea and swamp fever, "a fatal disease of congestive symptoms," threatened "to take off almost as many victims." The camp was situated on Metairie Ridge, "where every particle of earth appears to be made of decayed vegetation, and alligators and crawfishes appear to be the rightful owners of the land, as swarms of mosquitoes are proprietors of the air."[24] Humans, Bacon implied, did not belong to such a place, one that harbored dangerous animals and emitted deadly airs.

Bacon was not far off on his assessment of the perils of the lower Mississippi's environment. Topography, weather, climate, and the region's endemic diseases all presented significant problems. In May 1861 Winfield Scott admitted to Maj. Gen. George B. McClellan that he feared that patriotic zeal to crush the rebellion would send untrained troops down the Mississippi at water levels too low to safely carry their transport ships, only to have them arrive at places where frost had not yet had the opportunity to "kill the virus of malignant fevers below Memphis."[25] Haste, in other words, would imperil Union soldiers, not only because of incomplete training but also by exposing them to the natural hazards the Lower Mississippi Valley harbored.

Like Scott, residents of the area knew that their landscape contained dangerous elements and anticipated a vicious struggle between the Union troops and forces within the lower Mississippi's environment. In August 1861 the editors of the *Weekly Vicksburg Whig* scoffed at a *New York Times* report that campaigns against the Gulf Coast "could be safely conducted in the Summer season." The *Times* suggested, "Any number of men may be maintained in health on shipboard in Southern waters, and may safely make raids into the interior, if not too lazily or sluggishly conducted." The *Times* claimed an advantage, even noting that "the forces that would be required to oppose our [U.S.] Naval aggressions would all the time be employed in the swamps, and inevitably subjected to the deadly miasmas and destructive fevers that they occasion." The *Whig's* editors replied, "If they land on the coast they will find little else to fight except mosquitoes and alligators, and on these we hope they will try their hand. If they do not get the worst of it, we are mistaken."[26] The following April a Mississippi woman predicted that "an ally will rise up to assist us who will make their [the Yankees'] dastard hearts to quail. The yellow fever I mean."[27]

While efforts to combat disease were greatly hampered by the state of medical knowledge and technology at the time, the Union troops seemed perfectly prepared to confront another obstacle—the river itself. The science of engineering promised to eliminate the dangers posed by the river's unpredictability and by the Confederate fortifications strung along its banks. One potential means of turning the river from an enemy to an ally was by reshaping it through cutoffs and canals.

Canals in particular epitomized nineteenth-century notions of improving and commanding nature and became an integral part of the Union's victory-through-engineering strategy along the Mississippi River. These "artificial rivers" stretched across the eastern third of the nation at the start of the Civil War, providing relatively quick and easy transportation routes for commerce and travel, and had become to some degree "naturalized" parts of the landscapes through which they ran.[28] Moreover, they were a proven technology, one that could easily be adapted to military needs during wartime, and controlling access to the extant canals in the border states and throughout the South became a primary objective of both sides throughout the conflict. As prominent as canals were in the antebellum landscape, it is not surprising that planners and strategists, Union and Confederate, understood and exploited their military potential. Most wartime use of canals relied on preexisting ones, but Union troops also had to build new canals where older ones were unavailable. Early in their campaign against the Mississippi River, Union forces gained invaluable experience digging just such a canal to bypass Island No. 10.

Islands dotted the course of the Mississippi River, creations of the stream's unique hydrology and underlying geology. During the Civil War such islands became strategically important, none more so than Island No. 10, which took its name from being the tenth island south of the confluence of the Ohio River and the Mississippi. In August 1861 Confederate forces took possession of the island, located slightly upriver (east) from New Madrid, Missouri. The island, approximately 1 mile long by 450 yards wide, was in one Confederate officer's opinion "the strongest position for the defense of the Mississippi Valley."[29] The Confederate forces erected fortifications on the island and along the Tennessee shore in hopes of defending the river from Union incursion.

In March 1862 Gen. John Pope, commander of the Union forces in the area, ordered his chief engineer, Col. J. W. Bissell, to determine whether a way

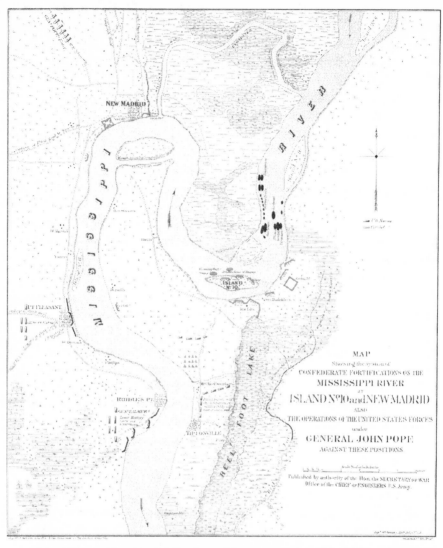

Island No. 10: Map showing Pope's canal (top center) above Island No. 10 (center of map). The cutoff connected the Mississippi with Wilson's Bayou through a heavily wooded area northeast of New Madrid, Missouri. Civil War Maps Collection, Geography and Map Division, Library of Congress, g4042m cw0301000.

around the island fortifications existed. He directed Bissell to "make an examination of the peninsula opposite Island No. 10, to ascertain whether a short canal, not to exceed 2 miles in length, cannot be dug, so that boats can enter above Island No. 10 and come out into the river below it." Pope believed that a "mere ditch, through which the water of the river can be started, will at this stage of the river wash into a deep channel in one night."[30] He hoped that the river would do most of the work for him. Pope's plan was further validated by his superior's approval. In an official letter to Pope, Gen. Henry Wager Halleck wrote, "I heartily approve of your plan. Impress all the negroes you can find to assist in the work. If you can in this way turn and capture the enemy, it will be one of the most brilliant feats of the war."[31]

Bissell identified a potential route that took advantage of a crevasse in the levee that had flooded the nearby land deeply enough for boats with three-foot drafts to pass through. Heavy woods to the west of the crevasse, however, impeded direct access to Wilson's Bayou, which was the intended bypass route around Island No. 10. Bissell recalled after the war that maneuvering the boats "through the submerged corn-field and the half-mile of road was easy enough, but when we reached the timber the labor of sawing out a channel commenced." The soldiers first cut the trees above the waterline, then either hauled them out with winches and pulleys or used an underwater swinging saw to cut the stumps farther below the water's surface. Bissell reported, "Here was where the ingenuity of the officers and men was exercised; as the saws were working four and a half feet beneath the surface, and the water was quite turbid, the question was how to ascertain what was interfering with the saw, and then to apply the remedy. But I found Captain Tweeddale equal to the most obstinate stump." Bissell's men may have been able to best a stump, but falling water levels and fast-moving currents posed greater challenges. "In one of the bayous for about two miles the current was so swift that all the men who were out on logs, or in exposed places, had safety-lines tied around them; and as the timber was slippery, some were indebted to these lines for their lives." Remarkably, Bissell's force of six hundred sustained no casualties.[32]

In early April Pope's men successfully finished the canal, which connected the Mississippi with Wilson's Bayou and then St. John's Bayou, which emptied back into the Mississippi west of New Madrid, downstream from Island No. 10. In a report to Halleck, Pope wrote, "Our canal has been a gigantic work; it has been infinitely more difficult than at first supposed." Once complete, the canal was fifty feet wide, four feet deep, and six miles long, providing Pope's men access "through a great forest of immense trees, [. . .] and then through cypress swamp thickly studded with cypress knees."[33] Rather than taking the expected twenty-four hours, the canal exacted "great labor" and had taken nearly three weeks to complete.[34] Pope reported that "the work was prosecuted with untiring energy and determination, under exposures and privations very unusual even in the history of warfare" and "will long remain a monument of enterprise and skill."[35] He discovered that fighting nature could be as difficult as a direct assault against his human enemy and that nature's obstacles could prove more challenging to overpower than the rebel forces. Nonetheless, the plan worked, and on April 7, 1862, the Confederate forces abandoned their positions and Union transport ships steamed toward the island.

The victory at Island No. 10, followed shortly by the capture of Memphis, freed the river for Union control south to Vicksburg. Further Union success at New Orleans and Baton Rouge opened navigation of the Mississippi from the Gulf of Mexico to Port Hudson, Louisiana, one hundred miles south of Vicksburg.[36] In response to these developments, Moses Gage, a chaplain with the Twelfth Indiana Volunteer Infantry, effused, "From the mouth of the Ohio to Vicksburg, and from the Gulf to Port Hudson, the pulsations of a new life were beating with constantly increasing vigor, and before us was the final accomplishment of the great work of opening the Mississippi." Transported to their battle posts by the very river they hoped to control, Gage recalled, "Gladly did noble hearts respond to the beautiful language of nature dressed in all her beauty, as she welcomed us to the honorable duty of bringing back to the paternal arms of the Government the broad and luxuriant Valley of the Mississippi, with all its garnered wealth of beauty and fertility."[37] He continued,

> Nature, science, law, morals, and religion are all arrayed on the side of truth, in whose defense we were engaged. Hence the difference in the value of motives by which men are impelled to action. Sincerity in error is not the equal of integrity in truth, and even the silent influence of nature impresses the heart of him who is engaged in a noble cause. Hence the dwellers in the lovely valleys among the mountains, before whom nature spreads a scene of mingled beauty and sublimity, are regarded as the firm adherents and defenders of truth. The mighty river, with its beautiful scenery, is also adapted to inspire noble sentiments and give new courage to those who maintain the right.[38]

According to Gage, victory on the Mississippi was not just a patriotic duty; it was an act in accord with nature.

What the troops discovered when they arrived at Vicksburg and Port Hudson, however, was a landscape arrayed against Union aims. Each location boasted rough terrain that would make frontal assaults perilous and fortifications that took advantage of those natural lines of defense. While both strongholds would have to be taken to completely free the Mississippi for Union navigation, Vicksburg was arguably the more important because it served as the Confederacy's only direct link to the vast resources of the trans-Mississippi West.[39] Confederate policy early in the conflict ensured that cotton would continue to dominate agricultural production in the Deep South for another year at least, so beef and other supplies from Texas, New Mexico, and Mexico were required to feed and support the Confederate armies in the western theater.[40] If Vicksburg fell into Union hands, a vital link for the Confederacy would be cut.

Vicksburg's built and natural environments provided strategic advantages for whoever controlled the city. The Vicksburg and Jackson Railroad linked the city to points east and the Vicksburg and Shreveport Railroad, accessible by ferry to De Soto Point across the Mississippi, connected Vicksburg with the trans-Mississippi West. By 1862 these transportation routes, which had been so essential to commerce and society in peaceful times, had been co-opted to serve military needs. In addition, numerous navigable streams served the city, including the Mississippi, Big Black, and Yazoo Rivers, as well as myriad bayous. Under peaceful conditions these waterways facilitated transportation and communication, but during the contest for control of the city they became important lines of protection for its Confederate defenders and significant barriers to Union operations.

The Yazoo and Big Black Rivers carved deep, twisting ridges into the erosion-prone loess soil surrounding the city to its north and east and were part of a complex system of swamps and bayous that further fractured the landscape. The tops of the ridges often served as roadways, but their tortuous nature meant slow progress and vulnerability to attack for any army moving across them. The city's western boundaries, made up of solid limestone and shale bluffs rising two hundred feet above the Mississippi River, were equally formidable and provided the city with the military benefit of high ground. The Confederates took advantage of these geographic assets and built an expansive system of forts, batteries, and redoubts in every suitable location. "Art," thus, "was brought to the assistance of nature in order to render the city impregnable."[41] Well aware that attacking a position so strongly fortified—by whatever means—could be costly, if not disastrous, Union leadership at Vicksburg attempted to neutralize nature in order to render art meaningless.

Union attempts to capture Vicksburg began with a naval assault led by Rear Admirals David Glasgow Farragut and Charles Henry Davis, two seasoned veterans noted for their earlier successes in the war and the senior naval officers on the Mississippi. But against the fortified bluffs and riverbanks, the attempt was a dangerous and potentially fruitless mission. Another option, however, existed. Rear Admiral Farragut and Maj. Gen. Benjamin Butler, put in charge of Union army efforts in the lower Mississippi after the capture of New Orleans, believed that Vicksburg could be taken out of commission, and therefore made irrelevant, if it no longer had access to the river. Together they developed a plan to divert the river entirely away from the city, leaving Vicksburg high and dry.[42]

Farragut and Butler found a willing partner to the scheme in Brig. Gen. Thomas Williams, trained at the U.S. Military Academy at West Point and a member of the Corps of Engineers. Much like his contemporary colleagues, he viewed nature as an obstacle to be overcome, a problem to be solved. Under Butler's orders, Williams developed a plan to force the river into a new channel—a canal his troops would dig across De Soto Point, the spit of land created by the horseshoe bend in the river across from the city—thereby creating a safe passageway for U.S. naval boats and opening the river to Federal navigation.

In light of the spectacular coup at Island No. 10, cutting a canal seemed the answer to the final sticking point in the Union's Mississippi River campaign. De Soto Point provided an ideal place for a river cutoff, a fact both Union and Confederate officers recognized. Lt. Col. Edward Fontaine, chief of ordnance for the Confederacy's Mississippi Army, suggested in December 1861 that an additional battery be built above Vicksburg to "prevent [the Federals] from cutting a canal and turning the river through the narrow neck between the bends, which a small army could do in a single day." Although Fontaine believed the Union forces capable of undertaking such a task, he was hopeful "that their designs will be thwarted by a kind Providence."[43] Four months later, Confederate general Pierre G. T. Beauregard warned Captain Harris, chief engineer at Vicksburg, that "the peninsula opposite Vicksburg should not be susceptible of being canaled across from the river above to the river below" and ordered that an additional battery be built "to command the ground over which said canal might be made."[44] These new defenses failed to deter Union plans.

On June 6 Butler sent Williams his orders: "You will send up a regiment or two at once and cut off the neck of land beyond Vicksburg by means of a trench across [. . .]. The river itself will do the rest for us."[45] Williams viewed the canal as both a military challenge and an ingenious solution for a problem posed by nature. Like Butler, he believed that if given the proper direction, the river would do most of the work, though he did acknowledge he needed the proper conditions to prevail. Early in the process he told his wife, "It's a great work and not of certain execution, for the river is falling rapidly. If the canal succeeds, Vicksburg is cut off and the Mississippi river turned, and Vicksburg and its defenses and batteries are conquered by the shovel." As an engineer,

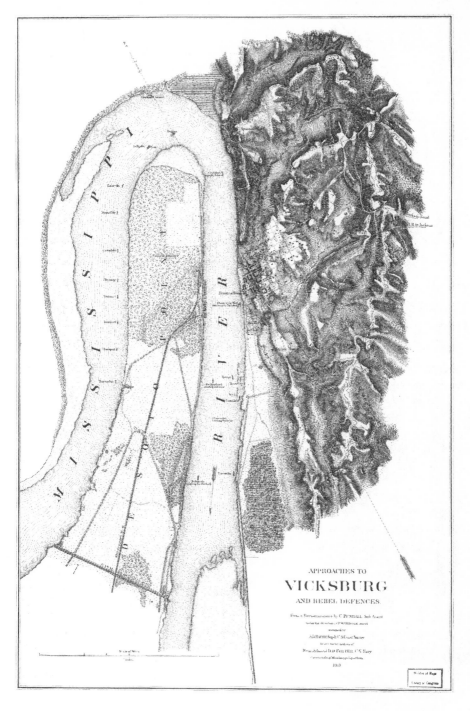

Vicksburg and environs: Map showing the city of Vicksburg, De Soto Point—across
which Union forces attempted to create a cutoff (see lower left of the map)—and
the city's rugged terrain. Civil War Maps Collection, Geography and Map Division,
Library of Congress, g3984v cw0278000.

Digging the canal: This illustration by Theodore R. Davis for *Harper's Weekly* (vol. 6, no. 292, August 2, 1862, p. 481) shows a contingent of slaves commandeered from nearby plantations digging the first attempt at the De Soto Point canal. Prints and Photographs Division, Library of Congress, LC-USZ62-138120.

Williams put great stock in the idea that the city could be decommissioned without a shot fired. He reiterated his point a second time in the same letter to his wife, noting that if his plan succeeded, "the Mississippi will take the course of the cut off and Vicksburg becomes an inland town with a mere creek in front of it. So the batteries will be made useless, and Vicksburg will fall with the spade."[46]

Winning a war with excavation implements proved more difficult than expected, largely due to environmental obstacles. The soils along the Mississippi River are vertisols.[47] The silt and loess deposited by flooding sit on top of these heavier, clay soils. Thus, to dig the canal the Union soldiers, in conjunction with over one thousand slaves commandeered from surrounding plantations, had to contend with tenacious clay, as well as thick vegetation, unpredictable water levels, and mosquito-borne illness.

In July Williams reported to the assistant adjutant general, Capt. R. S. Davis, that at least eleven hundred slaves, "gathered from the neighboring plantations by armed parties," were put to work excavating, felling trees, and grubbing roots. "The labor of making this cut is far greater than estimated by anybody," Williams acknowledged, noting that hard clay ten to eleven feet deep made up the top layer of soil. The work crew had an arduous task ahead of them, because they had to reach sand "before the cut can be pronounced a success." Williams knew from his engineering training that the river's current, "however great, will not wash the clay."[48]

Two weeks into the laborious project, and only twelve hours away from sure success, in Williams's estimation, "sudden caving began at several points, and thereby so arrested the excavation remaining to be made that the rapidly falling river had in the next left the bottom of the cut-off some feet above the river's level." Williams was "chagrined to report that, after the great labor of an average excavation of 18 feet in width and 13 feet deep, we have encountered at least a temporary failure." Not easily deterred, Williams proposed to expand his labor and tool resources and "make a real canal, carrying it, if necessary, to the depth of the greatest fall of the river at this point, say some 35 to 40 feet." No small project, Williams estimated that "with sufficient force—that is, with as much force as can be profitably worked—[the canal] will take three months."[49]

Few people shared Williams's optimism for the expanded project. Capt. David Dixon Porter of the U.S. Navy wrote a letter to his superior, Rear Adm. David Farragut, criticizing Williams's canal: "You may depend, sir, that General Williams is frittering away his time on that grand canal, which will never amount to anything while the river is falling." Porter believed that Williams's time would be better spent raiding the countryside, taking or destroying enemy stores and stock. Foreshadowing what was to come, he argued that such action was the only way to "in fact open this river; for I speak within bounds when I say that it is nearer to being closed up at this moment than it has been since we came into it."[50] Porter concluded that, as the three thousand troops under Williams's command "attempted nothing important, their presence was perfectly useless."[51]

Williams's subordinate officers also recognized the futility of the project. Lt. Col. Edward Bacon opined, "The Mississippi has proved too much for General Williams, and the Hill City is not yet made an inland town." Bacon criticized Williams's final plan as a "vain effort to overtake the falling waters of the river, and lead them where he willed them to go." He recalled that a "little trickling stream got through feebly" but failed to produce any real results, despite the efforts of a stern-wheel steamer employed "to force the water, by the action of the wheel, to obey the General's will."[52] Bacon laughingly derided Williams's ditch, "where the insubordinate water would not run up hill."[53]

The media offered criticism of the ill-fated project as well. Each time, it was not a failure of engineering but an uncooperative nature that thwarted the Union's attempts to take Vicksburg out of commission. The editors of *Harper's Illustrated History of the Great Rebellion* echoed Bacon's sentiments. Calling the canal "a failure," they noted that "the Mississippi, which had so often been known to change its channel in a single night on the slightest occasion, refused by a singular caprice to take the course which General Williams had opened for it, and Vicksburg, instead of becoming an inland city, had a joyful occasion for self-congratulation and for laughter at the foiled project of 'the Yankees.'"[54] The river's "caprice," not human hubris, caused the failure.

The river was not the only environmental factor that undermined Union operations at De Soto Point. Lamenting the turn of events, Williams wrote to his wife, "it would not surprise me if the decimation of troops and sailors by disease did not compel the abandonment of this Expedition until the return of frost and cool weather." He mistakenly believed that his men saw the canal as "something worth suffering for, and as long as that prospect was before us, officers and men kept back disease by the mere force of resolution. But now that the prospect has failed, the disposition is generally to give way."[55] While unfavorable water levels may be attributed to strictly natural causes—seasonal fluctuations, changes in precipitation—the Union army's battle against disease was the result of a confluence of human and environmental factors. In commandeering slaves from nearby farms and plantations to help dig the ditch, the Union army all but guaranteed increased incidence of malaria among its troops. Recent floods created puddles ideal for mosquito breeding, and the slaves "were almost certainly carrying plasmodium parasites when they were recruited to work alongside Williams' non-immune New Englanders."[56]

Hearing of the canal's failure and having a long relationship with the area's disease environment, the locals believed they were safe from Union advances for the time being. The *New Orleans Daily Times Picayune* published a report from Jackson, Mississippi, dated August 22, 1862, that stated, "As September is the most unhealthy month of the season, the miasma being particularly fatal then on the Mississippi river, it is quite probable that no regular attack will be made on Vicksburg again until October, or at least the return of cold weather."[57]

The Union army did indeed wait for cooler weather. After the failure of both Williams's canal and the initial naval campaign, the Union regrouped and made new attempts on the fortress city beginning in December 1862. Gen. Thomas Williams died in battle near Baton Rouge in August of that year, so the assault on Vicksburg fell to Maj. Gen. Ulysses S. Grant. The ranking officer in the western theater once Halleck transferred to Washington as commanding general of Federal forces, Grant had orders to capture Vicksburg at once. Relying on established military theory, he believed that taking the city would require two separate armies, one attacking from the west and another from the east. He sent his trusted junior officer, Brig. Gen. William Tecumseh Sherman, to command the western flank. Grant led the eastern column himself.

Grant planned on marching south through northwestern Mississippi from Corinth through Granada to Vicksburg. He followed standard military practice, establishing a stationary base behind his army from which supplies could easily be transported to the moving column. Leaving a garrison to guard the supplies, Grant marched toward Vicksburg. Gen. Earl Van Dorn of the Confederate cavalry sneaked to Grant's rear, however, and destroyed the supply depot at Holly Springs on December 21, leaving Grant and his army in hostile country with no provisions. Grant recalled the Mississippians' reaction to the news: "They came with broad smiles on their faces, indicating intense joy, to ask what I was going to do now without anything for my soldiers to eat." Grant informed them that he was taking care of the problem, collecting all food and forage to be found in a fifteen-mile area. "Countenances soon changed," Grant wrote, "and so did the inquiry. The next was, 'What are *we* to do?'" Grant told them, "[W]e had endeavored to feed ourselves from our own northern resources while visiting them; but their friends in gray had been uncivil enough to destroy what we had brought along, and it could not be expected that men, with arms in their hands, would starve in the midst of plenty. I advised them to emigrate east, or west, fifteen miles and assist in eating up what we left."[58]

Unaware that Grant's column could not assist him, Sherman marched south from Memphis on December 19 to attack Vicksburg from the northwest near the confluence of the Yazoo and Mississippi Rivers. Sherman knew he was at a disadvantage, forced to attack heavily fortified heights, but the landscape was even more of an obstacle than expected. As his opponent, Gen. John C. Pemberton, noted, "Swamps, lakes, and bayous, running parallel with the river, intervene between the bank and the hills, and leave but four practicable approaches to the high ground from Snyder's Mills to the Mississippi River."[59] Pemberton understood that he and his men were well protected from an attack.

Despite the obstacles, Sherman followed through on his orders and on December 29 attacked the Chickasaw Bluffs, named after the bayou that ran between the Yazoo and the Mississippi and emptied at the apex of the hairpin curve above Vicksburg. Sherman recalled that his army "met light resistance at all points," skirmishing along Vicksburg's bluffs, "which were found to be strong by nature and by art, and seemingly well defended."[60] The Confederates had supplemented their natural defenses with man-made defenses taken from the landscape's bounty. David Dixon Porter, now an acting rear admiral providing Sherman naval assistance in this operation, recalled, "Acres of wood had been felled, the trees overlapping one another and forming a *chevaux de frise* which extended through the swamp for several miles."[61] Much of the land on which the battle was fought had long ago been cleared of large swaths of its thick forest and vegetation for agricultural purposes, but plenty of tree cover remained. While it provided cover for the Union army, it also proved to be an impediment, as did the swampy land that dominated the landscape. Brig. Gen. George W. Morgan described the problems of moving an army through such territory. In addition to facing the enemy's guns, the troops "had to wade the bayou and tug through the mucky and tangled swamp, under a withering fire of grape, canister, shells and minié-balls, before reaching dry ground."[62] The Confederates held the high ground, well protected by their batteries and by natural defenses. Sherman and his men struggled against the swampy ground, a landscape ill suited for military actions.

The failure of these operations proved a crucial turning point in Grant's approach to strategy. The lessons learned in his first attempt at capturing Vicksburg led him to more innovative tactics that targeted not just the military defenses around the city but also the city's supporting landscape. He learned that all elements of a landscape could be used to military advantage, a lesson that he did not soon forget, and one that would revisit the southern populace time and again during the remainder of the war.[63]

For the time being, however, Grant had to pull back and adjust his plans for taking Vicksburg. Grant's fellow officers recommended that he move his army back to Memphis, regroup, and attempt another attack from the north. Grant knew, however, that such action would be seen as a retreat and that the northern people, already discontented with the war's progress, would not stand for it. He also knew that he had to keep his men busy for their sake, as well as for public appearances. Thus, he reopened work on Williams's abandoned canal.

The initial efforts seemed promising, as one Confederate officer noted in his diary: "There is a Strong probability that the canal opposite here will be made effective in the end—Dredge boats have nearly passed through it."[64] "If the river is not a secesh [secessionist]," a Union soldier remarked, "it will still rather more comfortably enlarge the canal according to our wishes. Judging by how it rises, it will be on our side in the end."[65] But Grant enjoyed no better favor from the Mississippi than his predecessor had. As U.S. general Lucius Hubbard recalled, "a sudden and almost unprecedented rise in the river" broke the dam at the entrance to the canal. "It was hoped notwithstanding this accident that the action of the water as it flowed through the excavated work might aid in securing a navigable channel, but the elements consistently maintained their unfriendly attitude in this case as in those of like efforts previously employed."[66] The same could be said, and was, about Grant's other attempts at engineering success along the Mississippi River.

In addition to the De Soto Point canal, Grant ordered similar projects to be undertaken nearby. In his memoirs, Sherman wrote, "The Mississippi River was very high and rising, and we began that system of canals on which we expended so much hard work fruitlessly: first, the canal at Young's plantation, opposite Vicksburg; second, that at Lake Providence; and third, at the Yazoo Pass, leading into the head-waters of the Yazoo River."[67] Each of these projects was intended to provide a water route around the batteries at Vicksburg, and each involved major manipulation of the landscape though engineering.

The most extensive of these secondary operations was the Yazoo Pass expedition. Grant sent a joint contingent of army and navy under the command of Rear Admiral Porter and Gen. Leonard F. Ross up the Mississippi River to just south of Helena, Arkansas, to determine whether a navigable route through the pass to the Tallahatchie-Yazoo River system could be found, thus providing a northern approach to Vicksburg. To access the pass, Union troops had to destroy the man-made levee obstructing its entrance to the Mississippi. Lt. J. H. Wilson of the Corps of Engineers commanded the troops entrusted with the work. After making two cuts in the embankment fifty feet apart, Wilson exploded a mine "under the mass of earth between the two cuts, simultaneously, shattering and loosening it so that the rapid rush of water, which ensued, soon carried it entirely away."[68] By eleven that night, a crevasse forty yards wide allowed the Mississippi to once again connect to Moon Lake, several miles to the east.

Anticipating this action, the Confederate forces in the area cut the timber alongside the Yazoo Pass to obstruct navigation. This was an effective defensive strategy, according to Lieutenant Wilson, as the "forest being very dense and the growth luxuriant, the trees were of the largest and heaviest kinds." Cut to fall across the stream, the enormous trees, some nine feet long and four feet in diameter, "rendered the barricade of no trifling nature." But the trees were not the only obstacles facing the expedition, as Wilson explained in his official report: "To add to the difficulties of the work the rapid rise of the water from the crevasse at the entrance overflowed the entire country except a very narrow strip of land next [to] the bank, not to exceed in any place fifty yards wide, and frequently not half that."[69] The expedition cleared the stream with the help of cables, windlasses, and other machinery but was ultimately foiled at the well-defended Fort Pemberton, located at the fork of the Yazoo and Yalobusha Rivers.

Frustrated at every turn, the Union forces made a final assault, thinking they could turn their erstwhile nemesis, water, into their ally. Grant recalled that Fort Pemberton "was so little above water that it was thought that a rise of two feet would drive the enemy out. In hope of enlisting the elements on our side, which had been so much against us up to this time, a second cut was made in the Mississippi levee."[70] This plan, too, failed, and the contingent returned to Milliken's Bend (approximately ten miles upriver from De Soto Point) to rejoin Grant's command.

Grant ordered another canal excavated near Duckport, Louisiana, just east of Milliken's Bend. This canal would run west from the Mississippi to Walnut Bayou, providing a water route to New Carthage downriver from Vicksburg. Lt. W. L. B. Jenney was the engineer in charge of that operation. In his report to Capt. Frederick E. Prime, chief engineer of the Department of the Tennessee, he described his methods for clearing the bayou of its vegetal obstructions: "I found it impracticable to pull the willows, (which were numerous,) up by the roots and therefore adopted the method [. . .] of sawing them off below the surface by means of swing saws—hanging from rafts." Jenney was pleased with the saws, as they "answered the purpose well—sawing from 50 to 70 willows (3 in. to 8 in. diameter) per day," requiring only eight men per raft to operate them.[71]

Jenney and his men, however, quickly discovered that their task "was rendered especially dangerous by an enemy that did not carry rebel guns. Poisonous snakes were very numerous that season of the year in that region."[72] The snakes fell from the overhanging branches onto the rafts holding the men and the saws. Despite the success of his crosscut saw contraption (similar to that used in cutting the channel around Island No. 10), the overall expedition seemed to Jenney less promising because the water "had fallen some seven feet, leaving the bottom of the Duck Port Canal some three feet above the surface of the water in the Bayou[,]" and had made the bayou "so narrow near the Canal as to render it useless [. . .] until another high water, not reasonably expected before next winter."[73] Once again, nature—in a variety of forms—thwarted Union plans.

According to Gen. Lucius Hubbard, the Duckport canal was "undertaken with a somewhat subdued enthusiasm." He, like Jenney, noted that the project was nearly complete "when the waters of the Mississippi began to recede and soon seemed to shrink with a rapidity that had characterized their previous propensity to swell." Hubbard was not surprised, nor, he argued, were the men working on the canal. He noted in his memoirs that many of those engaged in the project hailed from northern states along the Mississippi "and were therefore familiar with the erratic habits and sometimes capricious conduct of the old Father of Waters."[74]

The work on the canal was futile, according to Hubbard, and it was neither "soldierly" nor healthy. "Standing in the water up to one's knees and delving in the mud with a spade did not appeal to them as ideal soldierly duty, and the probable results, which seemed to them so clearly apparent, as hardly commensurate with the effort and sacrifice imposed upon them." Describing the "exposures to which the men were subjected," Hubbard suggested that the area "generated all known species of malarial poisons." Furthermore, because the camps occupied low ground, they "became thoroughly saturated by the heavy rains that for a time occurred almost daily, and as a consequence all the scourges to human life that accompany such conditions were an ever present enemy to be met." Smallpox, Hubbard said, "contributed its quota of horror with which the army had to deal. The death rate was excessive, and the floating hospitals along the river banks constituted a large percentage of the fleet that was held in the vicinity for army use."[75] Obviously, Hubbard was no fan of Grant's delaying tactics. He believed that they not only were a waste of time but also wasted valuable resources and men. He was not content to fight against the various elements of the southern environment and wanted instead to fight the Confederate troops.

In this second attempt to turn the river, water, and lots of it, posed the most immediate threat. Sherman recalled that in digging the canal they had to fight "the water of the Mississippi, which continued to rise and threatened to drown us. We had no sure place of refuge except the narrow levee, and such steamboats as remained abreast of our camps." Even Sherman's headquarters "had the water all around it, and could only be reached by a plank-walk from the levee, built on posts."[76] One Union soldier vividly predicted that if the river "rises ten feet more, then everything here will stand under water. The mountain [levee] that is about 12 feet high would protect us but only as long as it would cut us off from the enemy and until the river would flow through wildly, embracing us with its irresistible arms until it had made drinkers of so many with its caresses and cajolery, and then irretrievably given them the draught in which death is found: in a word, 'drowned.'"[77]

But the levees were no sure source of protection. "The war," Grant recalled, "had suspended peaceful pursuits in the South." At De Soto Point this meant that the levees were in disrepair and the "whole country was covered with water."[78] The levees, in their neglected condition, could not withstand the pressure from the river's increased current and broke in several places. James Crozer, a soldier from Company C of the Twenty-Sixth Iowa, described the consequences of one of these breaks: "[A]bove here about 8 miles is a crevass in the Levee. the water is pouring through nicely. they are trying to stop it up with Bags of Sand. if they don't stop it soon they will drown us out."[79]

The Mississippi was not the only source of water Union forces battled. The winter of 1862–63 was a wet one. The frequent rains captured Crozer's attention. In a diary entry dated February 15, 1862, he described a violent storm: "[L]ast night it seemed as though the Mississippi was turned loose instead of a shower. the lightening would fairly blind one[.] after every flash the rain seemed to come down harder & harder[.] I thought it was coming down by the Pailful the way it battered on the tent. I expected every minute that the water would move me as we are camped on low ground[.]"[80] Thomas Barton, a hospital steward with the Fourth West Virginia Volunteer Infantry, recalled that "the rains had been almost incessant along the lower Mississippi, and the low ground was submerged with water." This meant the troops had to camp along the levee, which put them in direct line of the batteries at Vicksburg. To reduce that danger, they were not allowed "any shelter from the heavy rains except the broad canopy of the heavens." The men innovated, however, and "many of the soldiers dug holes in the levee, and covered them with gum blankets, thus living more like wild animals than Union soldiers fighting to maintain the best government on earth." They "bore it patiently," however, "for they knew it to be a dire necessity."[81] Weather and warfare combined to make the Union efforts on De Soto Point difficult at best for the soldiers involved.

Furthermore, Grant noted, "Malarial fevers broke out among the men. Measles and small pox also attacked them."[82] Whether Grant attributed the increased incidence of disease directly to the watery environment is not clear, but his implied link between the decline of "peaceful pursuits" like levee maintenance and the high rate of fevers among his men was not entirely misplaced. Without constant repair, artificial and natural levees are susceptible to erosion, which can lead to flooding in the surrounding area, and stagnant water is prime breeding ground for the *Anopheles* mosquito. Historian Gregg Mitman has suggested, "Rather than consider the mosquito as an entity whose action upon the landscape exists apart from humans, we might instead regard its being and action as dependent upon a relational network of people, things, and forces at any given historical moment in time. Nature is an outcome, not the cause of changes in the land. Like health, it is a product of the interrelationships between and among human and nonhuman actors."[83] Thus, the watery landscape created by the vagaries of war may very well have led to increased rates of malaria among Grant's "unseasoned" soldiers.

Complicating the challenges of the high river and the nearly constant rains even further, the meager protections the men did have against the rising water levels often failed. By February 18 the rain had stopped, but it left a sticky landscape. "Mud [—] you that live in Iowa know nothing about that Article. There is no bottom to the Mud here in Louisiana & it sticks like *Glue*. if one's boots were large enough they might take a whole plantation along with them," Crozer wrote. At times it seemed to Crozer and his comrades that they were fighting the landscape instead of their Confederate enemies. When the sun came out the next day, Crozer wrote, "the boys gave him a rousing cheer."[84]

Crozer, like most of his fellow soldiers, was eager to get on with the real reason he was there. On March 11, 1863, Crozer wrote home about his restlessness to leave the swampy land across from Vicksburg. His regiment had orders to be ready to move immediately to Milliken's Bend, "and there Wait untill our Generals get ready to attack Vicksburg which I hope will be soon, for we are losing more men by Camping around in the Swamps & low land then we would to take half dozen Cities." Crozer suggested that he and his fellow soldiers "would rather pitch in & end this war and go home rather than stay in the *Sunny South* this summer." One reason for this was the weather. Crozer speculated that the summer would be hot, "for we have had a foretaste of it already." He acknowledged that he was "very comfortably fixed," with a "good cot[,] three blankets & a *feather pillow*," but despite the amenities, the rain irritated him. "[W]ho cares how long the *war* last," he wrote, "but somebody does care how much it rains. I think we get more than our fair share of it down here in the good for nothing country[.]"[85]

Finally, in April 1863, the rains let up and the Mississippi calmed its waters, enough so that Grant could make his move. As Sherman stated in his memoirs, "By this time it had become thoroughly demonstrated that we could not divert the main river Mississippi, or get practicable access to the east bank of the Yazoo, in the rear of Vicksburg, by any of the passes; and we were all in the habit of discussing the various chances of the future."[86] The future held uncertainty and risk, but Grant knew that he had to take those risks or fail trying.

In the first season of the Vicksburg campaign, the Mississippi River was both object and obstacle for the Union army. In order to gain control of the river, Federal forces needed to gain control over it, and Grant, like Williams before him, believed in his ability to do just that. But he failed to turn the river, just as Williams had. His men became ill by the thousands and died by the hundreds from diseases endemic to the area. The warm climate and abundance of stagnant water made the swamps around Vicksburg ideal breeding grounds for the mosquitoes that carried deadly fevers. Furthermore, filth and crowd diseases like dysentery, measles, and smallpox ran rampant due to unsanitary and crowded conditions. The troops camped around and laboring in those swamps thus had little chance of escaping infection. Nature—as water, mud, and microbes—stopped Grant and his various canal projects, perhaps more effectively than the Confederates could have. As David Dixon Porter so eloquently and accurately stated, "An Army of thirty thousand men can accomplish a great deal when well directed but it cannot convert swamps into dry land."[87]

In its first attempts to capture Vicksburg, the Union labored under the widely held assumption that much of the natural world had long been subdued and could be made to bend to human will. To be sure, many examples seemed to prove this point, including the canal above Island No. 10, cited in Benson Lossing's *Pictorial Field Book of the Civil War* as "a wonderful monument to the engineering skill and indomitable perseverance of the Americans."[88] But as Edward Bacon observed, "insubordinate" nature refused to obey.[89] Rather than follow the Union drummer boy's beat, nature instead followed its own rhythms, ebbing and flowing according to the seasons.

The landscape was not pro-southern, despite its seeming alliance with the Confederates entrenched among Vicksburg's hills. It was a neutral if active agent in war, one that provided great assistance if approached correctly. Drawing on the lessons learned at Holly Springs and on De Soto Point, Grant's next campaign against Vicksburg would take an entirely different approach both to the landscape and to warfare. By the end of the Union campaigns along the Mississippi, the Union leadership would embrace the hybrid nature of the river's landscape and use it to their advantage.

CHAPTER TWO

Broken Country

Union Campaigns at and around
Vicksburg, 1863

AS WINTER GAVE WAY TO SPRING in 1863, renewed energy infused the Union forces just as it did the verdant Louisiana countryside. The men were eager to leave their camps at Milliken's Bend and De Soto Point and distance themselves from the places they associated with floods, illness, and seemingly futile hard labor. Sherman lamented that after four months of being within sight of the city, they still had not "got at Vicksburg. We have not got on Shore." Sherman reasoned that "no man can wade the Mississipi or the deep sloughs and marshes that surround it." He noted at the time that in order to take Vicksburg, the Union forces would "have to overcome not only an equal number of determined men, however wrongfully engaged, but the natural obstacles of a most difficult Country."[1]

Instead of taking control of the eastern Louisiana landscape, Union efforts to improve that "most difficult Country" transformed it into a deadly environment. Compounding this, by late March the weather had already become quite warm, with at least one soldier complaining in a letter home that as he wrote "the sweat just drops off me."[2] Another soldier reported home from camp at Milliken's Bend that he and his friends were "all well at present, but it is very, very sickly about here."[3] The heat enervated the men, led to dehydration, and further facilitated the spread of fatal illnesses. The floodwaters of the Mississippi, near their peak in March that year, contributed to the sickly conditions and created other logistical problems. When the Mississippi was in flood, the tangled, forested backswamps filled with water and became navigable only by pirogues, the small canoes locals used. For an individual this was not such a problem, but for an army with horses, wagons, and artillery, the swamps and bayous posed an almost insurmountable obstacle.

Grant's best option was to utilize the narrow roads that ran atop the interconnected levee system—the only consistently dry land in the region. One of these roads snaked its way south from the Union camps at Milliken's Bend and

De Soto Point, following the contours of the natural levees along the Round-away Bayou between Richmond and New Carthage, Louisiana. There it joined another levee road along Bayou Vidal and Lake St. Joseph that led through Hard Times, Louisiana, to Disharoon Plantation, where Grant planned to cross the river and finally enter Mississippi. Though Hard Times was less than thirty miles south of De Soto Point as the crow flies, it was a more than seventy-five-mile circuitous march. The route potentially left the army vulnerable to a Confederate attack from the west and stretched the Union supply lines treacherously thin, but there was no viable alternative.

As long as the river remained in flood, however, Louisiana's geography for once would support Union actions. This was clear to Grant after an early reconnaissance mission revealed that the land surrounding the road "was so low and wet that it would not have been practicable to march an army across [it]." The levee, on the other hand, "afforded a good road to march upon."[4] The road followed the dry, cultivated natural levees, with the flooded and forested backswamps on one side for protection and the bayous on the other. The rains that had plagued Grant's army over the winter proved, in at least this instance, a blessing rather than a curse, pushing the Mississippi's level ever higher and creating a nearly impassable barrier between Grant's marching troops and the Confederate forces under Gen. Kirby Smith in western Louisiana.

Despite its potential benefits, the ubiquitous precipitation continued to be a source of discontent for Grant's army. On March 28, 1863, 3rd Sgt. Taylor Peirce of the Twenty-Second Iowa penned the following to his wife: "This is a nice country here but I would not like to live here on account of the water. The land is flat and low. And at this time if it were not for the levees thrown up along the river it would all be under water the surface of the river being higher than the surrounding country."[5] A week later he wrote again to his wife, complaining once more of an excess of water. "We are lying on the levee on the Missi[ssippi] with a mile of water on each side of us and it rained nearly all night last night and such a rain as it puts down here. It is none of your fine northern rains driving before the wind in fine drops and taking a half hour to wet you through but comes down just like pouring it out of a tub."[6]

A good drenching was nothing compared to the problems that stemmed from the rain-generated mud. When Grant finally gave his troops their marching orders on March 29, the levee was a saturated, boggy mess. Manning Force of the Twentieth Ohio recalled that after "six days of plodding" they finally reached their destination nearly seventy miles distant. One day's march took Force six miles over a road "strewn with wrecks of wagons and their loads, and half buried guns. At a halt of some hours the men stood deep in mud, for want of any means of sitting. Yet when we halted at night, every man answered to his name and went laughing to bed on the sloppy ground."[7] Few officers shared Force's amusement, including General Sherman, who despaired of the muck and its likely effect on army supplies. In a letter to his wife, Sherman predicted that the route was a disaster waiting to happen. "The road used is pure alluvium, and three hours of Rain will make it a quagmire over which a wagon could no more pass than in the channel of the Mississipi."[8] The prospect so concerned Sherman that he wrote in a second letter to Ellen a week later, "I look upon the Whole thing as one of the most hazardous & desperate moves of this or any war," complaining about the "narrow difficult Road, liable by a shower to become a quagmire."[9]

The high water levels frustrated Grant's plans at nearly every turn. Lt. S. C. Jones of the Twenty-Second Iowa remarked, "We started our march early on the 16th [of April], marching along the levee with the roaring Mississippi on one side and the submerged swamp on the other. The whole country is a water waste."[10] Floodwaters inundated the lowlands on either side of the levees, and large, impassable crevasses ripped through portions of the levee system, dashing any hope of following a continuous dry route through the region. Grant's engineers kept busy improving the route by building bridges and corduroy roads to facilitate the army's march, but persistent rains throughout April made the work slow and difficult. Thus, the water that protected Grant and his troops from a major Confederate attack also prevented quick and steady progress of the Army of the Tennessee toward its own goal of capturing the elusive Confederate stronghold across the river. The changing environmental conditions required constant adaptation and effort on the part of the engineers to create, even temporarily, a terrain conducive to Union military action.

Union troops were not the only ones affected by the continuous rains, however. As Sherman noted in a letter to his brother John, "All the lands are overflown and [the local farmers] cannot Cultivate."[11] Another Union soldier wrote home that "all the levees on the Mississippi, as well as on the tributaries, are neglected and broken through in several places or even ripped out completely for miles, so that the waters of the mighty stream stretch for a large part, indeed the greater part of the shore and render cultivation of the fields impossible."[12]

In addition to problems caused by water, Grant's troops also endured irritating insects and rising temperatures. Manning Force, who had found levity in the mud earlier in the campaign, failed to find humor in the swarming gnats of Louisiana's swamps. On April 20 he served on a road-building contingent seven miles south of the main camp at Milliken's Bend. "When the sun set," Force wrote, "the leaves of the forest seemed to exude smoke, and the air became a saturated solution of gnats." The insects made eating and sleeping unbearable. Force recalled that the gnats invaded every unprotected orifice and any uncovered bit of flesh: "They swarmed upon our necks, seeming to encircle them with bands of hot iron. Tortured and blinded, we could neither eat nor see." Attempting to bring some relief, the men put cotton around the perimeter of their camp and set it on fire. "The pungent smoke made water stream from our eyes but drove the gnats away. We then supped in anguish, but in peace." Force obtained some mosquito netting, hoping it would protect him as he slept that night. Somewhat successful, Force was one of the few who did sleep; more unfortunate soldiers "set by the fire all night fighting the gnats, and slept the next day."[13]

The gnats Force and his men endured likely were nothing more than a persistent irritation. Heat, on the other hand, posed a real danger. Paired with the humidity of the region and the wool uniforms that were standard issue, the rising thermometer caused some among Grant's men deep concern. Sherman somewhat sardonically quipped, "The weather is becoming hot here, and soon marching will be attended with the risk of sunstroke & fever. The enemy counts on our exhausting ourselves without their taking the trouble to shoot us."[14]

Despite the other threats to his soldiers' health and comfort, Grant's foremost problem was the watery conditions of the Louisiana countryside, which could leave him without a steady source of supplies once he finally got across the Mississippi. Nevertheless, he pushed forward and on April 28, 1863, Union troops began crossing the mighty river that had kept them at bay for over four months. Charles Wilcox of the Thirty-Third Illinois Volunteers recalled the momentous occasion in his diary. That morning he wrote, "The sun arose throwing an impressive splendor upon the exciting scenes of the early morn. [. . .] Every heart here is full of anxiety and emotion; wondering eyes and eyes not altogether tearless, gaze ever and anon upon the *Father of Waters* where lie the formidable fleet of gunboats and rams, transports and barges, the latter heavily loaded with troops whose courage and valor are sufficient when combined with that of the rest of this mighty army, to redeem this lovely valley of the Mississippi from fiends and traitors who are desecrating it."[15]

Over the course of the next twenty-four hours, twenty-two thousand Union troops crossed the Mississippi and began preparing for an arduous overland campaign. The troops were elated and, according to Wilcox, adopted "Onward to Vicksburg!" as their rallying cry upon reaching the eastern side of the river.[16] After nearly four months of being within sight of the city but still unable to approach it, the Army of the Tennessee was eager to make it crumble. Grant realized that the task before him was still dangerous and difficult: "I was now in the enemy's country," Grant recalled in his memoirs, "with a vast river and the strong hold of Vicksburg between me and my base of supplies." His situation was militarily precarious, but, he pointed out, he "was on dry ground on the same side of the river with the enemy."[17]

Simply crossing the river was not enough, however; the city lay thirty miles directly north-northeast of Bruinsburg, the plantation community that served as the debarkation point for the Army of the Tennessee. The most direct route from Bruinsburg to Vicksburg required marching through the swampy lands fronting the Mississippi River, crossing no fewer than four major waterways, and climbing up and down the continuous line of bluffs edging the river's banks, including those protecting the Confederate fortifications at Grand Gulf and Vicksburg. This would have been challenging from a logistical perspective in any case, but because no road followed this path, it was impossible. Thus, Grant had to take a more circuitous route that made the most of existing roads, as poor as they were.

In crossing the Mississippi River, Grant traded one troublesome landscape for another. The new challenge arose not from miles of standing water, as it had across the river in Louisiana, but rather from past hydrological activity. Wherever water raced across the loess highlands of Mississippi, it carved into the landscape an irregular system of ridges and deep ravines. Grant described the territory as a country that "stands on edge," where the roads took the path of the ridges "except where they occasionally pass from one ridge to another." Where left to its own devices, Grant recalled, the local vegetation covered the hills with "a very heavy growth of timber and with undergrowth, and the ravines are filled with vines and canebreaks, almost impenetrable." Unlike the swamps, however, which could and did provide some protection from enemy attack, the erratic terrain of the Mississippi's eastern bank made it "easy," Grant opined, "for an inferior force to delay, if not defeat, a far superior one."[18] The rugged and unfamiliar environment posed as great a threat to Grant's operations as the armed Confederates did.

In addition to the treacherous geography and the entrenched Confederate forces scattered along the path to Vicksburg, another threat forced Grant to divert from his original objective. Gen. Joe Johnston had begun amassing his forces near Jackson. Grant set his course toward the state capital, over sixty miles to the northeast. He had to act quickly, before Confederate reinforcements arrived to support Johnston. Loud clamoring in the North spurred Grant toward decisive action.

Unwilling to slow his progress any more than the difficult terrain required, Grant ordered his men to carry no more than three days' worth of provisions with them "and make the country furnish the balance."[19] Logistically and tactically, cutting loose from his supply line allowed Grant the best advantage; in doing so, however, he risked stranding his entire army in hostile territory with-

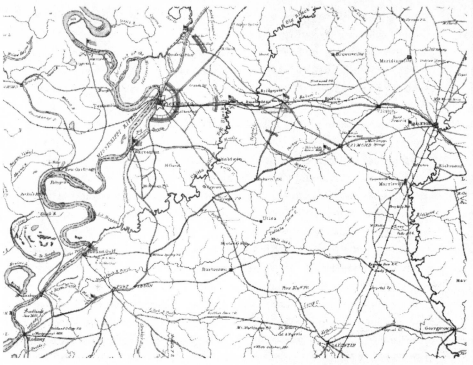

Grant's route to Vicksburg: Detail from "Map Illustrating the Operations of the U.S. Forces against Vicksburg," by J. W. Maedel, U.S. Coast Survey Office. The small U.S. flag in the upper left marks Milliken's Bend, where Grant's troops began their circuitous route to Vicksburg. In the lower left, near an oxbow lake, is Bruinsburg, the debarkation point. Jackson is in the center right and Vicksburg, circled by fortifications, is left of center. Civil War Maps Collection, Geography and Map Division, Library of Congress, g3984v cw0288000.

out adequate supplies. Grant knew the dangers of being without a solid supply line—the Holly Springs debacle the previous year had taught him a difficult but important lesson—but nevertheless, he took the risk that the surrounding countryside would keep his men well supplied.

Grant had good reason to believe his plan to live off the land would work. In contrast to the watery landscape on the western banks of the Mississippi, the higher ground east of the river promised ample provisions. Sherman had noted early in April that at Haines Bluff, just above Vicksburg, he "saw every where cattle, hogs, sheep, poultry and vast cribs of corn. We have Consumed much, and destroyed more," but the Confederate "soldiers are well clad & fat."[20] In deciding to make some of that abundance work to his advantage, Grant hoped to overcome the military limitations the landscape imposed—

primarily the narrow roads perched atop the precarious ridges—and gain increased maneuverability by exploiting the improvements locals had made.

The decision inspired derision and concern from a variety of sources. Confederate president Jefferson Davis and Vicksburg's commanding officer Gen. John C. Pemberton gave the Union forces only a few days until they would have to return to the river for supplies.[21] Grant's officers also questioned the wisdom of the plan, including his most ardent defender. "Even Sherman, who afterwards ignored bases of supplies other than what were afforded by the country [. . .] wrote me from Hankinson's ferry, advising me of the impossibility of supplying our army over a single road," Grant recalled.[22] Grant's plan to live off the land had two goals: to provide necessary provisions for his forces and to undermine the ability of the rebellion to supply the Confederate army.

While on the surface a valuable asset, the Confederacy's agricultural reserves and potential were also a chink in its armor, vulnerable to attack and destruction. One way Union forces exploited this weakness was through raids, in which cavalry troops destroyed or confiscated livestock, produce, tools, and vehicles—anything, that is, that could be useful to the enemy either directly or indirectly. In attacking a region's agricultural productivity, these raids in essence served to undermine its agroecological system more broadly. While early raids were typically small scale, with limited and temporary effects, they would serve as examples for later, more dramatic Union raids in which the consequences would be more profound.

Grant and Sherman saw raids, decried by their victims as savage acts, as acceptable actions in war. In his assessment of Union general Frederick Steele's raid against Greenville, Mississippi, in April 1863, Sherman noted, "The destruction of corn or forage and provisions in the enemy's country is a well-established law of war." He worried, however, that the Union soldiers would become "lawless" if their pillaging was not curbed and that "it injures our men to allow them to plunder indiscriminately the inhabitants of the country." Nevertheless, he asserted that "these devastating expeditions are the certain and inevitable consequences" of rebellious actions. In this particular case, he applauded Steele for trying to spare the populace from utter starvation. "I most heartily approve of your purpose to return to families their carriages, buggies, and farming tools, wherewith to make a crop. War at best is barbarism, but to involve all—children, women, old and helpless—is more than can be justified."[23] Sherman would later become less accommodating, but in early 1863 he believed that only those directly engaged in supporting the enemy or opposing the Union forces deserved to be targets of such actions.

Foraging quickly revealed itself to be a powerful tool in Grant's arsenal. He wrote to Sherman one week into the march that his men "started from

Bruinsburg with an average of about two days' rations, and received no more from our own supplies for some days. Abundance was found in the mean time. Some corn meal, bacon, and vegetables were found, and an abundance of beef and mutton."[24] In ordering his troops to live off the land, Grant effectively initiated a *chevauchée*, turning the improvements locals had made to his advantage while simultaneously reducing the Confederacy's control over the same.

In wars past, the *chevauchée* was used to take the horrors of war to enemy civilians. In reviving the strategy, however, Grant explicitly forbade his troops from molesting private citizens and from requisitioning property with no military potential. Grant urged Gen. Stephen A. Hurlbut, who conducted supporting operations in the northern part of the state, to "[i]mpress upon the cavalry the necessity of keeping out of people's houses or taking what is of no use to them in a military point of view." Anything that could be used against Union troops, however, was subject to confiscation or destruction. The cavalry, Grant ordered, "must live as far as possible off the country through which they pass, and destroy corn, wheat crops, and everything that can be made use of by the enemy in prolonging the war. Mules and horses can be taken to supply all our wants, and where it does not cause too much delay, agricultural implements may be destroyed." "In other words," Grant wrote, "cripple the rebellion in every way, without insulting women and children."[25]

Crippling the rebellion required destroying the means by which southerners, Confederate or not, managed and improved their environment. Destroying agricultural implements and taking or destroying agricultural products was not just an attack against Confederate resources but one against the agro-ecological foundations on which the Confederacy rested. Grant's orders to undermine the Confederate war effort in these ways potentially decreased his own chances of success in that they transformed the very landscape on which he himself proposed to depend.

A further complication was the very nature of the region's hybrid landscape. The swamps and bayous that intersected cultivated land made cavalry raids like Hurlbut's particularly difficult. A similar operation, led by Col. B. H. Grierson, was one of the most effective operations conducted under Grant's raiding orders and "one of the most thoroughly successful cavalry raids of the whole war."[26] Grierson's cavalry ran from La Grange, Tennessee, south and east to Starkville, Mississippi, through Newton Station (near Meridian), then west toward Grand Gulf, and finally to Baton Rouge, Louisiana, where he joined the Union forces camped there. Though Grierson did encounter some Confederate forces along his path, the geography was the worst impediment he faced. Swamps, mud, rivers, and rain made movements difficult. Grierson reported on May 5, 1863, that his troops maneuvered "through a dismal swamp nearly belly-deep in mud, and sometimes swimming our horses to cross streams." He also reported that outside of Louisville, Mississippi, they "struck another swamp, in which, crossing it, as we were obliged to, in the dark, we lost several animals drowned, and the men narrowly escaped the same fate."[27] Nevertheless, in just sixteen days, Grierson's cavalry covered nearly six hundred miles, destroying two major railroads, telegraph lines, and other property along the way and capturing "a number of horses and mules."[28] His raid, though not intended to collect supplies as later raids would, was of crucial importance to Grant's ultimate success and served as a prime example of the raiding strategy's utility. The raid diverted Confederate attention from Grant's intended target, even if only temporarily. He made good use of this lesson later in the Vicksburg campaign and the war.

As Grierson's and Hurlbut's forces drove through the northern and eastern sectors of the state, Grant left his erstwhile nemesis, the Mississippi River, behind. Moving east from Bruinsburg on the Port Gibson Road, Grant's troops scaled the bluffs at Windsor and encountered terrain that geographer Warren Grabau has called "a tactician's nightmare."[29] The system of ridges and ravines stretched from Bruinsburg to Port Gibson, where the first battle of the campaign took place on May 1. After that engagement, Grant reported to General-in-Chief Henry Halleck that the fighting at Port Gibson "continued all day, and until after dark, over the most broken country I ever saw." The irregular topography and dense vegetation made it "impossible to engage any considerable portion of our forces at any one time."[30] One Union soldier in the thick of the action recalled that the Confederates "had the advantage of knowing the ground and kept hid in the cane breaks all the time just standing far enough in to keep out of sight so that they could fire out at us." The tangled vegetation provided the Confederates little protection, however. "The slaughter on their side was dreadful for the number engaged," the soldier wrote, noting that "our English rifles sent their Leaden messengers in and thinned their ranks as if the plague was amongst them."[31] Port Gibson ended as a Union victory, with the Confederate forces falling back toward Jackson.

As they pressed onward toward Jackson across the tangled, tortuous ridges, the Union forces left behind very little to attest to the region's successful agroecological system. Historian James McPherson noted, "Although civilians were going hungry in Mississippi, Grant was confident that his soldiers would not."[32] In his memoirs, Grant recalled, "Beef, mutton, poultry and forage were found in abundance. Quite a quantity of bacon and molasses was also secured from the country, but bread and coffee could not be obtained in quantity sufficient for all the men." While every plantation had mule-powered mills, only those troops nearest the mills reaped the benefits, and "the majority of the command was destined to go without bread until a new base was established on the Yazoo above Vicksburg."[33] Responding to a report from Sherman, who was concerned about the lack of food for his own troops, Grant wrote, "You are in a country where the troops have already lived off the people for some days, and may find provisions more scarce, but as we get upon new soil they are more abundant, particularly in corn and cattle."[34] While this may not have reassured Sherman about his prospects for feeding his own troops, Grant's observation attests to the efficacy of the tactic.

The two armies met again at Raymond, a settlement about fifteen miles southwest of the capital. Torrential rains delayed the Federal attack and made maneuvering over the now muddy and broken ground almost impossible.[35] Despite the weather delays, this encounter, too, was a victory for the Federal troops. Grant ordered his troops to move quickly to Jackson and destroy the main railroad and any war-related industry in the city. Once again, rain impeded Union progress. Grant recalled that it "rained torrents during the night of the 13th and the fore part of the day of the 14th. The roads were intolerable, and in some places on Sherman's line, where the land was low, they were covered more than a foot deep with water. But the troops never murmured."[36] Likewise, Gen. John McClernand reported to Grant, "Everything seems to be going on well, though the tremendous rain-storms of last evening and today have made the march laborious and less expeditious than it would have been under more favorable circumstances."[37]

Despite the rain and the perilous terrain, Grant accomplished his goal at Jackson, left the city destroyed and in disarray, and turned due east to his ultimate aim, Vicksburg. His march would not go unobstructed, either by human or by natural forces. The Union troops had to cross numerous bayous and rivers and get around Confederate troops on Champion's Hill. The hill was a "considerable eminence," nearly one mile wide, with steep sides "roughened by knobs, gullied by ravines, and covered with forest."[38] Although "not more than 70 or 80 feet in height," Union general Francis Vinton Greene noted, it was "quite a prominent feature in an otherwise flat landscape."[39] The Confederate forces under General Pemberton had control of the hill, which, as Grant stated, "whether taken by accident or design, was well selected." Grant noted that the hill "commanded all the ground in range."[40] Nevertheless, the Union troops once again defeated the Confederate forces, pushing them back to the Big Black River, the final obstacle between Grant and Vicksburg.

Union and Confederate soldiers collided where the river turned west from a generally southerly direction. The Confederate forces had crossed the bridge

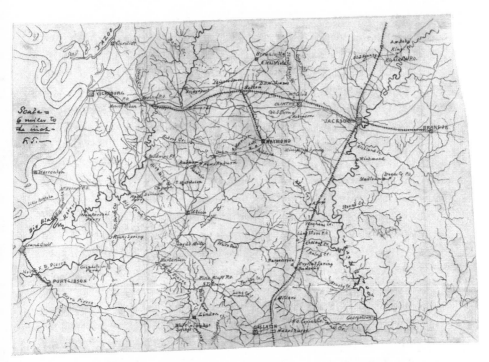

Waterways between Jackson and Vicksburg: Map showing the myriad rivers, streams, and bayous, as well as transportation routes, in the area of U.S. operations in Mississippi between Vicksburg (upper left) and Jackson (center right). Grand Gulf and Port Gibson are in the lower left of the map. Civil War Maps Collection, Geography and Map Division, Library of Congress, g3984v cws00117.

and were well positioned on the western side of the river. The Union troops were on the east side, which Grant described as "a low bottom, sometimes overflowed at very high water." A bayou ran through the area as well, but at the time of battle it held only one or two feet of water. To retard Union advance, Pemberton's men cut down some of the thick timber that lined the bayou, obstructing it. They also built a parapet out of cotton bales and dirt and "thoroughly commanded [the terrain] from the height west of the river." In contrast, the Union soldiers had only "a strip of uncleared land" at the upper end of the bayou for cover from Confederate fire.[41] Despite these obstacles, the Federal troops succeeded in pushing the Confederates farther back toward Vicksburg. Once again victorious, the Army of the Tennessee crossed the Big Black and marched toward the city that had taunted them for months as they sat across the Mississippi digging ditches.

When Federal forces reached Vicksburg, less than three weeks after crossing the Mississippi, they were little worse for wear despite several heated battles along the 108-mile march. Capturing the fortified city, however, would prove no easy task. Sgt. Maj. E. Paul Reichhelm of the Third Missouri Volunteer Infantry noted in his diary, "Vicksburg—a fortress by nature—strengthened on all in any way accessible points by a year's hard and skillful labor of the rebels, may well defy any sort of 'brilliant dash' or sudden attack. [. . . It] can only be taken by means of gradual and skillful siege. Not by sacrificing thousands of the brave sons of their country in vain and destructive battle."[42] Gen. Francis Greene likewise recalled, "The advantages of position were all on the side of the Confederates, they being in their own country, with which they were perfectly familiar, and which afforded admirable opportunities for defence." The Union forces, on the other hand, "were entirely ignorant of the country," according to Greene, "and were dependent for supplies upon seventy miles of wretched road, through overflowed lands, passing within a short distance of the Confederate position, and thus open to attack at all times."[43] Grant and his officers were not ignorant of Vicksburg's geography, nor did they rely solely on a distant supply depot for provisions. The Union forces were still at a disadvantage, however, as Greene and others suggested. Just as they could not scale the imposing bluffs that protected Vicksburg from a river attack, the Union army could not simply storm the fortifications surrounding the eastern edge of the city, try as they did.

In building the city's defenses, the Army of Vicksburg made excellent use of the topography. S. H. Lockett, Pemberton's chief engineer, described the terrain that served as his template: "The series of irregular hills, bluffs, and narrow, tortuous ridges, apparently without system or order, that constitute the strong defensive position of Vicksburg, raised some two hundred feet above the level of the river, owe their character, with all their strangely complex arrangement and configuration, to the natural erosive action of water on the fine, homogeneous, calcareous silt peculiar to the lias of bluff formation."[44] Lockett stated that he spent a month "reconnoitering, surveying, and studying the complicated and irregular" landscape. "No greater topographical puzzle was ever presented to an engineer," he declared, noting that the "difficulty of the situation was greatly enhanced by the fact that a large part of the hills and hollows had never been cleared of their virgin forest of magnificent magnolia-trees and dense undergrowth of cane." Lockett remembered that initially "it seemed impossible to find anything like a general line of commanding ground surrounding the city; but careful study gradually worked out the problem."[45]

As Grant recalled, the Confederate defenses ran "from near the head of one gully nearly straight to the head of another, and an outer work triangular in shape, generally open in the rear, was thrown up on the point; with a few men in this outer work, they commanded the approaches to the main line completely."[46] Gen. Lucius Hubbard also recognized the strength of Vicksburg's defenses: "The topography of the locality rendered Vicksburg naturally very strong as a defensive position, and to this advantage were added the most complete artificial works that experienced and accomplished military engineers could devise. Monster forts, connected by elaborate earthworks, crowned the heights of Walnut Hills, and impenetrable abatis of fallen timber guarded all approaches."[47] Even the common soldier could appreciate the natural benefits Vicksburg's defenses claimed. One noted, "It is certainly the roughest country I ever seen. The hills are not so very high, but the whole country is nothing but a succession of hills and hollows [. . .]. The Rebels have forts thrown up about 200 or 300 yds. apart all along their line, with heavy guns mounted and forts in the rear of these, making the place almost impregnable. I do not believe that another place in the country could be found that is so naturally fortified. [. . .] The hills in places rise abruptly, and look almost as though they had been drawn up purposefully for a fort."[48] Despite these heavy defenses, on May 19 and again on May 22, Union troops rushed Vicksburg's fortifications, hoping to capture the city in a blaze of glory.

The assault was one of the most fruitless of the war. It verged on the suicidal and resulted in widespread casualties. Some regiments suffered comparatively little, like the Fifth Minnesota Volunteers, which, according to Hubbard, "made its assault under circumstances that saved it from very serious loss." He attributed this to the "broken nature of the ground in its front, with its entanglement of fallen timber and dense thicket, [which] made it impossible to move in line of battle." Marching along a road obstructed by earthworks and *chevaux de frise*, the regiment made up the rear of the line and therefore was not exposed to the blistering fire from Vicksburg's Confederate defenders. Other regiments were not as fortunate. The Eleventh Missouri, led by Gen. Joseph Mower, marched at the front of a column that also included the Fifth Minnesota. Mower's regiment suffered terribly and looked "as if melted down, by the fire in front and on both flanks that was concentrated upon it." Hubbard recalled that in addition to the obstacles posed by terrain and fortification "[t]he heaps of dead and wounded men of themselves formed an obstruction difficult to surmount." The advancing troops eventually were ordered to "desist and seek cover," most finding safety "among the ravines and behind the felled timber on either side of the road."[49]

Sherman, too, commented on the futile nature of the attack. "The Forts are well built to command the Roads," he observed in a letter to his wife, "and the hills and valleys are so abrupt and covered with fallen trees, standing trunks and Canebrake that we are in a measure confined to the Roads. We have made two distinct assaults along the Line, but the heads of Colums are swept away as Chaff thrown from the hand on a windy day." Soon after the assault ended, the Union troops were "hard at work with roads and trenches, taking all possible advantage of the Shape of the ground," preparing for a different approach at toppling the fortress city.[50]

Reporting to Halleck, Grant noted, "The nature of the ground about Vicksburg is such that it can only be taken by a siege."[51] He reiterated as much in a letter to Gen. Stephen A. Hurlbut. "Vicksburg is so strong by nature and so well fortified that a sufficient force cannot be brought to bear against it to carry it by storm against the present garrison. It must be taken by a regular siege or by starving out the garrison."[52] Grant emulated his Confederate opponents and made excellent use of the topography around the city in laying out his forces for the operation. Using the ravines as ready-made trenches and the ridges as natural earthworks, he put all his engineer officers to work fortifying the Union positions and "directed that all officers who had graduated at West Point, where they had necessarily to study military engineering, should in addition to their other duties assist in the work."[53] The task was dangerous as well as difficult because the Union and Confederate lines were never more than six hundred yards apart.

Such proximity also presented other engineering opportunities. "Given the closeness of the opposing lines and the very hilly terrain at Vicksburg," historian David G. Martin wrote, "it is not surprising that enterprising Yankee engineers determined to dig a tunnel (or mine) under Confederate lines in an attempt to blow them up."[54] At about three thirty in the afternoon on June 25, after a month of digging, the Union forces exploded the mine underneath the Great Redoubt that guarded the Jackson Road. Brig. Gen. Andrew Hickenlooper, chief engineer of the Seventeenth Corps, recalled the mine's explosion: "At the appointed moment it appeared as though the whole fort and connecting outworks commenced an upward movement, gradually breaking into fragments and growing less bulky in appearance, until it looked like an immense fountain of finely pulverized earth, mingled with flashes of fire and clouds of smoke, through which could occasionally be caught a glimpse of some dark objects,—men, gun-carriages, shelters, etc."[55] Though the explosion destroyed the center of the Confederate fort, it did not open a breach in the larger fortifications, nor did it cause many Confederate casualties. The Vicksburg mine, according to Martin, "was more notable for its construction and expectations than for any military advantage it gained."[56]

More effective than Grant's attempts at engineering a victory were his tenacity and perseverance in siege operations. Preparing for a long investment

Siege of Vicksburg: An illustration showing Federal siege operations against Vicksburg. The flag on the hill indicates a Confederate position. Note the difficulty of approach, not only because of terrain but also due to vegetation. Prints and Photographs Division, Library of Congress, LC-DIG-pga-01871.

of the city, Grant wrote a series of orders instructing various divisions to scour the countryside for provisions and any outlying Confederate forces. Grant sent Maj. Gen. Frank P. Blair's division into the area between the Yazoo and the Big Black Rivers, where the "country was rich and full of supplies of both food and forage," and instructed the men to "take all of it." Grant ordered the cattle "to be driven in for the use of our army, and the food and forage to be consumed by our troops or destroyed by fire; all bridges were to be destroyed, and the roads rendered as nearly impassable as possible."[57] Likewise, Grant's orders to Brig. Gen. Joseph Mower read, "Destroy or bring in for your own use all the forage, provisions, and transportation you can reach."[58] And to Brig. Gen. Nathan Kimball: "Collect all the forage, cattle, and provisions you can, and destroy what you cannot bring away. It is important that the country be left so that it cannot subsist an army passing over it. Wagons, horses, and mules should be taken from the citizens to keep them from being used with the Southern Army."[59] Summing up his plans, Grant wrote to Henry Halleck, "I will make a waste of all the country I can."[60]

Under these new orders, the Union troops enjoyed ample supplies, as wild fruits and cultivated crops were plentiful. The soils around Vicksburg were some of the most fertile in the area. In the course of its frequent floods, the Mississippi River laid down the thick, black alluvial soil at the base of Vicksburg's hills, and winds coming from places farther west dropped the yellowish loess topsoil on the heights when they hit the uplift of the Mississippi ridge. Alexander Abrams, a Confederate soldier turned journalist, noted in the *Vicksburg Whig* that the city's outlying areas were "very fruitful" and that a "very extensive crop of corn and other cereals had been planted."[61] A local woman reported in June 1863 that "the whole wheat crop is splendid every where in this immediate Neighborhood, many have never had as good, not a partical of rust & hardly a faulty grain, and every where in Texas, Alabama, Georgia, it is good. The corn is beautiful thus far and although so many horses have been taken still the ploughing is going on as usual."[62]

In a letter home soldier William Henry Harrison Clayton wrote about the figs, peaches, blackberries, and corn he found nearby.[63] Sherman, too, remarked that "[b]lackberries are now as abundant as ever an army could ask, and are most excellent—Apples & peaches & figs are ripening, and of all these there will be an abundance even for our host. Corn too is in silk & tassel."[64] Confederate captain Gabriel M. Killgore had great confidence in his home landscape's fertility and the Confederacy's ability to feed its troops and people. He noted in his diary on April 6 and again on April 30 that Pemberton's army would withstand the siege, and the Confederacy the war, because supplies would be replenished from the coming year's crop.[65]

Grant had no intention of allowing this to occur. Requisitioning all food, forage, and equipment in the country surrounding Vicksburg was the basis of his operations and accomplished several things. First, although the Union army established a secure supply base on the Yazoo River upon reaching Vicksburg, the provisions taken from the region supplemented the standard rations with fresh meat and produce. Second, by appropriating all available provisions, the Army of the Tennessee left the Confederates in Vicksburg no means of replenishing their own stores. Finally, it sent a powerful message to the civilian population both in and around Vicksburg that the Federal forces were in control.

The Union troops may have had command over the fruits of the landscape, but other aspects of the environment remained unharnessed. The locals, especially, were well aware of the dangers posed by Mississippi's climate, environment, and disease regime and predicted Grant's ultimate failure. According to the *Natchez Weekly Courier*, "Gentlemen owning plantations on which Grant's army was encamped before Vicksburg, declared that his soldiers would perish for the lack of water, or die like sheep with the rot, from drinking such as they could obtain." Furthermore, the paper reported, "[W]e were told that the malarious diseases of the climate would decimate his army, and compel him to raise the siege."[66] Similarly, the *Vicksburg Daily Citizen* reported that the Federal troops "are considerably on the sick list. Fever, dysentery and disgust are their companions, and Grant is their master." The *Citizen* claimed the "boys" were tired of "the earth delving, the burrowing, the bad water and hot weather."[67]

Although the *Citizen's* report was mostly bluster, such challenges did in fact exist for the Union soldiers investing the city. George Remley reported home, "This is a beautiful country and were it not for war & its ravages, I would like to live here." However, he wrote, "The water we have here is very scarce and of an inferior quality. I hope we will not have to drink it long."[68] Taylor Peirce wrote, "The days are no hotter here than in Iowa but every day is hot alike. The nights are quite cool and if it was not so we would be unable to do anything at all. For the heat is so weakening that it seemes impossible for a man or at least one of us to muster up energy enough to cook a little victuals."[69] J. W. Greenman of the Eighth Wisconsin wrote in his diary on June 10, "The weather was very warm and as we marched across fields and through the Corn which was as high as our heads many of the men were overcome with the heat. The Brigade that was with us was composed of men who had no experience of the Southern climate and many of them died of sunstroke."[70] Another wrote, "Indeed unless you have experience[d] it, you can not *even imagine* the enervating effect that the hot and sultry weather of this Southern climate, has upon one's system. The entire system—mental, physical and nervous—is weakened and prostrated to such a degree that I never felt, nor even had any idea of before."[71]

Despite the dire predictions of the Confederate sympathizers and the complaints of Union soldiers, the besiegers fared much better than the besieged. In cooperation with Rear Admiral Porter's Mississippi fleet, Grant kept up an almost constant shelling and prevented any supplies from reaching the Confederate garrison—and the civilians—trapped in the hill city, thus turning the erstwhile advantages into severe limitations. Many of Vicksburg's civilian residents took refuge in caves carved out of the loess hillsides on which the city was built, but their homes, businesses, and material possessions enjoyed no such protection from the mortars and shells pummeling the city.

As early as 1862, Confederate troop strength in the city reached over ten thousand men. The city's resources could not support such large numbers, and the strain on them began to take a larger toll than Union shelling. Drinking water and adequate accommodations were the first shortages to arise; food and medicine followed shortly after.[72] The situation grew worse as the siege wore on and additional troops—ultimately numbering around twenty-five thousand—moved behind the city's fortifications. According to Vicksburg historian Pamela Lea Grillis, "Diseases ran rampant. Measles, dysentery, lice and horrible skin diseases were epidemic."[73] In mid-July 1863 Sherman commented that he saw "dead animals lying unburied" and "acres of hospital tents," almost all flying the yellow quarantine flag.[74]

Starvation, too, took its toll. *Harper's Weekly* reported that "Pemberton had expressed his determination never to surrender the town till the last dog had been eaten and the last man slain." By the first of June that was not a far-off possibility: the Confederate soldiers' rations had been reduced by then to a mere fourteen and a half ounces of food per day.[75] By the end of the month, again according to *Harper's Weekly*, the city's beef supply was gone "and mule-meat was resorted to as a last expedient."[76] Civilians had to fend for themselves in the face of dwindling provisions. One woman wrote in her diary on May 28, 1863, that she believed "all the dogs and cats must be killed or starved: we don't see any more pitiful animals prowling around." On July 3 she wrote, "provisions so nearly gone, except the hogshead of sugar, that a few more days will bring us to starvation indeed. Martha says rats are hanging dressed in the market for sale with mule-meat: there is nothing else."[77] The July 2, 1863, edition of the local paper, printed on scavenged wallpaper, reported on a party hosted by some enterprising citizens who had found a new source of meat, not for sale at local stores: cats.[78] The paper made light of the situation, warning local cats to beware. Whether meant to bring some levity to an otherwise bleak period or as a true account of what Vicksburg's citizens were reduced to, the story reveals the extent of deprivation those behind the city's fortifications suffered.

Just seven weeks after the siege began, and one day after the Union victory at Gettysburg, Vicksburg capitulated. The *Natchez Weekly Courier* reported, "In spite of water, climate, disease, and repeated repulses, Grant compelled Pemberton to surrender."[79] The white flag "was a glorious sight to officers and soldiers," Grant recalled. "The troops felt that their long and weary marches, hard fighting, ceaseless watching by night and day, in a hot climate, exposure to all sorts of weather, to diseases, and worst of all, to the gibes of many Northern papers that came to them saying all their suffering was in vain, that Vicksburg would never be taken, were at last at an end and the Union sure to be saved."[80] In a poignant note to his wife in Iowa, Union soldier Taylor Peirce wrote, "To day no sound occurs to break the stillness. All is quiet and it seems as if all nature felt relieved."[81]

Peirce was not the only person to recognize that nature was as much involved in the conflict as its human participants were. As the Army of the Tennessee set out to conquer Vicksburg, Sherman remarked that they "had to fight a senseless clamor at the North, as well as a determined foe and the obstacles of Nature."[82] Time and again the human actors invoked nature to protect, assist, and obey them. It was alternately cursed for being obstinate and troublesome or praised for its bounty and beneficence. Nature actively participated in the war, but it sympathized with neither the Blue nor the Gray. Heat, weather, disease, terrain—each affected Union and Confederate alike, though whether as enemy or ally depended on perspective. Vicksburg's steep bluffs and eroded loess hills initially served Pemberton's army as a sort of ready-made fortress, handily keeping the Union forces out. In the end, however, those same features became prison walls, trapping the Confederates inside.

Vicksburg felt the consequences of war acutely, as did its surrounding hinterland. Whether intentionally or inadvertently, armies affect the environments through which they pass. Grant recalled on the eve of crossing the Mississippi that his army "had nearly exhausted the country, along a line drawn from Lake Providence to opposite Bruinsburg."[83] Taylor Peirce recorded in one of his many letters home, "We live on the fat of the land. I tell you the fair part of rebledom looks black at us yankees when we make them shell out their good things for our benefit." Peirce noted that the area was "being laid waste so that there will be nothing raised here this year and what the people is to do for something to eat is more than I can tell. They say that their is not more than two weeks provisions here and some of them is being fed by Govt now." The devastation disturbed Peirce, enough for him to claim, "Truly war is a terrible calamity to any land when it exists and I pray god that it will soon end in our beloved country and that we may once more enjoy the blessing of Peace."[84]

Throughout the Vicksburg campaigns, troops cut down trees for firewood and defensive fortifications and splintered them with rifle and cannon fire. Manning Force recalled a scene at the battle of Raymond: "I remember noticing the forest leaves, cut by rifle balls, falling in thick eddies, still as snow flakes."[85] Similarly, Grant recalled the fate of a stunted oak tree that witnessed Pemberton's surrender: "It was but a short time before the last vestige of its body, root and limb had disappeared, the fragments taken as trophies."[86] In the face of such destruction, however, daily life retained some semblance of normality. In a moment of lyrical sentiment, Sherman juxtaposed the beauty of nature's resilience with the violent character of war. "The trees are now in full leaf—the black & blue birds sing sweetly and the mockingbird is frantic with Joy—the Rose and violet, the beds of verbina and Mignonette, planted by fair hands now in exile from their homes occupied by the Rude Barbarian, bloom as fair as though Grim war had not torn with violent hands, all the vestiges of what a few short months ago were the homes of people as good as ourselves."[87] Similarly, a soldier from Missouri wrote home about nature's persistence. "The weather is very fine," Nehemiah Davis Starr wrote in February, "and just like spring should be. The ground is beginning to be covered with grass and trees are out in bud, the wild magnolias with their heavy foliage green as can be make a magnificent shade, so that the scenery here is rather more romantic than war like."[88] One Vicksburg resident noted in her diary that during the siege a pair of chimney swallows took up residence in her parlor chimney. "The concussion of the house often sends down parts of their nest," she wrote, "which they patiently pick up and reascend with."[89] As the chimney swallows' persistent rebuilding attests, human wars can be more disruption than catastrophe for much of the nonhuman world. During and after the conflict, alligators continued to slink silently through the swamps, and blackberries still grew wild along the deep ravines.

The toll of the Vicksburg campaigns was less a wholesale destruction of nature than a reorganization of the city's landscape. More than most cities, Vicksburg depended on the Mississippi River for its survival. It identified with, built on, and actively developed a working relationship with the river. The agreement between the city and the river was inherently tenuous, as the river frequently and without warning shifted its course. Union attempts to hurry this process along met with fierce opposition from the city and the river, but had they succeeded, Vicksburg would have been forced to reevaluate and redefine its relationship with the Mississippi.

The river was only one element of nature with which Vicksburg negotiated, however. The land, too, provided the city with wealth and meaning, and Vicksburg's residents and outlying population firmly grasped the importance of the land to their lives. The day Vicksburg capitulated Sherman wrote to Grant, "The farmers and families out here acknowledge the magnitude of this loss, and now beg to know their fate. All crops are destroyed and cattle eaten up."[90] In the aftermath of the siege Sherman made quick work of the region between the river city and the state capital. In a telegraph report to Grant, Sherman recounted his "fine progress," assuring his superior that not only was the population "subjugated" and "cry[ing] aloud for mercy" but also that "the land is devastated for thirty miles around."[91]

More injurious even than the physical destruction to the landscape was the dismantling of the system that created that landscape. The South was a slave economy, its productive capacity dependent on the continuance of the "peculiar institution." Slavery infused every aspect of southern society, impinging even on the lives of those who owned no slaves. Disruption of the slave system produced obvious, widespread, and lasting effects on the relationship southerners had with the land. Signs of this manifested early on in the campaigns against Vicksburg, especially on the Louisiana side of the river. In March 1863 Union soldier Taylor Peirce noted, "The whole farming country here seems deserted. I do not think there will be enough raised here this year to support anything. The negroes are all run off and the plantations deserted and are fast being laid waste by the soldiers."[92] Another soldier commented from New Carthage, Louisiana, in April, "When 'massa runs away,' the negroes do not pretend to put in crops or do any kind of work. The cotton crop is entirely neglected and the planters seem to have been giving corn their undivided attention, but now even that is interrupted in this section of the country."[93]

Although emancipation had only recently become a formal goal of Lincoln's administration, disruption of the slave system promised to be a productive avenue toward destroying the Confederacy. One Confederate officer from Mississippi told his wife, "[I]f the negroes are freed the country, as a general thing, is not worth fighting for at all. We will be compelled to abandon it and seek some more congenial climate." Later that year he wrote, "I know that this country without slave labor would be wholly worthless, a barren waste and desolate plain—we can only live and exist by this species of labor: and hence I am willing to continue to fight to the last."[94] On March 31, 1863, Henry Halleck informed Grant of the government's policy "to withdraw from the enemy as much productive labor as possible." The rationale for the policy maintained that as long as slaves labored in the fields, white men were free to support the armed rebellion. "Every slave withdrawn from the enemy," Halleck explained to Grant, "is equivalent to a white man put *hors de combat*."[95]

Halleck saw a direct military correlation between the productive labor of slaves and the strength of the Confederate army. Without slaves to grow the cotton that financed the Confederacy's war efforts, or the grains and other comestibles that fed the Confederate troops, the Confederacy would crumble. Halleck's opinion stemmed not from a humanitarian point of view sympathetic to the plight of slaves but rather from a purely pragmatic perspective. Halleck asserted, "[I]t is the policy of the Government to use the negroes of the South, as far as practicable, as a military force, for the defense of forts, depots, &c." He urged his officers to take advantage of the slaves' labor and perceived acclimation to the climate and diseases of the South; if the slaves "can be used to hold points on the Mississippi during the sickly season, it will afford much relief to our armies." Halleck postulated that slaves were like any other resource and "may be made instruments of good or evil. In the hands of the enemy, they are used with much effect against us; in our hands, we must try to use them with the best possible effect against the rebels."[96]

Grant wasted no time in implementing the policy, including it in his orders to Frederick Steele on April 11, 1863. "It is our duty," Grant exclaimed, "to use every means to weaken the enemy, by destroying their means of subsistence, withdrawing their means of cultivating their fields, and in every other way possible." In case the procedure for accomplishing these goals was unclear, Grant explicitly spelled it out. He ordered Steele to "destroy or bring off all the corn and beef-cattle" and to "encourage all negroes, particularly middle-aged males, to come within our lines."[97] In June Grant ordered Lt. Col. Samuel J. Nasmith to "destroy all bridges and corn-cribs, [and] bring away all negroes disposed to follow you." Grant admonished Nasmith to keep his troops in line and to prevent plundering but instructed him to make it clear to the locals that if Confederate troops "make raids necessary, all their crops and means of raising crops will be destroyed."[98] Grant was directly ordering his troops to attack the agroecological foundations of the area, thereby undermining the local residents' (and, by association, the Confederate government's) control over the natural environment.

The results of this policy were not lost on those who suffered from it, nor on those who implemented it. In a letter written during the siege, Sherman admired the southerners' "heroic courage," but he recognized that "they cannot stay the hand of destruction, that is now setting adrift their Slaves, occupying with fruitless muskets the adult whites, consuming and wasting their fields and improvements, destroying their roads, bridges, and the labor and fruits of near a century of undisturbed prosperity."[99] Agriculture was the cornerstone of the South's relationship with the natural world, its success the result of constant and delicate negotiation between humans and their environment. Grant's revival of the *chevauchée* preyed on the tenuous nature of this arrangement, bringing chaos to what had been (albeit imperfectly) under control. "We have ravaged the Land," Sherman reflected, "and have sent away half a million negros so that this country is paralyzed and cannot recover its lost strength in twenty years."[100] Despite its obvious hyperbole, Sherman's assessment was based in truth. In targeting everything southerners employed in pursuit of agricultural productivity—tools, storage buildings, animals, and slaves—the Army of the Tennessee attacked the Confederacy's most visible symbol of power: its agroecological system. It proved a very effective strategy against Vicksburg and became one that Union military leadership would endorse in subsequent campaigns.

Grant's victory at Vicksburg earned him national acclaim as well as the command of all Union forces. In March 1864 Congress revived the rank of lieutenant general, previously held only by George Washington, and conferred it on Grant. As the new general-in-chief of the Union army, he lost no time in formulating a comprehensive master plan for winning the war, concentrating on defeating the four major Confederate armies remaining in the field. Grant joined Gen. George Meade and the Army of the Potomac in a full-bore effort to defeat Gen. Robert E. Lee's Army of Northern Virginia in Richmond and ordered Benjamin Butler at Petersburg, Virginia, to put pressure on Lee from the south. At the same time, Grant sent Sherman from his base in Chattanooga to oust Joe Johnston from Atlanta, ordered Nathaniel Banks from New Orleans to Mobile and into Alabama's interior, and commanded Franz Sigel to destroy the several rail links in the Shenandoah Valley. Though raiding operations in Virginia and Georgia would soon overshadow those in Mississippi, it was during the campaigns along the great river that Grant demonstrated the efficacy of such a strategy. Grant's contest with the landscape of the Lower Mississippi Valley initiated the Union's battle against the Confederacy's agroecological foundations and demonstrated that a fertile landscape could be as much a liability as a benefit in war.

CHAPTER THREE

Ravaged Ground

Sheridan in the Shenandoah Valley, 1864

THE SHENANDOAH VALLEY's peaceful, pastoral reputation obscures its violent past. Powerful collisions of tectonic plates thrust the Appalachian Mountains into existence millions of years ago, then wind and water besieged the mountains' exposed flanks of limestone and shale, separating the Alleghenies from the Blue Ridge and creating an open plain two hundred miles long and, on average, twenty miles wide. Fast-flowing rivers further penetrated the mountains' defenses and formed narrow passes, or gaps, as the water fought its way to the sea. Thomas Jefferson described such a battle as "one of the most stupendous scenes in nature." He explained, "On your right comes up the Shenandoah, having ranged along the foot of the mountain an hundred miles to seek a vent. On your left approaches the Potomac, in quest of a passage also. In the moment of their junction, they rush together against the mountain, rend it asunder, and pass off to the sea." This was evidence for Jefferson that "the most powerful agents of nature" had formed the Shenandoah Valley and established its character. In his estimation, however, nature's "finishing" muted the region's tumultuous orogenic and hydrologic origins and made the Valley into a "placid and delightful" counterpoint to the "wild and tremendous" mountains that surrounded it. Jefferson believed the landscape was "worth a voyage across the Atlantic" and bemoaned that few, even those who lived nearby, had "been to survey these monuments of a war between rivers and mountains, which must have shaken the earth itself to its centre."[1]

That ancient battle between nature's forces set the stage for the conflict that convulsed the Shenandoah Valley in 1861. The more recent conflict was political, not elemental, but it, too, would remake the Valley's landscape. Throughout the Civil War, control over the Shenandoah Valley held a central place in both Union and Confederate strategy, making it some of the most contested terrain of the war. Though early military operations there had limited impact on the civilian population, in the summer of 1864 residents of the Shenandoah Valley faced a new style of warfare, one aimed at their most important relationship to the natural environment. That year the Union implemented a strategy that attacked the means by which the Shenandoah Valley had become "the granary of the Confederacy," setting fire to fields, barns, and mills, taking or killing livestock and draft animals, and spreading news of emancipation to slaves. These acts targeted the symbols and artifacts of the residents' control over nature and left the Valley's agricultural landscape fundamentally altered.

To those who witnessed them, the consequences of constant struggle and, more importantly, of the attack against the Valley's agroecological foundations were plain: a once idyllic landscape became a virtual wasteland. Though apocalyptic descriptions of the Valley's destruction are likely exaggerated, they should not be discounted entirely. In fact, they provide valuable insight into nineteenth-century ideas about nature and warfare. The 1864 Shenandoah Valley campaign is especially instructive because individuals, regardless of affiliation, used the language of wilderness to describe the effects of a kind of warfare they saw as "uncivilized." According to that trope, civilized people had improved nature prior to the war, transforming the Valley into a civilized landscape; during the conflict, savage men turned it back into a wilderness.

Long before the Civil War, nature's original handiwork in the Shenandoah Valley had been modified through human efforts. Native American tribes had used and managed the Valley's resources for centuries, burning woodlands to improve hunting and farming and thereby creating a patchwork of grassland and forest. By the mid-1800s, however, disease, warfare, and the arrival of permanent white settlers resulted in a dramatic decrease in Native American influence in the area. The new arrivals began their transformations of the Valley in the 1730s, carving the grasslands into small, mixed-crop farms. Subsequent settlers introduced plantation agriculture and slavery to the Shenandoah, making it into a prosperous tobacco-producing region.[2] Despite this later development, a significant proportion of the Valley's residents eschewed the institution of slavery, so it did not take as firm a hold there as it did in the coastal and piedmont regions of Virginia. According to historian Michael Mahon, in 1850 slaves made up about 20 percent of the Valley's population. A decade later that number had decreased to less than 18 percent. In terms of the state's slaveholding population, William G. Thomas noted that the Valley "boasted 17 percent of Virginia's slaveholding households and 10 percent of Virginia's slaveholders." These numbers were not consistent throughout the Valley, as John L. Heatwole pointed out; slavery was more prominent in the lower (northern) portion of the Valley than in the upper (southern) area, where Mennonites and Dunkers made up significant portions of the population.[3] Nonetheless, slavery was an important element in Valley society and economics and a part of the region's agroecological development.

On the eve of the Civil War, the Shenandoah Valley epitomized the ideal nineteenth-century landscape: productive, well managed, and idyllic. The "beautiful prairie" had been "improved" by 1860 into a fertile agricultural countryside that also supported a wide variety of light industrial works.[4] Its rich soils produced wheat, corn, and other grains in addition to quality to-bacco. Dense woodlands provided habitat for wildlife and timber for build-ings, fences, and firewood. Livestock thrived in the Valley's lush meadows and pasturelands. Clear streams cut through and served as the motive power for the region's mills and diverse manufactories, which included numerous flour mills, several sawmills and iron furnaces, some tanneries, a few saltpeter works, one powder mill, and a woolen mill.[5] Well-maintained macadam and plank roads linked farms to local markets and, where they passed through the mountain gaps, to larger markets farther afield. The towns of Staunton, Strasburg, and Winchester boasted major railroad connections. Lexington and Harpers Ferry provided access to Virginia's two most important rivers, the James and the Potomac, respectively, as well as the canals that skirted the banks of those rivers. The Valley's residents thus enjoyed the benefits of nature—rich soil, plentiful forests, navigable streams, a gentle climate—as well as those of culture—roads, railroads, canals, manufactories—and they made the most of their good fortune.

During the war, the Valley's improved landscape evoked a sense of awe and reverence, no matter the observer's allegiance. In 1862 Confederate officer Richard Taylor crossed the Blue Ridge Mountains and saw the Shenandoah Valley for the first time. "The great Valley of Virginia was before us in all its beauty," he wrote. "Fields of wheat spread far and wide, interspersed with woodlands, bright in their robes of tender green. Wherever appropriate sites existed, quaint old mills, with turning wheels, were busily grinding the pre-vious year's harvest; and grove and eminence showed comfortable homesteads. The soft vernal influence shed a languid grace over the scene."[6] Pvt. Wilbur Fisk of the Second Vermont Volunteers noted of the area around Berryville, "The wide fields showed a fertile soil, and are fair to look upon. They are just such as would please the eye of a practical farmer."[7]

Taylor Peirce from Iowa remarked that he had "never seen so beautiful a country. On the South stands the Blue Ridge rearing its peaks far above the Valley. And Streaching away off towards the North East is lost to view towards Carlisle Pa. [O]n the North is seen the Spurs of the Alleghany. While laying like the land of rest is the beautifull valley of Virginia." He further noted, "The land has been heavily timbered and has been cleared out for the farmes, leaving the whole face of the country covered with skirts of timber, and many of the

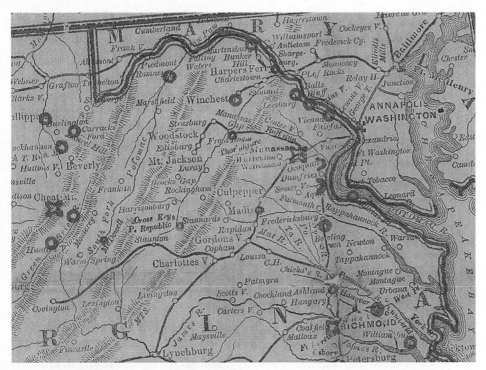

The Shenandoah Valley: Detail from "The Historical War Map," 1863. Richmond is in the lower right corner, Washington is in the center right. The Shenandoah Valley runs diagonally across the left side of the map, with Winchester and Harpers Ferry at the top center and Staunton, Lexington, and Covington in the lower left. The circular markings indicate areas of engagement. Civil War Maps Collection, Geography and Map Division, Library of Congress, g3701s cw0023000.

farms have been fitted up in a style of luxury and comfort that I have seen no where in the south." Villages "are scattered over the country 2 or 3 miles apart and the most of them have a church spire rising above the surrounding trees which gives the landscape a most beautiful appearance." The view made "the lover of his country feel indeed as if this was a nation and a country worth risking his life for."[8] Peirce also thought that the Valley was "truly a place to awaken thought of times past. The grand old woods, the mountains in the distance with their rocks and rugged peaks carrys one back to the times when the red man walked through the groves and traversed the mountains the owner of all he could see. The Eagle wheeling o'er his head Proclaimed that all around was free." Unable to ignore his reason for being in the Valley, Peirce concluded, "[A]las, the mind will imediately come from the thought of perfect freedom to the State of Slavery that has existed here between that period and the present." He lamented that "the nation is now paying out in blood for the sins it has permitted to lay and fester around this most beautifule part of Gods earth."[9]

The Valley did pay out in blood, and in other ways, for its nominal allegiance to the Confederacy. Though the Valley was tied closely to the North socially, politically, and economically before the war, loyalty to Virginia trumped these connections when the state voted to secede in 1861.[10] This was a fateful decision for Valley residents, as their home would become "the theatre of a series of campaigns at once picturesque and decisive."[11] Over the course of the war, it "saw more than a dozen pitched battles, hundreds of skirmishes, and chronic guerrilla activity."[12] One eyewitness mourned the effects of these events on the Valley's landscape. Writing to his wife in September 1864, Confederate general Stephen Ramseur told her that he had "travelled over & sojourned in the most beautiful part of the valley" and wished she "could see this magnificent Valley—at this beautiful season of the year." Although "the blackened remains of once splendid mansions [could] be seen on all sides," Ramseur was consoled that "nature is triumphant—magnificent meadows, beautiful forests & broad undulating fields rich in grass and clover! Truly it does seem sacreligious to despoil such an Eden! by the ravages of War."[13]

Sacrilegious though that destruction may have seemed, by 1864 it had become necessary if Union war aims were to be achieved. Historian Gary Gallagher has argued, "The logistical importance of the Valley during the conflict scarcely can be overstated. Its agricultural riches promised sustenance for Southern forces in Virginia. The most important wheat growing area in the entire Upper South through most of the antebellum period, it also led Virginia in production of other grains and cattle and contributed substantial quantities of leather, wood products, woolen textiles, and whiskey." Strategically, the Valley served as an "avenue whence either side might mount a threat to the western flanks of Washington or Richmond."[14] These attributes together made the Valley, according to Thomas Lewis, the "lynchpin of the Southern Cause and a primary target of the Northern war machine."[15]

From the outset of the war until its final six months the Valley remained a Confederate stronghold and storehouse for needed food, forage, and other supplies. For the Confederate troops operating in Virginia, the Valley "was in such a prosperous condition that the rebel army could march down and up the valley billeting on the inhabitants."[16] This they did, first under Thomas "Stonewall" Jackson, then under Jubal Early. Under these two able commanders, the Confederate Army of the Valley protected the fertile Shenandoah from all Union incursions.[17] In addition, John Mosby's Rangers obstructed Union goals in the Valley and in neighboring Loudoun and Fauquier Counties. An early chronicler of the war wrote that the Valley "had yielded so many captures of Union garrisons and so many disasters in the field, as to be called the Valley of Humiliation."[18]

Historian Jeffry Wert explained that the Valley's geography worked in concert with its Confederate defenders, contributing "significantly to Union frustration and defeat in the region." The Alleghenies and the Blue Ridge guarded its flanks as though they were, in one soldier's estimation, breastworks thrown up by "a race of titans [that] had been at war."[19] Union general Wesley Merritt noted that the lay of the land favored Confederate movements on Washington, Maryland, and Pennsylvania and that the Valley "led away from the [Union] objective, Richmond." This left the Federal troops "exposed to flank attacks through the gaps from vantage-ground and perfect cover." Merritt recalled that until "the summer of 1864 the Shenandoah Valley had not been to the Union armies a fortunate place either for battle or for strategy."[20]

Part of this misfortune was due to Union reliance on traditional military tactics in a landscape that benefited its defenders. Grant initially instructed his subordinates to use direct engagement with the enemy to diminish their operational strength and to employ tactical maneuver to gain control over key lines of communication and transportation, as well as over the gaps, passes, and rivers that provided access to the Valley. Furthermore, the Federal troops were to dismantle the Valley's railroads in order to deny their use to Confederate troops and suppliers. Each of these required the Union forces to take the offensive in terrain that favored defensive maneuver. The mountain passes could be defended by limited numbers of troops. Furthermore, the Massanutten Range, which separated the Luray (or Page) Valley from the main part of the Shenandoah between Front Royal and Harrisonburg, also provided cover for small contingents of cavalry that could move back and forth between the two valleys to harass a larger enemy force.

Despite these obstacles, Grant ordered Maj. Gen. Franz Sigel to clear the Valley of Confederate forces. In early May 1864 Sigel moved tentatively up the Valley from Winchester toward Harrisonburg until he met with resistance at the town of New Market on the fifteenth. Orchards skirted the lovely pastoral town nestled against the massive Massanutten Mountain, and green meadows posed the only barrier between Sigel's men and his enemy. Former U.S. vice president John C. Breckenridge, now a Confederate general, led the opposing forces, including 247 eager cadets from the nearby Virginia Military Institute. The young rebels routed Sigel, who quickly retreated back down the Valley.[21]

After Sigel's ignominious defeat, Grant realized that offensive maneuvers alone were ineffective in the Valley and decided that more drastic measures were necessary. In addition to attacking whatever Confederate forces defended the Valley, he ordered his soldiers to destroy the area's resources. This decision had a solid basis in logic, as General Merritt explained: Grant "reasoned that the advantage would be with us, who did not want it as a source of supplies, nor as a place of arms, and against the Confederates, who wanted it for both."[22] Undermining an area's ability to support its military forces—psychologically or materially—was a tried-and-true method for Grant, and he determined that the Shenandoah Valley posed an excellent opportunity to prove the strategy's efficacy once again. Drawing on his experiences in Mississippi, Grant's new strategy made the Valley's landscape, in addition to its Confederate defenders, the object of operations.

In mid-1864 the war that had raged across the Shenandoah Valley for three years became a war waged *against* the Valley, one that attacked the agricultural and industrial improvements that previously had sustained its citizens and supplied the Confederate army. Grant made destruction of the Valley's greatest asset—its awesome productivity—into its most damaging liability. Ten days after Sigel's retreat, Grant ordered that the Shenandoah Valley be laid waste, rendering it useless to the Confederacy. Innovating on the ancient strategy of the *chevauchée*, such operations effectively undermined the Valley's agroecological foundation and neutralized it as a source of support for Lee's Army of Northern Virginia. In attacking the improvements the Shenandoah Valley residents had made, and in destroying the means by which those improvements were maintained, Union operations in the area not only brought the war home to civilians but significantly diminished their abilities to manage nature and support the Confederate war effort.

On May 25, 1864, Grant issued orders to Maj. Gen. David Hunter to renew Federal operations in the Valley, "living upon the country and cutting the railroads and canal as he went."[23] With these orders, what became known as "The Burning" commenced, bringing with it dramatic changes not only to the Shenandoah's landscape but to Union strategy in the Valley.[24] By mid-June Hunter had reached Lexington, where he "enlarged upon the burning operations begun at Staunton. On his way, and in the surrounding country, he burnt mills, furnaces, storehouses, granaries, and all farming utensils he could find, besides a great amount of fencing, and a large quantity of grain."[25] Hunter's destructive foray earned him the scorn and hatred of the local residents (some of whom were his own relations) but successfully threatened the Orange and Alexandria, the Virginia and Tennessee, and the South Side Railroads at Lynchburg, farther up the Valley. In July Grant expanded his orders, indicating to Halleck that he wished Hunter and his troops to "eat out Virginia clear and clean as far as they go, so that crows flying over it for the balance of the season will have to carry their provender with them."[26] Although ultimately a defeat and a failure, Hunter's raid established a precedent for future Union operations in the Valley and formally initiated Grant's strategy of toppling the Confederacy by attacking its agroecological foundations.

Although Hunter successfully attacked the Valley's means of production, he was no match for Lt. Gen. Jubal A. Early and the Second Corps of the Army of Northern Virginia (the same corps Stonewall Jackson led to numerous victories in the Valley in 1862). Hunter eagerly destroyed, but he hesitated to fight. Faced with attacking what he believed to be a superior force protected by Lynchburg's defenses, Hunter withdrew on June 19 and sought refuge in the Alleghenies. By July 6 Early and his Army of the Valley had cleaned the Shenandoah of all Federal troops and made an audacious movement down the Valley, across the Potomac, and toward Washington. Early defeated Lew Wallace at Monocacy Creek, just north of the Federal capital, and threatened the capital city on July 11. Though Early withdrew back to the Valley four days later, the Confederate point was made: the Shenandoah still protected and supported the Confederate cause.[27]

Gravely disappointed by his commanders' failures, Grant became convinced that the conquest of the Valley needed to be a top priority and redoubled his efforts to make that happen. He authorized the creation of a new department of the army, the Middle Military Division, which melded several smaller units into one. To command the new Army of the Shenandoah, as it came to be known, Grant turned to the man he knew could finish the job: Maj. Gen. Philip H. Sheridan. At the time of his appointment, Sheridan had been the commander of the cavalry forces of the Sixth Corps of the Army of the Potomac. Although he had proven his mettle in such vital battles as the Wilderness and Chancellorsville, only Grant among the Union high command was confident that the brash, young Sheridan could successfully command an entire military department. As commanding general, however, Grant enjoyed considerable influence, and Sheridan received his orders on August 7, 1864, to take charge of the Shenandoah campaign and its namesake command.

Sheridan, a "little terror of a man with an unholy aptitude for the arts of war," subsequently conducted the most devastating of the Valley campaigns.[28] His philosophy matched Grant's in that he believed "it was time to bring the war home to a people engaged in raising crops from a prolific soil to feed the country's enemies, and devoting to the Confederacy its best youth." Sheridan argued, "[T]he stores of meat and grain that the valley provided, and the men it furnished for Lee's depleted regiments, were the strongest auxiliaries he possessed in the whole insurgent section." Furthermore, territory like the Shenandoah Valley "is a factor of great importance, and whichever adversary controls it permanently reaps all the advantages of its prosperity."[29] Sheridan was eager to make the Valley residents feel the effects of the war, and he was ruthless in the execution of his duties. On August 26 Grant sent Sheridan the following orders: "Do all the damage to rail-roads and crops you can. Carry off stock of all discreptions and negroes so as to prevent further planting. If the War is to last another year we want the Shenandoah valley to remain a barren waste."[30] In essence, Sheridan's orders were to destroy the means by which Shenandoah Valley residents managed the natural environment, transforming it from a civilized, improved landscape into a virtual wilderness.

In one sense, Sheridan had his work cut out for him. "Nature had been very kind to the Valley," Sheridan recalled, "making it rich and productive to an exceptional degree, and though for three years contending armies had been marching up and down it, the fertile soil still yielded ample subsistence for Early's men, with a large surplus for the army of Lee." Destroying such fecundity was nearly impossible. Sheridan's task was mitigated, however, by the Valley's long history of management and by the gentle character of its terrain. "The ground had long been well cleared of timber," Sheridan recalled, "and the rolling surface presented so few obstacles to the movement of armies that they could march over the country in any direction almost as well as on the roads, the creeks and rivers being everywhere fordable, with little or no difficulty beyond that of leveling the approaches."[31]

The campaign would not be without its obstacles, with hot weather being the most notable. Orderly Sgt. John Hartwell peppered his diary and letters home with complaints about the adverse environmental conditions he and his fellow soldiers endured. In late July he noted, "Very hot today & little or no air stiring. the heat from the Sun is very oppressive. [. . .] Men fell out by the hundreds and many died by the way. Great Suffering & it rearily seemed almost *brutal* to urge men to march when it was so hot."[32] Two weeks later he wrote to his wife, "We have suffered greatly from heat & rapid marches. This is killing us slowly but surely, our once large & good looking Corps of men are sadly thinned, the men all or nearly looked haggard & worn out."[33]

Despite the heat, Sheridan determined that he would confiscate or destroy all crops and agricultural implements in the Valley, leaving the area an agricultural void. On August 10 Sheridan began his march into the lower Valley from his base in Halltown (just west of Harpers Ferry), skirmishing with Early's troops all the way to Cedar Creek, just north of the town of Front Royal. The night of the sixteenth, Sheridan turned his cavalry back toward his base, "driving all the cattle and livestock in the Valley before it, and burning the grain from Cedar Creek to Berryville," just east of Winchester.[34] Pvt. Norval Baker of the Eighteenth Virginia Cavalry noted in his diary, "The lines of battle could be seen along the roads right and left. The dead horses lay in lines as they were killed and little mounds of fresh earth marked the resting places of dead soldiers. The weather was sultry and the dead animals were in all stages of decomposition and millions of buzzards gathered to the Lower Valley. We could always tell when the Yankees were coming by the birds raising high up and sailing around."[35] Jubal Early frustrated Sheridan's plans to do the same farther up the Valley, confining him to the lower Valley for the rest of August and into September. Although limited geographically, Sheridan continued his destructive raids as autumn approached. As the *New York Herald* reported on September 15, "Sheridan is now gathering in his harvest."[36]

Early's men, too, busily scoured the countryside for provender, balancing their tasks of harassing Sheridan and feeding themselves. One Union soldier observed, "This is splendid country, the best I ever saw." However, "the country has been pretty well 'laid waste' by both armies."[37] Where Sheridan's orders were to destroy the Valley's resources, saving only what the Union troops could use along the way, Early's task was to protect the harvest and requisition it for distribution to the various Confederate forces in Virginia. Writing from the vicinity of Winchester, Major General Ramseur noted on September 11 that his Confederates were "gathering all of the wheat in this wonderfully productive valley enough to supply ourselves & to send large supplies to Gen'l Lee's Army."[38] Despite having divergent motivations, the Union and Confederate forces each wanted the same thing: ultimate control over the productive capacity of the Shenandoah Valley.

Local farmers, caught in the middle, struggled to maintain some semblance of normality and to enjoy the benefits of their labor. For some families, the task was a difficult one. Robert Barton, a native of the Valley, noted that his family's wheat crop that summer "had been a splendid one," but with all the Barton men off at war, it had not yet been threshed as of September 17. On the eighteenth General Early, "who wanted the wheat for his army [. . .] sent a lot of men and a machine to thresh it." The following day a major battle took place all around Springdale, the Barton property, which was located just south of Winchester. Sheridan's army routed Early's, pushing it back up the Valley. As the Union forces pursued the retreating rebel troops, they set fire to the barn where the Bartons' newly threshed grain was stored. "The wheat was all consumed except the few bushels which had been put in the grainery," and the Bartons' barn and buildings "were saved with great effort."[39]

The contest over the Bartons' wheat epitomized the larger struggle in the Valley and, indeed, the war itself. The Valley's civilian residents—some Unionists, some Confederate sympathizers, and others who tried to remain neutral—continued to work their land, coaxing from the fertile soil the very thing that brought the war to their homes. The Valley's agricultural wealth was the product of generations of negotiation with the natural environment, and control over that bounty was the crux of the military engagements there in 1864. Control did not simply entail military dominance over the territory, however. It included the power to determine how the area's resources were to be used and by whom. Sheridan sought to destroy the results of the farmers' labor; Early sought to use them. By sending Sheridan to the Valley, Grant intended to wrest power over the Shenandoah and its abundance from Lee's grasp, thereby crippling the Confederate war effort and ending the rebellion.

Sheridan's progress in the Valley began slowly, but after the third battle of Winchester (in which the Bartons' wheat crop was destroyed), he gained unstoppable momentum and made visible progress toward his goal of destroying the Valley's improvements. One Union soldier described the scene after the recent battle: "The country has been pretty well devastated, fences destroyed (rails burned and stone fences thrown down) stock all driven off, orchards stripped of fruit and altogether it was the most desolate looking picture I ever saw. Dead horses along the roadside and new made graves gave evidence that it had lately been the scene of strife."[40] Pursuing Early's retreating forces, Sheridan marched three columns of his army up the Valley along the turnpike, passing once again Robert Barton's home. Barton recalled that two columns flanked the road, marching in the fields and "destroying everything before them. Hogs, sheep, cattle &c. were shot down and left to rot and horses were taken and carried away, whether needed by the army or not. Springdale was left like a wilderness, almost every living animal on the place either being driven off or else killed and left in sheer deviltry and wickedness."[41] Another soldier remarked, "Nobody who has witnessed the ravages of an army would ever applaud the system of Living off the country. When it means anything, it means un-restrained plundering and robbery and rascality."[42] With equal venom and disdain, Confederate general John Gordon claimed that after Winchester, Sheridan "decided upon a season of burning, instead of battling; of assaults with matches and torches upon barns and haystacks, instead of upon armed men who were lined up in front of him."[43]

Although Gordon's assessment of Sheridan's main tactic—destroying all agricultural and industrial assets in the Valley—was largely correct, he grossly understated "Little Phil's" will to fight. After the battle at Winchester on September 19, Gordon noted that Sheridan "graciously granted" the Confederates "two days and part of a third to sleep and rest and pull [themselves] together." The Confederates retired to the shelter of the Blue Ridge Mountains, stopping briefly at Fisher's Hill, a small outcropping at the base of the Massanutten Range. There they "[s]pread [their] banners on the ramparts which nature built along the Shenandoah's banks."[44] Nature may have built the defenses, but

Sheridan in the Shenandoah Valley: Alfred R. Waud, an illustrator for *Harper's Weekly* assigned to document the operations of the U.S. Army of the Potomac, titled his drawing "Sheridan's army following Early up the Valley of the Shenandoah." While it does not depict destruction of the Valley per se, the number of men gives an idea of the capacity for devastation. Morgan Collection of Civil War Drawings, Prints and Photographs Division, Library of Congress, LC-DIG-ppmsca-21001.

it did not protect the rebel lines from Sheridan's quick flanking movement. On September 22 Sheridan roused the Confederates from their respite and forced them farther up the Valley toward Staunton. Early's troops regrouped near Front Royal at Brown's Gap—"Jackson's 'old campground,' which kind nature seemed to have supplied as an inspiring and secure retreat for the defenders of the Valley"—where they remained, waiting for Sheridan's next attack.[45]

After the rout at Fisher's Hill, Sheridan focused on achieving his primary purpose in the Valley: the systematic destruction of its productive landscape. Sheridan "went to work with his command," Grant reported in his memoirs, "gathering in the crops, cattle, and everything in the upper part of the valley required of our troops; and especially taking what might be of use to the enemy. What he could not take away he destroyed, so that the enemy would not be invited to come back there."[46] Jedediah Hotchkiss, Stonewall Jackson's famed mapmaker, wrote home on two occasions to report on Sheridan's actions across the Valley. He told his wife of the "great deal of burning" in the area and reported to his brother Nelson that in Rockingham County "they have done a vast amount of damage, burning mills, barns, wheat and hay stacks, and robbing houses."[47] Union lieutenant colonel Jacob Weddel recalled, "The army settled itself down in and around Harrisburg and for some time lay there, foraging off the country all there was at that time to forage. Finally marching orders were given, and then we started to fall back nearer our old base. This was the time that Sheridan laid waste the valley by fire."[48]

The devastation led many Union soldiers to consider the fate of the civilians left in its wake. One wrote, "This is nice country here and has the appearance of wealth but the boys are cleaning it up now and if we retreat no army can subsist in this vally again for another year at least."[49] Another commented that he did not "know how the citizens are going to live this winter. They say we have taken away from them everything they have—their wheat, their corn, their cattle, and everything we could find, and now as winter is coming on they are entirely destitute." He felt some sympathy, acknowledging, "Part of their woes no doubt, are real, but we cannot depend upon all they tell us. Whether justifiable or not, the damage we have inflicted upon them has had its effect in teaching the people to have some respect for Yankee power."[50] That power extended not only over Confederate forces but also over civilians' abilities to manage their environment and to take from it the means of survival.

Officers, too, commented on their role in the Valley's predicament. Brig. Gen. James H. Kidd wrote to his father, "How the people of Virginia will live this winter I cannot imagine. Nothing is left where we have been but corn and not much of that. Barns and mills are all destroyed. Hay and grain has been given to the flames." Calling their tactics "relentless war," Kidd believed "it may be the best speediest way."[51] One of Sheridan's staff officers echoed these sentiments. J. H. Wilson wrote to Grant, "The measures he is taking in the valley will effectively render it useless to the enemy—and impossible as a theatre of further operations against us this year."[52] Destroying the means by which locals derived sustenance from their environment—that is, their "improvements"—was the most expedient path to Union success in the Valley.

In a report to Grant, Sheridan noted, "[T]he whole country from the Blue Ridge to the North Mountains has been made untenable for a rebel army." He then proceeded to inventory what his army had destroyed or confiscated in the Luray, Little Fork, and Main Valleys: "I have destroyed over 2,000 barns filled with wheat, hay and farming implements; over seventy mills filled with flour and wheat; have driven in front of the army over 4,000 head of stock, and have killed and issued to the troops not less than 3,000 sheep. [. . .] A large number of horses have been obtained, a proper estimate of which I cannot now make." He reported that the "people here are getting sick of the War, heretofore they have had no reason to complain because they had been living in great abundance." Sheridan concluded with a promise to Grant: "Tomorrow I will continue the destruction of wheat forage &c. down to Fisher's Hill. When this is completed, the valley from Winchester up to Staunton (ninety-two miles) will have but little in it for man or beast."[53]

As Sheridan moved back down the Valley, destroying anything he had missed on his first pass through, Early determined to make one last effort to oust the Federals. On the morning of October 19, one month to the day after the Confederate rout at Winchester, Early ordered his men to attack Sheridan's forces encamped at the base of the Massanutten Range near Strasburg, on the banks of Cedar Creek. Gordon recalled, "It was unmistakably evident that General Sheridan concurred in the universally accepted opinion that it was impracticable for the Confederates to pass or march along the rugged and almost perpendicular face of Massanutten Mountain and assail his left." He was less convinced that Sheridan's flank, protected only by the "natural barriers" of the "impassable" mountain and the gentle Shenandoah River, was so secure. Gordon found a "dim and narrow pathway" that allowed his entire corps to cross the mountain in a single night, putting them in position for a surprise flank attack on Sheridan's left. Gordon's plan succeeded beyond all expectations, forcing the entire Union army to retreat from its position. On the verge of a complete victory, however, Jubal Early called off the attack, believing they had had "enough glory for one day." It was a fatal mistake, one that would transform the victory into defeat. Rallying his retreating soldiers, Sheridan rode to the front line and turned the tide of the battle.[54]

A rousing Union victory, Cedar Creek "was the last of the great conflicts in the historic Valley which for four years had been torn and bloodstained by almost incessant battle."[55] The *New York Herald* reported in October 1864, "Hitherto that valley has been justly styled the rebel granary. It has fed the rebellion at Richmond, it has been a harbor to hordes of guerillas, and it has furnished a convenient avenue for the invasion of the North; for the rebel armies could advance down that valley when starved out of Richmond and find food all the way to the Potomac." But, the paper declared, "General Grant has wisely determined to put a stop to all that."[56] Six months later the same paper reported, "Between Sheridan and Early, the fertile Shenandoah valley has been thoroughly cleaned out; the country east of the Blue Ridge, from Leesburg to Richmond, has been left exhausted and desolate by the spoils of both armies."[57]

In his official report at the end of the campaign, Sheridan accounted for everything his men appropriated or destroyed. Though military equipment composed part of the list, the majority focused on the agricultural damage the

Middle Military Division exacted: 435,802 bushels of wheat, 77,176 bushels of corn, 20,397 tons of hay, 10,918 beef cattle, 12,000 sheep, and 15,000 hogs. Not only did Sheridan's troops take or destroy what the Valley had already produced, but they undermined the area's productivity for the immediate future by burning twelve hundred barns, killing or taking over four thousand horses and mules, and destroying farm implements and any industrial facilities that had survived to that point.[58]

Furthermore, part of Sheridan's strategy was to attack the means by which the Valley's residents had transformed it into "the granary of the Confederacy." Thus, despite the institution's limited hold on the Valley, slavery became a target of Union operations there. According to historian Michael G. Mahon, "Aware of how important slaves were to a farmer in working his land or keeping his house in order, the [Federal] soldiers made certain not to leave them behind."[59] Recognizing an opportunity for freedom, slaves also acted on their own behalf, freeing themselves. William Hoxton wrote to his sister, Sallie Randolph, in September, "Mary received your letter together with one from Aunt Julia yesterday, and she gave a dreadful account of their suffering down at Locust Farm by this last Raid of Sheridan's. Joe and all the rest of the servants having run away[,] carrying everything with them and leaving them in a state of perfect destitute."[60]

Even when the slaves remained, many refused to work for their former masters, resulting in major changes to what had once been deemed an idyllic landscape. Another of Sallie Randolph's correspondents, her mother-in-law, Mary Randolph, wrote from her estate Eastern View in the lower Valley:

> I can't describe the scene of ruin and desolation that met my view when I got here. I just cried heartily and felt as if it indeed never could be renovated. The naked frame of the dear old house loomed up before me looking so sad and ghostly—the yard overgrown with weeds and strewn with rubbish from the fallen chimneys [?] but more painful still the negroes in complete possession of everything[,] their tubs and pots setting all around and clothes hanging about on the bushes—the smoke house and lumber house doorless and torn practically to pieces, pigs moving about everywhere and not a glimpse of comfort to be seen—I cant tell you how I felt.

All signs of a civilizing influence, in Randolph's opinion, had been removed from the plantation landscape with the ascendancy of the slaves. Further evidence of this was the condition of the grounds under the care of the newly free men and women. "You *never* saw *such a garden* [—] nothing to be seen but grass up to my waist almost and weeds, with patches of corn and tobacco belonging to the possessors of the soil, the negroes."[61] The grounds had returned to a weedy wilderness, devoid of the signs of improvement or civilized society.

Without labor, either that of slaves or of family members taken by the war, residents of the Shenandoah could not maintain the landscape they had spent generations creating. What three years of combat and maneuver through the Shenandoah Valley could not accomplish, a summer and fall of raids, foraging, and burning could. Sheridan's rampage through the fertile Valley "constituted the first large-scale demonstration that the strategy of exhaustion could accomplish the psychological and logistical damage envisioned by Grant."[62] In attacking the agroecological foundations of the region, Sheridan effectively subdued the Valley and took control over it for the Union.

Reactions to Federal operations throughout the summer and fall of 1864 in the Valley and neighboring counties, where "The Burning" spread in order to contain John Mosby's Rangers, reveal a fear of unmanaged landscapes and what they represented.[63] Both participants in and those subjected to Hunter's and Sheridan's destruction turned to the powerful metaphors of desert and wasteland to describe the war-torn landscape and to images of savagery to describe the men who created it. Thomas Ashby, a boy of sixteen at the time, noted that "Hunter destroyed everything in his path and left sections of the Valley along his route as bare as a desert."[64] Henrietta B. Lee wrote to Hunter himself, complaining of the cruelty she felt he committed when he gave orders for her house to be burned. "Hyena-like, you have torn my heart to pieces, for all hallowed memories are clustered around that homestead, and demon-like, you have done it without even the pretext of revenge, for I never saw or harmed you." Her final words condemned Hunter absolutely:

> Your name will stand on history's page as the Hunter of weak women and innocent children, the Hunter to destroy defenseless villages and refined and beautiful homes; to torture afresh the agonized hearts of widows; the Hunter of Africa's poor sons and daughters, to lure them on to death and ruin of soul and body; the Hunter with the relentless heart of a wild beast, the face of a fiend and the form of a man. Oh Earth, behold the monster! Can I say, 'God forgive you'? No prayer can be offered for you. Were it possible for human lips to raise your name heavenward, angels would thrust the foul thing back again, and demons claim their own.[65]

In Lee's estimation, Hunter was not merely beyond the pale of civilization, he was the epitome of savagery, both a fiend and a wild beast.

The use of such metaphors is revealing. It demonstrates the persistence of American unease with unmanaged landscapes, places seemingly devoid of positive human influence. While war-scapes are the products of human action, they reflect the destructive, rather than the constructive, capacity of human agency. Thus they are reviled, not revered. Such language also illustrates the centrality of the perception of control in nineteenth-century American ideas about nature. Power over nature was linked to other kinds of power. When Union forces undermined the ability of Valley residents to shape and manage the environment around them, those civilians lost power in other areas of their lives.

In the end, the raids made their expected impressions on the civilians of the Valley and achieved their ultimate goal of undermining material and psychological support for the rebellion. Without the symbols and products of improvements, the Valley no longer presented the appearance of a civilized country. However, reactions to the raids were sometimes tempered by a belief in the Valley's resilient nature. Catherine Cochran, writing in September from The Plains in Fauquier County, recorded in her diary, "The whole country from the Rapidan to Loudoun has a desolate, forsaken look—fences all gone, houses burnt, dismantled or unoccupied—villages of log huts remain standing about Culpeper [Court House]. Tho hundreds have been hauled off for fire wood but the wonderful fertility of the country is seen in the sea of verdure that has obliterated the traces of military occupation. The eye takes in miles of luxuriant grass & every fruit tree was bending under its load of ungathered fruit."[66] Daniel K. Schreckhise of Rockingham, Virginia, reported to his brother James that "the yanks burnt a good many houses [so] the people in the lower valley will have to leave & go someplace this winter." However, he also noted that "almost every body was done seeding & the wheat is up & looks very fine."[67] Another resident took heart on seeing from atop Massanutten Mountain the main part of the Valley stretching before him "green and brilliant until the distances were lost in the haze. From far above no scars of war were visible; a sweep of the eye revealed innumerable fields where a new crop of [wheat] was being harvested."[68]

Although the Union soldiers "swept [the] country of everything that they could find in the way of food supplies" and set fires so that the skies "were red at night with the glare," Thomas Ashby yet found comfort in nature itself. "Fortunately for our citizens that were non-combatants, the bounty of nature is often more beneficent than man." Ashby recalled that despite the constant fighting and even the intentional destruction of agricultural supplies, Sheridan's men could not destroy the Shenandoah Valley's natural fertility. "Our country had never known such seasons as we had during the four years of war," he wrote. "Whatever was put into the ground grew in profusion. Wheat, corn, oats, rye, and grass yielded large crops, with little cultivation. The orchard bore heavily, small fruits and the nuts on the trees were in the greatest abundance; wild game was prolific and the poultry, hiding in the weeds and briars around the houses, gave abundance of food that could not be removed or burned." Furthermore, although the "lands had grown up in weeds and bushes, [. . .] the grass was in good condition; such live stock as was left could find good grazing all through the winter, and was kept alive by this fortunate condition." Nonetheless, Ashby had little hope for a productive spring. "If the war continued, little farm work could be done as the farm lands, labor, and implements necessary to cultivate the land were all in such a condition as to make farming operations impracticable, except on the smallest scale."[69] Even with the blessings of nature, without the means to control or at least manage them the Valley's residents would face lean times.

Retreating from the Valley, Confederate general John Gordon "could but contrast the aspect of devastation and woe which it then presented, with the bounty and peace in all its homes at the beginning of the war." He wrote, "Before the blasting breath of war swept over its rich meadows and fields of clover, they had been filled with high-mettled horses, herds of fine cattle, and flocks of sheep that rivalled England's best." After Sheridan's raid, "[h]eaps of ashes, of half-melted iron axles and bent tires, were the melancholy remains of burnt barns and farm wagons and implements of husbandry. Stone and brick chimneys, standing alone in the midst of charred trees which once shaded the porches of luxurious and happy homes, told of hostile torches which had left these grim sentinels the only guards of those sacred spots. At the close of this campaign [. . .] there was in that entire fertile valley—the former American Arcadia—scarcely a family that was not struggling for subsistence."[70]

This was precisely what Grant and Sheridan had hoped to accomplish through the raid. They intended to undermine the region's ability to support the Confederate war effort by attacking the Valley's landscape. The approach certainly had its critics. On October 10, 1864, as Sheridan and his men were completing their task of destroying the Shenandoah Valley, Confederate general Stephen Ramseur wrote home to his wife, "I feel that they have put themselves beyond the pale of civilization by the course they have pursued in this campaign. This beautiful and fertile valley has been totally destroyed. Sheridan had some of the houses, *all* of the mills & barns, every straw & wheat stack burned. This valley is one great desert. I do not see how these people are to live."[71] Even Union supporters commented on the seemingly drastic measures taken during the campaign. One of Sheridan's officers, Wesley Merritt, acknowledged after the war that the campaign was harsh "and appears severer now in the lapse of time; but it was necessary as a measure of war."[72] A Union soldier echoed Merritt's sentiments. "It not infrequently happens that barns and stacks of hay and grain are burned by our troops as we pass through country," he wrote. "This must seem pretty hard to the citizens but it is one of the invariable consequences of invasion no matter how civilized the people."[73]

Sheridan defended his actions, stating in his memoirs, "I do not hold war to mean simply that lines of men shall engage each other in battle, and material interests be ignored. This is but a duel, in which one combatant seeks the other's life; war means much more, and is far worse than this." Noncombatants, Sheridan argued, sit peacefully at home, secure in their perceived immunity from war's depredations. When "deprivation and suffering are brought to their own doors," however, "the case appears much graver, for the loss of property weighs heavy with the most of mankind; heavier often than the sacrifices made on the field of battle. Death is popularly considered the maximum punishment in war, but it is not; the reduction to poverty brings prayers for peace more surely and more quickly than does the destruction of human life, as the selfishness of man has demonstrated in more than one great conflict."[74]

The larger implications of Sheridan's actions are the subject of some debate among scholars.[75] There are two general camps: those who accept Sheridan's and other eyewitnesses' accounts as accurate depictions of the devastation and those who argue that the destruction has been exaggerated and should be placed into its proper perspective. The former often employ the same metaphors of wasteland and wilderness as those who participated in or were victims of the campaigns. One early historian wrote that after Sheridan's operations "the Valley felt the fury of war, and its fatal wealth of resources was laid waste."[76] Another, more sympathetic to the Confederate cause, wrote of Sheridan, "In fact nothing that devilish ingenuity could invent was left undone to transform the loveliest and most fertile valley in the world into a desolate and howling wilderness."[77] A later chronicler described Sheridan's actions as "a holocaust that spread from the Blue Ridge to the Alleghenies," crying, "Verily was the fertile vale left in desolation!"[78] Gary Gallagher argued, "Without an appreciation of why the Shenandoah Valley became first a battleground and then a wasteland, it is impossible to understand fully the last year of the war."[79]

Those who argue for a more tempered reading of the primary sources shy away from images of deserts and wasted landscapes. Michael G. Mahon suggested that "Sheridan's destruction of the Valley in 1864, colorful and dramatic as it was, did not deprive the Confederacy of any measurable amount of subsistence or help hasten the fall of Richmond."[80] Instead, the Valley's value to Lee's armies had been greatly diminished as early as 1862 due to the near-constant presence of competing armies and to poor weather. "The farmers could not even find an ally in the weather," Mahon wrote. "Snow and an inordinate amount of rainfall throughout the winter and early spring [of 1862] turned the countryside into a vast quagmire and prevented many from plowing and preparing their land in time for spring planting."[81] The wet weather gave way to drought in the summer of that year and again in 1864, limiting the area's productivity. Nature, not Union actions, was to blame.

Mahon also contended that because Sheridan's Middle Division had to fight Jubal Early's forces on a regular basis, Sheridan could not devote much attention to the targeted destruction that Grant's orders required him to conduct. Thus, the majority of Union efforts were against farms located along the main roads, leaving much of the interior portions of the Valley relatively untouched. For Mahon, the main importance of Sheridan's 1864 operations in the Valley was not that they destroyed a vital source of sustenance for the Confederate armies operating throughout Virginia but instead that they ultimately denied a significant proportion of the Valley's population the means of subsistence in the short term.

Mark Neely agreed: "The destruction visited on the Shenandoah Valley in 1864 was a secondary consideration for Sheridan and his army." Sheridan's agenda was instead to conduct "a military campaign, the major purpose of which was to defeat and destroy if possible Jubal A. Early's Confederate army."[82] Neely contended, "The valley was not scorched." Doing so would have been difficult, he noted, "without application of some potent fire accelerant, with which the army, trained and fitted for combat rather than for terror and sabotage, was not equipped." Furthermore, a large-scale burning was unlikely because "the roads, hedges, orchards, and forests of late summer, not to mention the brooks and streams, would act as impediments to scorching the earth in any literal sense."[83]

William G. Thomas also suggested that the 1864 campaigns "inflicted limited and targeted damage that neither destroyed the entire Valley nor subjugated its population." Rockingham County, which conducted a post-campaign census to determine the extent of its residents' losses, reported a less than 25 percent decline from 1860 figures. However, Thomas acknowledged that even through limited destruction, "Federal officers openly challenged the Confederate civilians' sense of security and faith in their government. They destroyed Confederate supplies and buildings and threatened Confederate men. They also visibly demonstrated the weakness of Confederate institutions."[84]

Edward Phillips concurred. He argued that through acts of destruction, the Union forces intended to demonstrate "that the power of the Confederacy to help or protect" its citizens "was gone" and "that the Rebel cause was itself hopelessly lost." Phillips added an important dimension to the debate when he suggested that "as the resources of the region dwindled, new acts of destruction became weapons of psychological warfare."[85] However, he too believed that

Sheridan's raids were limited in what they accomplished. "Man had demonstrated his genius for destroying man and the works of man," Phillips wrote, but he "had not yet developed the techniques for destroying the land."[86]

Such perspectives have merit, and their proponents make compelling arguments. It is true that neither Sheridan nor Hunter before him literally destroyed the land. Though the devastation wrought by their campaigns may have been limited geographically and even materially, however, Union actions in the Shenandoah in 1864 did in fact destroy the Valley's landscape. This is an important distinction. Landscape is the product of a community's relationship with the surrounding natural environment. It is the visible evidence of culture interacting with nature to create a representation of the society that claims that landscape as its own. So, regardless of whether Union operations in the Shenandoah Valley in the summer and fall of 1864 actually turned the fertile farms into wastelands (which they did not), those whose livelihoods depended on that agricultural landscape perceived that they had. What this short episode in the history of the Civil War illustrates, therefore, is an important aspect of environmental history: perception shapes relationships with nature just as physical interaction does. When residents lamented that their Eden had been turned into a desert, they not only revealed a deep-seated fear of uncontrolled landscapes but also indicated they had been forced to develop new relationships with their environment. This is the ultimate legacy of Sheridan's operations against the Shenandoah Valley.

CHAPTER FOUR

Devoured Land

Sherman's Georgia and Carolina Campaigns, 1864–1865

"WE HAVE DEVOURED THE LAND," wrote William Tecumseh Sherman in a letter to his wife, Ellen, in June 1864. "All the people retire before us, and desolation is behind. To realize what war is one should follow our tracks."[1] Sherman was reflecting on the damage wrought by the protracted battle for control over northern Georgia between his Union forces and Confederate general Joe Johnston's army. Neither side intended to destroy the landscape; the devastation was instead an unavoidable result of armies in motion and one of the inevitable costs of war. By November, however, Sherman implemented a strategy that shifted devastation from a regrettable, haphazard consequence into a deliberate weapon of war.

Sherman's campaigns through Georgia and the Carolinas from November 1864 to April 1865 focused on destroying the physical, economic, and cultural landscapes of the region. The campaigns succeeded in revealing the Confederacy's inability to militarily and politically control its own territory by undermining its capacity to marshal critical resources through managing nature in meaningful and productive ways. Like similar operations around Vicksburg and in the Shenandoah Valley, Sherman's marches displayed Union power over the Confederate government, its army, and its residents by denying them the ability to transform nature into culture, thus depriving them of a fundamental source of security. By imposing his own (and the federal government's) will over the fertile southern landscape, Sherman attacked and destroyed the agroecological system on which the Confederacy and its citizens relied and hastened the end of the conflict.

Although Sherman's operations in Georgia and the Carolinas have inspired an impressive array of critical analysis, few scholars have acknowledged or examined the operation's implications from an environmental perspective. Much of the scholarship focuses on the military and social issues surrounding the marches: it debates the novelty and efficacy of Sherman's strategy, questions

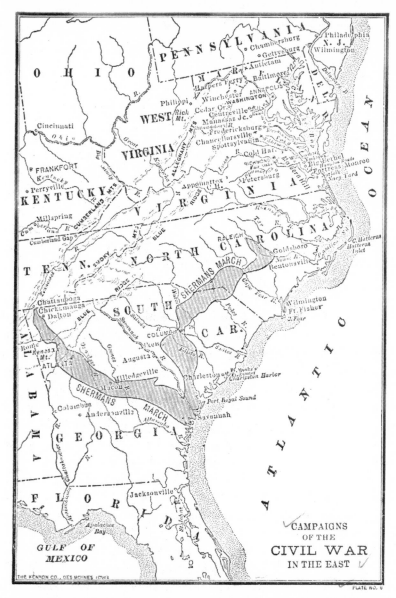

Sherman's March: The shading on this map indicates the areas affected by Sherman's operations in Georgia and the Carolinas. Civil War Maps Collection, Geography and Map Division, Library of Congress, g3701s cw0071c20.

whether the marches ushered in the modern era of "total war," and provides intricate details of the experiences of the common soldier and those who lived in the army's path. All of this is important, and the magnitude of the literature reveals the strategic, social, and psychological impact this single set of campaigns had for Americans during the war and since.[2] But equally important, and inextricably related to each of those other areas, are the ways in which American relationships with nature shaped and in turn were transformed by Sherman's operations in Georgia and the Carolinas. As historian Jacqueline Glass Campbell has argued, "Sherman's March was an invasion of both geographic and psychological space. The Union Army constructed a vision of the Southern landscape as military terrain."[3] Even more than reenvisioning the landscape in military terms, however, Sherman's operations were predicated on gaining control over the landscape. Control—over nature, labor, and territory—formed the basis of the campaign. In the end, Sherman's marches were not just expressions of political and military power as he envisioned them; they also revealed the Union's power to exert control over and shape the southern environment.

That environment, however, had power of its own and could be just as hostile as the people who fought to protect it. Terrain, weather, and disease proved to be as threatening as, or more threatening than, any human enemy Sherman's troops encountered. Taking power away from the local populace and the Confederate government thus required Sherman to assert control over various elements in the landscape, or at least minimize their hold over him. Union success was not always certain, but by deploying several weapons in their arsenal—foraging, fire, and the science of engineering—Sherman's army brought war upon the land, transforming gardens into wastelands and leaving a lasting imprint on the southern landscape.

Sherman's stated goal for his operations in late 1864 and early 1865 was to dismantle the industrial infrastructure and transportation networks that supported the Confederate army. Fire was one of Sherman's greatest tools, which he used to reduce the Confederacy's military assets to ashes. Sherman's men set fire to any building, warehouse, or structure that could be used for military purposes. They pried up the railroad tracks, set the ties ablaze, and melted the rails, twisting them into "Sherman neckties." Cotton stores, too, were burned, with the purpose of undermining the Confederacy's ability to finance its war effort.

The obliteration of the Confederacy's infrastructure was only part of the battle, however, as a surgeon in the Union army intimated in a letter home: "It seems now we will hold no interior point between Chattanooga and the Gulf, as all railways, foundries, and other public works will be destroyed before this campaign shall end, and much of the country effectually eaten up and desolated."[4] Over and above targeting the military landscape, Sherman's army would attack the agricultural base of the Confederacy, taking what it needed and destroying the rest. Sherman believed that he was fighting not only "hostile armies, but a hostile people" and that the war could not be won until both were conquered.[5] His plans for conquest centered on the *chevauchée*, a massive foraging raid that would not only destroy much of the region's military and agricultural potential but also would reveal the futility of civilian resistance to the Union army's overwhelming power.[6]

Sherman had some experience in these tactics, not only during the 1863 campaign against Vicksburg but also as commander of Union forces in the western theater after Grant was promoted to commanding general of all U.S. forces. Early in 1864 Sherman conducted a successful raid through central Mississippi, using local resources to support his troops.[7] While this arguably was not a full-fledged *chevauchée*, it did serve as a good model for Sherman's campaigns through Georgia and the Carolinas. These later raids would more powerfully strike at the heart of the residents' relationship with nature, eliminating their power to reorganize the environment to suit their—or the Confederacy's—needs. In November 1864 Sherman determined to march his army through the heart of Secessia, living off the land, leaving the local residents little except food for thought.

In conducting the *chevauchée*, Sherman commandeered or destroyed every vestige of the locals' agroecological system. Throughout the war, Union and Confederate forces requisitioned agricultural resources such as grain and livestock for their immediate use as a matter of military necessity; in the *chevauchée*, however, these same resources, as well as the tools and labor used to produce them, became viable military targets. They were the means by which southerners had molded the landscape into one that supported the Confederacy, so their destruction became tantamount to destroying the rebellion. Sherman understood, even if he did not articulate it in such language, that the power to shape the landscape was linked to other kinds of power. He suggested in a letter to Grant, "If we can march a well appointed Army right through his territory, it is a demonstration to the World, foreign and domestic, that we have a power which [Jefferson] Davis cannot resist. This may not be war, but rather Statesmanship," Sherman proclaimed, "proof positive that the North can prevail."[8] In order for that march to be successful, however, Sherman needed to go beyond simply crossing space on a map; he needed and intended to reveal the weakness of the Confederacy by illustrating that southerners' control over their landscape was precarious at best.

Key to the success of Sherman's "demonstration" were Special Field Orders No. 120, which set the parameters for the *chevauchée* and all other aspects of the 1864–65 campaigns. Issued at Kingston, Georgia, on November 9, 1864, these orders divided the Military Division of the Mississippi into two wings, each comprising two corps that would march along four nearly parallel roads between Atlanta and Savannah (in order to maintain flexibility in operation, Sherman did not announce his final target, even to his officers). Each wing could take only a limited number of wagons, reserved for transporting pontoons, hauling ammunition, and providing ambulance service. All other supplies, including the men's rations and forage for the animals, would be taken from the countryside. Such limitations on the supply train enabled Sherman's men to concentrate their efforts on the main purpose of the march—to exhibit Federal power to move within and transform the southern landscape at will.

In taking what his army needed from the areas through which he marched, Sherman revealed the Confederacy's inability to protect its most valuable assets: its agricultural wealth and the slave labor that made such bounty possible. In order for his efforts against these resources to be most effective, Sherman established strict protocols for the operation. Section 4 of Special Field Orders No. 120 directed the army to "forage liberally on the country during the march" and ordered each brigade commander to "organize a good and sufficient foraging party, under the command of one or more discreet officers, who will gather, near the route traveled, corn or forage of any kind, meat of any kind, vegetables, corn meal, or whatever is needed by the command, aiming at all times to keep in the wagons at least ten days' provisions [. . .] and three day's forage." The orders forbade soldiers from entering houses or "commit[ing] any trespass," but "during a halt or camp, they may be permitted to gather turnips, potatoes, and other vegetables, and to drive in stock in sight of their camp." Section 5 restricted to corps commanders the power to destroy buildings and instructed them to use that power only when "guerrillas or bushwhackers molest our march, or should the inhabitants [. . .] manifest local hostility." If such opposition arose, Sherman gave his commanders permission to "order and enforce a devastation more or less relentless, according to the measure of such hostility." Section 6 enabled the cavalry and artillery to appropriate horses, mules, and wagons "freely and without limit," although Sherman urged his men to discriminate between "the rich, who are usually hostile, and the poor and industrious, usually neutral or friendly."[9]

Taking and destroying were not the only ways Sherman had to express power. While he rarely needed to use military force along the marches, he regularly needed to reshape the landscape to facilitate his progress. Anticipating as much, Sherman included provisions for appropriating labor for engineering and other needs. The majority of this labor he hoped to acquire along the way, which would not only provide needed manpower but also serve to undermine slaveholders' control over their workforce and, therefore, the landscape. Section 7 read, "Negroes who are able-bodied and can be of service to the several columns may be taken along; but each army commander will bear in mind that the question of supplies is a very important one, and that his first duty is to see to those who bear arms." Section 8 provided for the "organization [. . .] of a good pioneer battalion for each army corps, composed if possible of negroes," which was responsible for repairing roads, "doubl[ing] them if possible, so that the columns will not be delayed after reaching bad places." The pioneer corps was also charged with building fortifications, corduroying roads, and other such tasks. Section 9 dealt with the engineering needs of the army.[10]

Many scholars of the campaign focus on the apparent shift away from "limited" toward "total" or "hard" war tactics implied in Special Field Orders No. 120 and analyze them for their military and social ramifications.[11] What these sources ignore, however, is that the provisions had important environmental consequences as well. In addition to waging "hard war" against the Confederacy's citizens, the orders directly attacked the agroecological systems those residents had struggled for decades to establish. The campaigns through Georgia and the Carolinas reasserted Federal power in the region by undermining or destroying the local population's ability to manipulate the landscape to generate sustenance and wealth. In taking away their slaves, tools, animals, and even their produce, Sherman's forces interrupted—or completely rearranged—the fundamental relationship with nature the local populace had established. In these final campaigns, Sherman attacked and destroyed the foundations of the Confederacy, causing it to crumble.

Two days before the great march began, one of Sherman's staff officers, George Ward Nichols, wrote, "I never heard that manna grew on the sand-beaches or in the marshes, though we are sure that we can obtain forage on our way; and I have reason to know that General Sherman is in the highest degree sanguine and cheerful––sure even of success."[12] Sherman had good reason to be optimistic; if knowledge equals power, then Sherman seemingly was blessed many times over. His education at West Point had inculcated in him a faith in humanity's ability to bring order from chaos, even in times of war. He had been well trained in the history and art of war; the latter, he suggested, was founded on principles "as true as the multiplication table, the law of gravitation, of virtual velocities, or any other invariable rule of natural philosophy." Sherman also had remarkable self-confidence: "Without being aware of it, I seem to possess a knowledge into men & things, of rivers, roads, capacity of trains, wagons, etc., that no one near me professes to have."[13]

Perhaps more important than even these esoteric insights, Sherman had firm practical knowledge that would serve him well in the forthcoming campaign. He was intimately familiar with the physical and cultural geography of the region through which his army would march, having participated in a detailed survey of the area as a young army officer years before.[14] Moreover, Federal foraging parties had reconnoitered around Atlanta in September and October, obtaining new intelligence about central Georgia's circumstances. He had discovered, according to the *New York Herald*, "that Central Georgia was filled with supplies; that her endless cottonfields of 1860 had become her inviting corn fields of 1864, for the subsistence of rebel armies."[15] All of this underlay Sherman's decision to cut loose from his supply base.

"They don't know what war means," Sherman wrote to chief of staff Henry Wager Halleck, "but when the rich planters of the Oconee and Savannah [Rivers] see their fences and corn and hogs and sheep vanish before their eyes they will have something more than a mean opinion of the 'Yanks.' Even now our poor mules laugh at the fine corn-fields, and our soldiers riot on chestnuts, sweet potatoes, pigs, chickens, &c." Sherman concluded that it would "take ten days to finish up our road, during which I will eat out this flank and along down the Coosa [River], and then will rapidly put into execution the plan."[16] Clearly, Sherman believed that destroying the symbols, artifacts, and means by which southerners had "improved" nature would cure "secession fever." Confident both in his plan and of ample provisions for his men and animals, Sherman set fire to the railroad depot, cotton warehouses, and armory in Atlanta and moved out with his sixty thousand men on November 15, 1864.

Leaving Atlanta was somewhat bittersweet—its capture had been hard won. Prior to that pivotal victory, Sherman's men had spent the summer of 1864 fighting heated battles in some of Georgia's most rugged territory. Their struggles in the 140-mile stretch of the Appalachians between Atlanta and Chattanooga, Tennessee, inured them to the hardships of war, however. Battles such as Resaca, Kennesaw Mountain, New Hope Church, and Peach Tree Creek pitted the seasoned veterans against an equally experienced foe that often had a distinct geographical advantage. The difficult operations in northwestern Georgia made the campaigns that followed—the "March to the Sea" and the subsequent forays through the Carolinas—seem mere picnics, pleasant marches through picturesque forests and over rolling, fertile hills. The ease of these campaigns was due largely to the lack of concerted Confederate opposition, but the end result of both the terrible battles and the less contested *chevauchées* was the same: the destruction of the Confederacy's cultural and agroecological landscapes.

On the first leg of the *chevauchée*, Sherman's route took his army through diverse landscapes ranging from the hilly terrain around Atlanta, through the slopes and ridges of central Georgia, to the marshy lowlands approaching Savannah and the Atlantic Ocean. Thick woods of oak and pine covered much of the territory along the path. Good roads facilitated the transport of wagons and artillery, and warm, dry weather ensured easy movement over the red clay and sandy soils of central Georgia.[17]

Marching through gently rolling country, Sherman's army seemed to have few natural obstructions to its progress. Maj. Thomas Ward Osborn, chief of artillery for the Eleventh Corps, noted in a letter to his brother Abraham that campaigning through the pine forests of Georgia was "pleasant. The roads are hard and solid to move the trains on except where the quicksand bottoms are found near the rivers and creeks. The general character of the country made the moving of the army easy."[18] Sgt. Rice Bull, a volunteer with the 123rd New York Infantry, recalled that the march "started under ideal weather, good roads and only a small force of the enemy in our front who could oppose or harass us. [. . .] The worst foes the soldier had to contend with on such a campaign were rain and mud," though he acknowledged that they "had only one day's rain until [they] were within seventy-five miles of Savannah."[19]

Maj. Henry Hitchcock also commented on the ease of the campaign through Georgia: "The perfection of this campaign just now consists in our marching through this 'pine barrens' country: good (sandy) road, fine pure air, no difficult hills, trains well up, forage of every kind in *super-abundance*, and our camp tonight superb. Tents are pitched in open space in fine grove of large pine trees, no undergrowth, water convenient, clear, and good (as is all the water in this region, even the swamps and ponds)."[20] Likewise, Maj. Gen. Jacob Cox noted that, except for two days of snow in late November, "[t]he weather had generally been perfect." "The camps in the open pine-woods, the bonfires along the railways, the occasional sham-battles at night, with blazing pine-knots for weapons whirling in the darkness, all combined to leave upon the minds of officers and men the impression of a vast holiday frolic," he wrote.[21] Even the Confederates noted the ease of the campaign. Maj. Gen. Gustavus Smith of the Georgia Militia recalled that the "face of the country was open, the roads were in good order, the weather was fine and bracing, the crops had been gathered, and were ready for use; in short, a combination of circumstances favored an easy march for Sherman's army."[22]

Accounts that focus on the ease of the operations can be misleading, however, and obscure the immense effort Sherman's engineers and pioneer battalion exerted over Georgia's terrain in order for the campaign to progress efficiently and effectively. According to Maj. Gen. Jacob Cox, commander of the Army of the Ohio (Twenty-Third Corps), "[T]he topography of the [campaign route] is determined by the river courses, which run in radiating lines from the highlands a hundred miles northeast of Atlanta." The Savannah River flows "in a very direct general line" southeast to the Atlantic, forming the border between Georgia and South Carolina. "The Ocmulgee and Oconee Rivers rise near Atlanta," Cox reported, "and flow in parallel valleys about forty miles apart in the same southeasterly direction nearly two hundred miles, when they unite to form the Altamaha, which enters the ocean a little north of the Florida line." The Ogeechee, which Cox described as the "only other stream of any importance in this part of the State," originates "midway between Milledgeville and Augusta, but gradually approaches the Savannah, so that for fifty or sixty miles from the ocean these rivers are nearly parallel and from fifteen to twenty miles apart."[23] Though the route mapped out by Sherman avoided crossing the major rivers unless absolutely necessary, at least a dozen smaller tributaries emptied into these main streams. In addition, as the columns pressed closer to the sea coast, they encountered swamps with much greater frequency.

All of this water posed enormous logistical problems. While the infantry and cavalry could traverse most of the rivers and swamps without great travail, the wheeled artillery pieces, livestock, and ammunition and supply wagons required bridges or other means of crossing them. Sherman, "a scientific soldier with a strong knowledge of engineering and its importance," foresaw such difficulties and made specific provisions in Special Field Orders No. 120.[24] Section 8 created a pioneer battalion, charged with providing manual labor for all engineering and fortification needs. Section 9 appointed Col. Orlando M. Poe, a fellow West Pointer, as chief engineer and assigned "to each wing of the army a pontoon train, fully equipped and organized," to be "properly protected at all times."[25]

According to Noah Trudeau, "The pontoon trains were Sherman's secret weapon, whose critical role in the coming campaign would be seldom recognized or acknowledged."[26] Furthermore, "Without the skillful hard work of the army's bridge makers and road fixers, the march would have become a dispiriting slog through Georgia. The fact that Sherman could plan a route across fifteen significant creeks, streams, or rivers, requiring bridging at an average 230 feet per crossing [. . .], along with nearly 100 miles of corduroy paths, most of which was accomplished without serious delay to the columns, speaks to the effectiveness of this arm of the General's operation." Indeed, Trudeau argued, the engineering and pioneer work "represented a logistical achievement of unparalleled accomplishment."[27]

Sherman's engineers and pioneers enabled the rest of his army to direct its full attention and energy to the primary task at hand—to attack and destroy or commandeer the very basis of the Confederate nation: its agroecological foundations. The means by which Sherman intended to accomplish this task was through the *chevauchée*. In accordance with section 4 of the special field orders, formal foraging parties accompanied each of the army's two wings. According to Thomas Osborn, a soldier on the march, the foragers "spread themselves over the entire country and every thing available for the use of the army was gathered in." They slaughtered food animals "where found" and brought horses, mules, wagons, provisions, and forage for pickup by the soldiers along the line of march. "Wherever cotton was found," Osborn wrote, "it was burned. I think but few houses were destroyed."[28] Pondering what might happen, George Bradley, a chaplain with the Twentieth Corps, noted in his diary, "No one, without being here, can form a proper idea of the devastation that will be found in our track. Thousands of families will have their homes laid in ashes, and they themselves will be turned beggars into the street. We have literally carried fire and sword into this once proud and defiant State."[29] Osborn's assessment of the infrequency of destruction of dwellings was more accurate than Bradley's exaggerated prediction; barns, mills, granaries, and other structures—not homes—were the main targets for Sherman's torches.

Jacob Cox noted that "from barn, from granary and smoke-house, and from the kitchen gardens of the plantations, isolated foragers would hasten by converging lines, driving before them the laden mule heaped high with vegetables, smoked bacon, fresh meat, and poultry." As the army reached evening camp, the soldiers "would find this ludicrous but most bountiful supply train waiting for them at every fork of the road, with as much regularity as a railway train running on 'schedule time.'"[30] On November 18 Henry Hitchcock wrote, "Plenty of forage, poultry, hogs, etc., and 'foraged liberally.' Camps all around us and frequent shots sound through the woods, each the death knell of some luckless secesh pig or rebel fowl."[31] Charles Belknap, one of Sherman's foragers, or "bummers" as they came to be known, recalled, "Everything on foot and wing, all the things of the earth and air, were 'contraband of war.'" Calling his fellow foragers "military agriculturalists," Major Belknap noted that they "prodded the ground with ram-rod and bayonet [. . .] punching the unoffending earth."[32] The landscape, even the ground itself, became the target of Sherman's raiding soldiers.[33]

The foragers had a great deal from which to stock their mobile larders. Sgt. Rice Bull noted that although the "country over which we moved on our first day's march had during the siege of Atlanta been overrun by both Armies and was completely stripped of everything in the way of needed supplies," once the troops passed Stone Mountain east of the city, they "crossed the boundary of the devastated and entered and continued through the richest farming section of Georgia. This region was filled with food for man and beast that could be used by the Army if collected as we marched along."[34] Sherman recalled that between Covington and Milledgeville they found an "abundance of corn, molasses, meal, bacon, and sweet potatoes" in addition to "a good many cows and oxen, and a large number of mules." He attributed this wealth to the state "never before having been visited by a hostile army; the recent crop had been excellent, had just been gathered and laid by for winter."[35] Others remarked on the region's abundance as well; on November 28 Henry Hitchcock described the army's surroundings in his diary: "Today's march on sandy roads, and through woods chiefly pine, though as yet we still see oaks and other trees. Good farms along the travelled roads, and crops have all been good. We see hardly any cotton—corn almost exclusively instead—*for which we are much obliged*."[36]

Few Georgians heard, or would have accepted, any sentiment of gratitude from the foragers. Dolly Lunt Burge of Newton County recorded the actions of Sherman's foragers on her plantation. She asked the soldiers for protection, "But like Demons they rush in. My yards are full. To my smoke house, my Dairy, Pantry, kitchen & cellar like famished wolves they come, breaking locks & whatever is in their way." Burge lost a thousand pounds of meat, most of her dry goods, and all of her poultry. The "young pigs [were] shot down in my yard, & hunted as if they were the rebels themselves." She felt "utterly powerless."[37] That, of course, was the point.

By the time Sherman began his march through Georgia, southern agriculture had changed to accommodate the Confederacy's war needs. Mobilization of the land resulted in increased focus, albeit temporary and scattered, on grains. Six days after he indicated gracious appreciation for southern corn, Henry Hitchcock wrote, "Abundance of forage—chiefly fodder—hardly ever twenty minutes together out of sight of cornfields, though land is sandy and unpromising. No cotton today, as usual. That monarch is evidently an exile for the present from where he once reigned."[38] George Nichols's journal entry for November 27 echoed Hitchcock's. "We had been told that the country was very poor east of the Oconee, but our experience has been a delightful gastronomic contradiction of the statement," he wrote. "The cattle trains are getting so large that we find difficulty in driving them along. Thanksgiving-day was very generally observed in the army, the troops scorning chickens in the plenitude of turkeys with which they had supplied themselves. [. . .] In truth, so far as the gratification of the stomach goes, the troops are pursuing a continuous thanksgiving."[39] The riches of Georgia, however, were quickly depleted. Sherman's army of sixty thousand could not tarry or it would risk the same fate as those left starving in its wake.[40]

That risk became reality as the army neared Savannah. The last seventy-five miles of the Union march passed "through a country so intersected with mirey swamps and deep morasses" that it slowed the army's progress, according to

George Cram, a soldier on the campaign.[41] Another of Sherman's soldiers, Theodore Upson, recorded in his diary on December 11, "This whole country is a marsh." The enemy had "cut the dykes," Upson observed, and "[e]vry thing is a black muck."[42] Sgt. Rice Bull recalled that Savannah "was circled by swamps, lagoons, canals, and rivers" and that "beyond all these water hazards were the enemy fortifications, manned by such forces as had been gathered together. When we reached the vicinity of the swampy ground west of the city, we halted and the investment of Savannah was begun."[43]

The task of taking the city was made more complicated by the surrounding environment. In addition to dealing with muddy roads and swampy rice fields, which made even nominal progress wearisome, the foraging companies had a difficult time acquiring food and fodder. With the rich cornfields of central Georgia behind them, the foragers had to rely on the rice fields of the coastal lowlands. Although Sherman noted that Savannah's rice plantations appeared promising, it was only a short while before the sixty thousand men encamped near them depleted those supplies.[44] "For awhile after we arrived here things looked blue enough," George Cram wrote. "We had taken with us only about eight or ten days rations, and had obtained the rest from the country during our march. This worked very well so long as we were changing camp daily [. . . but] when we came to a dead halt in front of an armed city and not a pound of bread or bacon in our entire army, our haversack empty, affairs looked alarming enough."[45] Rice Bull observed, "Savannah of necessity must be taken in a few days unless connection at some other place was made with our fleet; we must have food soon. Our foragers were all in, there was no place to forage; all we had to eat was what could be taken from the wagons and that supply was nearly exhausted." Luckily, Bull and his comrades found an untouched crop of rice on which they lived for two weeks. Describing it as "manna in the wilderness," Bull speculated that without that fortuitous discovery they "would have gone hungry."[46]

Hungry soldiers made poor soldiers, and if Sherman was going to capture Savannah, he had to reestablish a supply line and connect with the U.S. Navy's fleet covering Savannah's shore. On December 13 Union soldiers under Maj. Gen. William B. Hazen captured Fort McAllister—a Confederate outpost south of the city—thereby opening a secure base to which supplies from Union-held Port Royal, fifty miles to the northeast, could be transported. With a guaranteed supply line, Sherman could resume his movements against the city.

The city's geography, however, favored its defenders. Sherman told his wife, "The strength of Savannah lies in its swamps which can only be crossed by narrow causeways all of which are swept by heavy artillery."[47] A city of nearly twenty-five thousand residents in 1864, Savannah sits on a sandy plateau, approximately forty feet above sea level, between the mouths of the Savannah and Ogeechee Rivers. The surrounding land, according to Jacob Cox, sunk "almost to the level of the sea." The coast was "low and cut into islands by deep sinuous natural canals or creeks," which were "widely bordered by the salt marsh which is all awash at high tide." Savannah's location was "almost like an island in the swamps." The only landed approach to the city from the west consisted of a narrow tongue of land six to eight miles wide between the two rivers, dotted with plantations "in the midst of broad rice-fields which had been reclaimed from the surrounding marsh." These rice swamps edged the rivers, creating "a natural barrier around the city on the northwest, about three miles away." The Little Ogeechee River flows between the two larger rivers, providing yet another line of defense southwest of the city. To the north, "a series of suburban plantations with their rice-fields in front" made up a "natural line of defence for the town."[48] Surrounded by water—rice fields to the north, west, and south, large rivers to the north and south, and the Atlantic to the east—Savannah was a veritable fortress. As at Vicksburg, nature and culture coalesced to provide protection to the city's Confederate defenders.

The seventeen thousand Confederate troops charged with holding the city made good use of Savannah's natural defenses as well as the various elements of its managed landscape. As Cox noted, "Extensive dams, canals, and flood-gates were part of the system by which the artificial inundation necessary for rice tillage was made, and these works were easily modified so as to become an essential part of the military defence."[49] Savannah's "hydraulic landscape," as historian Mart Stewart has called it, was the result of decades of effort to wrest value from swampy landscape and became the means by which whites attempted to maintain control over both slaves and nature.[50] During the war, however, the complex irrigation system could be and was employed to flood the lands surrounding the city, making any approach difficult if not impossible. One soldier noted in his diary that "nature had helped them [the Confederates] very materially, there being swamp all along their line of works. In some places there were rice swamps, over which they had let the water at high tide and then shut down the gates. In charging their works, we should have been obliged to go right through these swamps in the face of a galling fire from both musketry and heavy guns."[51] The roads, too, benefited the defenders: they were "narrow causeways," Cox recalled, "heaped high enough to be out of water when the rice-fields were overflowed, as they often were, to a depth of from three to six feet."[52] Flooding the fields impeded traffic on the causeways, especially for heavy wagons and artillery pieces.

Sherman reported to Grant that his opponent Gen. William Hardee had "taken refuge in a line constructed behind swamps & overflowed rice-fields" between the Savannah and the Little Ogeechee, which, he observed, was "impassable from its Salt marshes and boggy swamps, crossed only by narrow causeways or common corduroy roads."[53] Nevertheless, Sherman was undeterred by the Confederates' seeming advantage. He had faced similar circumstances the previous year with Grant at Vicksburg and had confidence in his men to overcome the obstacles that humans and nature placed before them.

While his soldiers attempted to set up decent camp amid the swamps and rice fields, Sherman's engineers and pioneer corps worked hard to turn the sodden terrain into a traversable landscape, building bridges, corduroying roads, and removing wagons and cannon from the mud.[54] According to Jacob Cox, efforts to mend the breaks in the causeways and canals and to rearrange the floodgates "so that they should shut out the water from the rivers instead of shutting it in" succeeded, and "the depth of the inundations began to be sensibly diminished." Draining the water was of supreme importance. "Till the water should be a good deal reduced an assault could hardly be thought of, for narrow columns along the causeways and dykes would have little chance, and in the overflowed fields the certainty of all wounded men being drowned would make an unjustifiable waste of human life."[55] Sherman had to manage the landscape before he could attack the city.

While Sherman's engineers were attempting to transform the flooded landscape into one more suitable for sustaining an army, General Hardee in Savannah planned his escape. Not wanting to be trapped inside the city's defenses, Hardee evacuated his men on December 19, with only a nominal show of force. The Federal forces moved into the city on the morning of the twenty-first, and Sherman telegraphed President Lincoln, presenting Savannah to him "as a Christmas-gift."[56] Sherman's nearly bloodless campaign—his "demonstration to the world"—ended as a grand success.

Sherman and his men were well aware of the effects, both military and psychological, their recent campaign elicited. Henry Hitchcock wrote in his diary that the campaign proved "that a large army can march with impunity through the heart of the richest rebel state, after boldly cutting loose from all its bases, and subsisting on the country." Hitchcock concluded that the campaign was a "great and important success, full of significance for the future."[57] Another soldier predicted that the campaign "will be one of the really historical campaigns of the war, much more so than some where vastly more fighting was done. It was brilliant in conception and well executed, but practically one of the easiest campaigns we have had."[58]

In less than one month, Sherman had marched an army sixty thousand strong through the heart of enemy territory with little resistance. The Military

Division of the Mississippi left the foothills of Atlanta on November 15, 1864, traversed the rolling country near Milledgeville, crossed the swampy lowlands to the seacoast ("foraging liberally" along the way), and captured Savannah on December 21. Sherman understood that taking or destroying everything associated with agricultural production would bring the Confederacy to its knees. "I know my Enemy," he wrote to his brother Philemon Ewing, "and think I have made him feel the Effects of war, that he did not expect, and he now Sees how the Power of the United States can reach him in his innermost recesses."[59] The Confederacy's strength as well as its weakness stemmed from its power to transform the environment into a productive landscape, capable of meeting both military and civilian needs. By trumping that power, Sherman's March to the Sea struck a significant blow to the South's agroecological foundations and to the rebellion.

Sherman's men also recognized the consequences of such a strategy. The majority of Union soldiers and officers came from rural communities and nearly half were farmers or farm laborers. The destruction of the South's agrarian infrastructure resonated strongly with them. Recounting the damage done and the provisions taken, one officer noted, "We have torn up and destroyed about 200 miles of railroad, burned all bridges and cleaned up the country generally of almost every thing upon which the people could live." Sherman's army had "burned all cotton, took all provisions, forage, wagons, mules, horses, cattle, hogs and poultry and the many other things which a country furnishes and which may be made available for the support of an army. In fact, as we have left the country I do not see how the people can live for the next two years."[60] Others, too, made grim predictions about the region's future. "One thing is for certain," George Nichols wrote, "neither the West nor the East will draw any supplies from the counties in this state traversed by our army for a long time to come. Our work has been the next thing to annihilation."[61]

The damage done to the South's military resources—both provisions and materiel—was extensive. As Sherman told Henry Halleck, "[O]ur campaign of the last month, as well as every step I take from this point northward, is as much a direct attack upon Lee's army as though we were operating within the sound of his artillery."[62] He reported that his army had destroyed the Georgia State Railroad entirely and that it had consumed the corn, sweet potatoes, fodder, cattle, hogs, sheep, and poultry found "thirty miles on either side of a line from Atlanta to Savannah." His army requisitioned tens of thousands of horses and mules and ordered thousands more killed in order to prevent them falling into enemy hands. A "countless number" of slaves who were determined to seize their freedom joined the moving columns, despite Sherman's exhortations to stay put. Sherman estimated the damage at "$100,000,000; at least

$20,000,000 of which has inured to our advantage." The rest Sherman chalked up to "simple waste and destruction."[63]

Daniel Oakey, captain of the Second Massachusetts Volunteers, remarked that the Georgia campaign was seen as "a grand military promenade, all novelty and excitement." He believed it had a deeper significance, stating that its "moral effect on friend and foe was immense. It proved our ability to lay open the heart of the Confederacy, and left the question of what we might do next a matter of doubt and terror."[64] Emma LeConte, a young resident of Columbia, South Carolina, certainly wondered what lay in store for her native state. "Georgia has been desolated," she wrote in her diary on New Year's Eve, 1864. "The resistless flood has swept through that state, leaving but a desert to mark its track." LeConte had heard that Sherman's men were "preparing to hurl destruction upon the State they hate most of all, and Sherman the brute avows his intention of converting South Carolina into a wilderness."[65] For Sherman, his plan was clear. Exhilarated by his success in Georgia, he wrote to Grant in late December, exclaiming, "I could go on and smash South Carolina all to pieces."[66]

Grant's initial plan was for Sherman to move north from Savannah by water to join him in Virginia against Lee, but the success of the Georgia campaign and the lack of ready transports persuaded Grant that a foray through the Carolinas, "if successful," would promise "every advantage." With both Georgia and the Carolinas unable to provide supplies, Lee's forces at Richmond would have to rely on a small area of Virginia to feed and support them. Because that state, though "fertile, [. . .] was already well exhausted of both forage and food," Grant "approved Sherman's suggestion therefore at once."[67]

Sherman's army left Savannah on January 19, 1865, and arrived on the coast of South Carolina four days later. Sherman's plan for the Carolinas mirrored his actions in Georgia, with four corps organized into two wings marching north along nearly parallel lines from the coast toward Columbia. From there he would march to Goldsboro, North Carolina, and then to Raleigh. According to Capt. George Pepper, "The soldiers entered on this campaign with light hearts and exultant feelings. The very hope of treading the soil of the wretched State that inaugurated secession, fired every heart and brightened every eye. They looked forward anxiously to the issues of an expedition which would materially affect the interests of the whole country. They felt, however, that through the superb skill of Sherman and his Captains, the Confederacy would be shorn of its strength, and the rebel army so thoroughly broken that it would not be able again to regain its power."[68] Without the agricultural wealth—the products of improvement—the Confederacy could not survive.

Maj. Henry Hitchcock predicted that although the march through the

Carolinas would be more important than the one in Georgia, "it will very likely not be as much of a mere 'pic-nic,' because we may not go into so desirable or rich a country, nor will it, in all probability, be as *apparently* remarkable because the novelty is worn off."[69] Maj. James Connolly of Illinois wrote, "I am satisfied this will be a much harder campaign than that against Savannah, for this State of South Carolina is as full of swamps and bayous as a sieve is of holes, and they will make our marches tedious and difficult."[70] Daniel Oakey described the impending campaign as "formidable," one that would involve "exposure and indefatigable exertion." Oakey noted that the campaign's success depended on continuous forward movement, "for even the most productive regions would soon be exhausted by our 60,000 men and more, and 13,000 animals." He further remarked that, despite being fully prepared for "a pitched battle, our mission was not to fight, but to consume and destroy."[71] The battle was not against armed men but against a productive landscape created out of a specific set of interactions with nature.

The march through Georgia took Sherman's army across a rolling, fertile countryside; that through the Carolinas, South Carolina especially, covered less productive and more unforgiving terrain. "Our first impressions in regard to the country we had invaded, gave us no very exalted opinion of the State of South Carolina," George Pepper recalled. "Vast swamps, or barrens, where nothing but pine will grow, houses few and far between, no fence rails to burn, no living things in the fields to kill and eat, it was pretty generally conceded that we had not struck a very fine lead." The lack of improvements led Pepper to observe that the "soil is treacherous, like the people who own it. A thin crust of earth and fine cane, cover four or five feet of quicksand; and wo to the unlucky horseman or muleteer who leaves the beaten path for a short cut through the fields or woods. Heavy bodies were only safe on the corduroy."[72]

In addition to being a more hostile landscape, South Carolina was known for its secessionist fervor. Pro-Union sentiment in Georgia, while perhaps not widespread, exceeded that in South Carolina, and Sherman and his soldiers reserved most of their vehemence for the hotbed of rebellion.[73] Again, George Pepper had much to say on this:

> While the war of her creation has depopulated other sections, ravaging the fields, obliterating towns and cities, and filling whole communities with suffering and death, disaster has not yet come near her doors; her fields have not been devastated; her people have only now and then felt the pressure of calamity. But at last, to her lips also, the chalice is presented. The danger she has defied is upon her in fatal earnest. A hostile and irresistible army treads her soil, laying waste her luxuriant plantations, arresting her cultivation, breaking

Carolina terrain: The original caption for this photograph is "Terrain on the way from Savannah to Columbia." This wet, swampy ground and dense vegetation greeted Sherman's forces through much of the march through South Carolina, at least until near Columbia. Prints and Photographs Division, Library of Congress, LC-DIG-cwpb-03277.

down her haughty pride, and inflicting upon her people, with fullest measure, the losses and pains which they have braved and scorned through all the years of conflict.[74]

In order to make the people of South Carolina feel the full measure of their actions, the Union army would attack the heart of the state—its agroecological foundations.

Even the Union high command was not immune to wishing the worst for South Carolina. As Sherman was planning his campaign through that state, chief of staff Henry Halleck told him, "Should you capture Charleston, I hope that by *some accident* the place may be destroyed, and, if a little salt should be sown upon its site, it may prevent the growth of future crops of nullification and secession."[75] Sherman responded, "I will bear in mind your hint as to Charleston, and don't think salt will be necessary." However, he told Halleck, the "whole army is burning with an insatiable desire to wreak vengeance upon South Carolina. I almost tremble at her fate, but feel that she deserves all that seems in store for her."[76] South Carolina's incendiary politics provoked harsh treatment from Sherman's men, and it would suffer terribly at the hands of the Union troops.

South Carolina, in contrast to Georgia, struck back. Resembling the area around Savannah, where rice fields mingled with swamps and streams and rivulets meandered across the land creating islands out of higher ground, coastal South Carolina was wet and marshy with few good roads. Maj. Henry Hitchcock described them as "frequently bad," cutting through sparsely settled and "very uninviting country." They were "usually closely bordered either by the dense woods full of almost impenetrable underbrush, or marshes, swamps and wet rice-fields, on both sides."[77] David Conyngham, an army correspondent with the *New York Herald* attached to Sherman's command, noted that the natural obstacles "encountered through South Carolina, though of a different nature [than those before Atlanta], were no less difficult. True, we had no Buzzard Roost nor Kenesaw to scale, but we had to cross wide rivers, whose sedgy, oozy banks were covered for miles with dismal swamps. Through these we had to build roads or cross on single causeways, barely sufficient for four men abreast, and in many cases to dislodge an intrenched enemy at their heads."[78]

South Carolinians knew their terrain would be a major impediment to the advance of Union troops if it was properly utilized by Confederate defenders. William Gilmore Simms, the noted novelist, poet, and journalist, evoked the ancient battle of Thermopylae when he suggested that "in a thousand places of dense swamp, narrow defile, and almost impenetrable thicket" it "would have been easy to find spots where three hundred men, under competent commanders, who knew the country, might most effectually have baffled three thousand." There would be no such epic battle for South Carolina, however, despite many suitable locations. Poor military leadership, lack of resources, and, according to Simms, a flawed "system which insisted upon artillery as paramount—insisted upon arbitrary lines for defence, chosen without any regard to the topography of the country" failed to capitalize on the state's natural defenses.[79] Even so, those elements in the landscape, in conjunction with an unusually wet winter, effectively slowed the otherwise inexorable march of Sherman's army.

Heavy rains throughout January kept the Union troops practically immobilized. The left wing included the Fourteenth and Twentieth Corps and was delayed forty miles north of Savannah at Sister's Ferry, where it grappled with the flooded Savannah River. The Fifteenth and Seventeenth Corps constituted the right wing, which was stranded at Beaufort, South Carolina, unable to move its supply trains and artillery over the flooded terrain. Sherman's troops desperately needed solid ground, but the continued rains caused rivers and streams to swell beyond their banks, some spreading a mile or more.

From the beginning of the campaign, then, water—not rebel forces—posed the greatest challenge to Sherman's army. From Beaufort Thomas Osborn wrote his brother that "the low country along the coast is badly overflowed and the roads are exceedingly bad. When we move they will become as bad as roads can be. Those we shall have until we reach a higher country away from the coast."[80] Describing the problems faced by the left wing at Sister's Ferry, Jacob Cox noted that the "almost continuous rains" threatened the trestle and pontoon bridges and that the Union Causeway out of Savannah "was under water, and the whole region was more like a great lake than a habitable land."[81]

After nearly a week at Beaufort, Sherman pressed northward, only to be stopped again by rain and impassable muddy roads at Pocotaligo. On January 29 Sherman reported to Grant, "[T]errific Rains which caught me in motion, and nearly drowned some of my Columns in the Rice fields of the savannah, swept away our Causeway which had been carefully corduroyed, and made the Swamps here about mere lakes of slimy mud." Situated midway between the Coosawhatchie and Salkahatchie Rivers approximately ten miles in from the South Carolina coast, Pocotaligo was a small community where Union troops had captured a fort earlier that month. The final days of January brought a reprieve from the constant precipitation, so Sherman ordered his troops to move out on February 1, believing he was on "terra firma."[82]

Sherman discovered, though, that appearances could be deceiving and that even seemingly solid ground posed dangers. The route from Pocotaligo to Columbia was "practically determined by the topography of the country, which, like all the Southern seaboard, is low and sandy, with numerous extensive swamps and deep rivers widely swamp-bordered, only approachable by long causeways on which the narrow head of a column may be easily and long resisted by a small force."[83] These "made roads," as Henry Hitchcock described them, frequently required extensive corduroying to make them useable.[84] Thomas Osborn recalled that even in dry conditions "two hours use of the roads absolutely ruins them, and we are compelled to depend on rails and timber to get the trains along." Osborn ascribed the problem to the composition of the region's soil. He termed it "quicksand land," noting that the roads "cut through," or in local parlance, "'the bottom falls out,' long before a Corps and its trains can pass over."[85] The very nature of the ground did more to impede the progress of Sherman's troops than any Confederate force.

Mud was a significant factor throughout most of the campaign, hampering forward progress. Jacob Cox recalled the exertion required in dragging loaded wagons and heavy artillery "over mud road in such a country" and "the infinite labor required to pave these roads with logs, levelling the surface with smaller poles in the hollows between, adding to the structure as the mass sinks in the ooze." Multiply that work by the hundreds of miles the army had to cover, and one "will get a constantly growing idea of the work, and a steadily increasing wonder that it was done at all," Cox wrote.[86]

Much of the credit belonged to Sherman's chief engineer, Col. Orlando Poe, and the engineer and pioneer corps under his command. The pioneer corps often engaged in the most difficult, and at times most dangerous, labor of the campaigns. Frequently working in front of the line, these men endured enemy fire while building the bridges or roadways necessary for the rest of the army to progress. Thomas Osborn appreciated early on the difficult work done by the pioneer corps. He wrote, "Our superior pioneer organization is of great value to us now. It is composed mostly of negroes and is probably superior to that of any other Army."[87]

Trained at West Point to engineer nature into landscapes suitable for military operations, Poe focused on spanning the streams and swamps with pontoon and trestle bridges and on corduroying the muddy roads snaking through the Carolinas. A pragmatic man, Poe ordered his pioneers and engineers to take advantage of all local improvements to facilitate their efforts. He noted that corduroying "was a very simple affair where there were plenty of fence-rails, but, in their absence, involved the severest labor." Poe estimated in his final report that Union troops had corduroyed over four hundred miles of road and built fifteen pontoon bridges equaling a total of 1.25 miles.[88] In the end, Poe's "army of expert woodsmen," as Jacob Cox called them, overcame "difficulties in logistics commonly thought insurmountable."[89]

The purpose of Sherman's campaign through the Carolinas, however, was not to battle nature or to pave the area's roads; rather, the difficult labor was a prerequisite to the successful exhibition of the Union's power. As in Georgia, Sherman's primary goal was to disrupt the Confederacy's supply lines. The most effective way to accomplish that goal was to employ the same strategy he had in Georgia: Sherman attacked the states' agroecological foundations.

Special Field Orders No. 120 again provided the parameters for Sherman's strategy and enabled him to deliver a mortal blow to the Confederacy. Early in the campaign Confederate lieutenant general Wade Hampton, lately placed in charge of defending his home state of South Carolina, condemned Union foraging as against the rules of war.[90] "Of course you cannot question my right to 'forage on the country,'" Sherman responded. "It is a war right as old as history. The manner of exercising it varies with circumstances, and if the civil authorities will supply my Requisitions I will forbid all foraging." However, Sherman concluded, "I find no civil authorities who can respond to calls for Forage or provisions, and therefore must collect directly of the People."[91] Sherman's references to law and history obscured his true motive, to make the people "feel the hard hand of war."[92]

Sherman's men shared his convictions. One argued that the Union's task "was incomplete while the Carolinas, except at a few points on the sea-coast, had not felt the rough contact of war." He voiced concern, though, that "their swamps and rivers, swollen and spread into lakes by winter floods, presented obstructions almost impracticable to an invading army, if opposed by even a very inferior force."[93] George Nichols implicitly equated the hurdles nature presented with the challenge of fighting and defeating the rebel forces themselves. He recorded in his journal the "remarkable experience in floundering through these South Carolina swamps." Surrounded by water and sodden ground, "our tireless soldiers stop for nothing," Nichols wrote. "Yesterday afternoon the swamps were conquered, the Salkahatchie was crossed, and a force of the enemy who offered a determined opposition to our passage of the stream were driven back."[94]

That the threat posed by rebel forces seemed an afterthought to Nichols is telling but not surprising. As Sherman's army moved north through South Carolina toward Columbia, the greatest challenges it faced came not from armed men but from an inhospitable and generally uncooperative environment. In a rare moment of lyrical hyperbole, Jacob Cox summed up his impression of the South Carolina campaign. "If the march through Georgia remained pictured in the soldiers' memories as a bright, frolicsome raid, that through South Carolina was even more indelibly printed as a stubborn wrestle with the elements, in which the murky and dripping skies were so mingled with the earth and water below as to make the whole a fit type of 'chaos come again.'" In Cox's estimation, however, "the indomitable will of sixty thousand men, concentrated to do the inflexible purpose of one, bridged this chaos for hundreds of miles, and out-laboring Hercules, won a physical triumph that must always remain a marvel."[95] In an era when humanity's right and ability to control the natural environment were assumed, the obstacles of nature must have been great indeed to evoke the power of the gods.

At times, overcoming nature's challenges was merely unpleasant. "In a country where many of the rivers are known by the name of swamps," Cox noted, "continuous rains so raised the waters that scarce a stream was passed without deploying the advanced guard through water waist deep, and sometimes it reached even their armpits, forcing them to carry the cartridge-box at the neck and the musket on the head."[96] At other times the challenge turned dangerous. In a subtle irony, a region covered with water provided little that was safe to drink. Daniel Oakey recalled that soldiers suffering from thirst found it "hard to resist the temptation of crystal swamp water, as it rippled along the side of a causeway."[97] Thomas Osborn commented as well on the dearth of potable water. North of Columbia, at Muddy Springs, Osborn remarked in his journal that the army had "not found water enough within a dozen miles to keep the men from suffering."[98]

Sherman's men were not simply marching over South Carolina's territory; they were fighting it all the way. According to historian Russell Weigley, South Carolina's "best bet against [Sherman] seemed to be not a scattered army and either worn-out or inexperienced troops, but geography and weather."[99] Similarly, Joseph T. Glatthaar argued that Sherman's army "had to conquer Mother Nature and the topography of Georgia and the Carolinas, both of which seemed at times insurmountable."[100] George D. Harmon also remarked, "Through South Carolina the rains were incessant and the roads and streams were almost impassable. For several days there was almost no fighting, just marching against obstacles that were decreed by nature."[101]

South Carolina's landscape and climate did indeed seem prepared to aid the Confederates in blocking Sherman's advance. Rain fell on twenty-eight of the first forty-five days of the campaign (which lasted only fifty-five days total from Beaufort to Fayetteville, North Carolina), complicating the numerous stream crossings and turning the roads into quagmires. Furthermore, the swampy terrain precluded agricultural pursuits in much of the region, and as Weigley noted, even those "acres in the armies' path as happened to be dry were not much more hospitable to farming than the marshes."[102]

As Sherman's men were dependent on the fruits of the landscape, the limited agricultural production had significant consequences. Their reactions to the dearth revealed not only frustration over a genuine logistical problem but also their prejudices about the region as a whole. Historian Jacqueline Glass Campbell suggested that "Union soldiers saw not only a hostile territory, but also one that was vastly inferior by their standards. As they slogged through swamps and mud, the troops conflated the physical and ideological geography of the rural South in a way that convinced them of their own moral and cultural superiority." "In fact," Campbell argued, "soldiers were inclined to compare the landscape with their own back home. Many of Sherman's infantry came from the Western states of Ohio, Illinois, and Indiana where towns had been designed to impose a man-made order over nature." In contrast to the western towns laid out according to a grid, the more organic southern patterns of rural settlement, with their "small towns, poor roads, and inferior housing," revealed to the Union troops that "their preconception of Southern inferiority had been correct."[103]

This low opinion of southerners and their agricultural abilities disregarded important regional differences. The critical Union soldiers made no distinction between Georgia—which had provided well—and the Carolinas, which did not always do so. In December 1864 Sgt. William Bluffton Miller wrote, "This part of Georgia is very poor. The Soil is very Sandy and the timber mostly pine. I would not take the best plantation here as a gift and live on it."[104] Henry Hitchcock described a farm near the Coosawhatchie Swamp with a "large and good looking double frame house" in a setting that left much to be desired. A "dense tangled forest, with dead logs and underbrush, in apparently its primitive wilderness condition" enveloped the house, making for "surroundings [that] were not inviting." Hitchcock acknowledged that the farm was "in the swampy and least cultivable part of the State" but believed a "Yankee farmer would make the same place *look* far more comfortable."[105] From Robertsville, near Pocotaligo, E. D. Fennell wrote that he had never seen "a place as base for a little something to eate in my life. [. . .] They aint too [two] men out of a hundred can tell you any thing about the place and so ugly they would scare the Yankees[.] in short this was the last place made and there was not material enough to finish it."[106] Similarly, George Ward Nichols disparaged the landscape and people around Hickory Hill, also near Pocotaligo. "During the march to this point we have had opportunities of observing a barren agricultural region, and a population of 'poor whites' whose brain is as arid as the land they occupy."[107]

Criticizing the southern farmer for being ignorant or lazy obscured other, more fundamental reasons why agriculture was stymied in the area: soil fertility problems—due to both environmental conditions and the exhaustive agricultural practices of the past century—and the war itself.[108] Nearly four years of armed conflict had resulted in widespread deprivation across the South and in labor shortages, which further limited productivity. Decades of intensive cotton cultivation had depleted soil nutrients, forcing farmers to move to newer, frequently marginal, lands.[109] The abandoned tracts of land were often left to revert to natural growth, resulting in what many termed "waste" lands or old fields.

Several of Sherman's soldiers commented on the "wasted" land in their letters and diaries. Tom Taylor of the Forty-Seventh Ohio recorded in his diary on November 16, "Large quantities of land is worn out, although it has not been cleared more than fifteen years." Two days later, "The country exhibited a good state of improvement. The soil, however, is perfectly exhausted." Again, on the twentieth, "Roads wretched—country generally good—much worn out land. [. . .] Improvements very fair."[110] Moses Gage of the Twelfth Indiana Infantry recalled the landscape at McPhersonville, a small town five miles north of Pocotaligo. "This little town lay nestled among pines of almost a century's growth, which covered a large cotton plantation, abandoned on account of sterility. Tens of thousands of acres, once under cultivation, are now surrendered to the restoring hand of nature." Rather than seeing the benefits of leaving land in nature's hands, Gage saw it as a waste: "This is the Southern mode of cultivation, under the influence of slavery, the very ground being cursed in consequence of the sin of the people. No effort is made to recruit the waste of productive elements, in the light soil of the vast pine region of the Carolinas, by the use of fertilizers, but when old fields are exhausted they're given up to the invigorating power of nature, while new tracts are brought under cultivation, and after a long series of years the new growth of forest is again removed, and thus the careless round of unrequited toil goes on."[111] Farther north, near Shady Grove, North Carolina, another soldier noted, "The last five miles today was through beautiful country, fine houses, too." Despite these improvements, he remarked, "I think that not more than one-fifth of the cleared land so far in this State is under cultivation this year, and that fully one-fourth of all has been turned over to nature for refertilization from four to forty years."[112]

Gage called the process "a curious spectacle to eyes accustomed to scenes of beauty and fertility in the vicinity of rural villages of the North."[113] Not only did such scenes reveal a "curious spectacle," they posed a very real problem. In South Carolina Sherman's men frequently marched through marginal areas like those Gage and others described, which resulted in difficulties collecting supplies. This scarcity, when added to the animosity the Union troops held for South Carolina, meant foraging became an even more powerful weapon in Sherman's arsenal. On that leg of the campaign, Union foragers took everything they found—and they found everything, despite efforts by locals to hide

SHERMAN'S MARCH THROUGH SOUTH CAROLINA—BURNING OF M'PHERSONVILLE, February 1, 1865.—Sketched by William Waud.—[See Page 135.]

Sherman burning McPhersonville: Attributed to William Waud (likely Alfred Waud), this illustration was originally published in *Harper's Weekly* on March 4, 1865. McPhersonville is the town in southern South Carolina whose fields Moses Gage described as being "surrendered to the restoring hand of nature." Morgan Collection of Civil War Drawings, Prints and Photographs Division, Library of Congress, LC-DIG-ppmsca-21756.

food and valuables. Sgt. Rice Bull recalled, "Various ways were taken by the inhabitants along our way to conceal their property. The usual manner was to pack the food in boxes which were buried in the fields; horses and mules were driven into the swamps."[114] Attuned to any disturbance of the soil and wise to common hiding places, foragers left no stone unturned. "The fresh earth recently thrown up, a bed of flowers just set out, the slightest indication of a change in appearance or position, all attracted the gaze of these military agriculturalists," George Ward Nichols remarked. "It was all fair spoil of war, and the search made one of the excitements of the march."[115] The foragers made no distinction between rich and poor, black and white. Their determination to wreak havoc on South Carolina increased as they neared its capital city, Columbia. Their actions (and reputations) prompted Columbia resident Joseph LeConte to write, "The enemy, swearing vengeance against South Carolina, the cradle of Secession, is approaching step by step, consternation and panic flight of women and children in front, and a blackened ruin behind."[116]

On February 17, 1865, the four separate columns of Sherman's army converged and entered Columbia. The Confederate forces garrisoned there retreated quickly, setting fire to several cotton bales collected in the streets. High winds stymied efforts to douse the flames, and by evening much of the city was on fire. Full of vengeance, and in some cases liquor, Union troops did little to help matters, fanning the flames or setting new fires. Many of Sherman's men, however, attempted with minimal success (and, some at the time argued, minimal effort) to put out the fires. The winds shifted the following morning and the conflagration died, but not before over half of the city had been reduced to ashes. What cotton was found was either confiscated or destroyed.[117] As Sherman put it, cotton was "one of the chief causes of the war" and "it should help to pay its expenses." Sherman further stated, "all cotton became tainted with treason from the hour the first act of hostility was committed against the United States."[118]

After regrouping in Columbia, Sherman moved his four columns out of the capital city on February 20 toward North Carolina. Again, adverse weather conditions and unreliable sources of forage presented the biggest challenges for the Union troops. Rain continued to fall, turning the roads into quagmires, and spotty food supplies left the men hungry. "We left Columbia early this morning," wrote Thomas Osborn, "and found a fair country for about five miles, the remainder is the poorest country I have ever seen. It is quite hilly, covered with small pines, and scrub oaks. The soil is white, drifting sand and too barren for the meanest weeds to grow. We have collected no forage today."[119] Daniel Oakey noted the same: "After passing Columbia there was a brief season of famine. The foragers worked hard, but found nothing. They made amends, however, in a day or two, bringing in the familiar corn-meal, sweet-potatoes, and bacon."[120]

The ferocity with which Union foragers collected provisions in South Carolina diminished once they crossed the border into North Carolina. "The army burned everything it came near in the State of South Carolina," Maj. James Connolly wrote to his wife. "The men 'had it in' for the State and they took it out in their own way. Our track through the State is a desert waste. Since entering North Carolina the wanton destruction has stopped."[121] If the "wanton destruction" ended, the regular form of it did not. Charles Jackson Paine wrote to his father from Raleigh in April, "We take of course everything eatable from the inhabitants. [. . .] The country is cleaned out behind us—& it will be hard work for the people to live till fall."[122] Thomas Osborn recalled that Sherman's troops scoured clean both Carolinas, leaving the area "in no condition to supply another army which may need to pass over it, if indeed it can supply the necessaries of life for the people living in it."[123]

Fighting nature and finding adequate supplies were not the only problems Sherman's army faced, however. After fifty-five days of slogging through mud, swamps, and rain, Sherman once again faced the formidable Joe Johnston. For the first time since their bloody confrontations in northern Georgia, Sherman's and Johnston's armies clashed at Averasboro, North Carolina, on March 16 and again at Bentonville three days later. The Confederate army sustained heavy casualties, leaving Johnston only twenty-one thousand troops to defend Goldsboro against Sherman's sixty thousand hardened veterans. In the face of such odds, Johnston chose to retreat; Sherman captured Goldsboro, then moved on toward Raleigh. In Russell Weigley's words, it seemed that, "[a]gainst any possible human intervention, Sherman's armies were irresistible."[124]

Sherman's troops may have appeared invincible, but their resilience in the face of nature's onslaught diminished as the campaign dragged on. In a letter to his sister from Goldsboro, Lt. Samuel Mahon of Ottumwa, Iowa, reported, "The campaign just closed has thrown the Georgia Campaign far in the shade[.] I can give you no conception of the Swamps of South and North Carolina the army waded in water for days. [. . . T]his is about the way the whole Campaign has been performed."[125] Gen. Jacob Cox recalled that the days following the battle of Averasboro "are remembered by the officers and men [. . .] as among the most wearisome of the campaign. Incessant rain, deep mud, roads always wretched but now nearly impassable, seemed to cap the climax of tedious, laborious marching."[126] Averasboro was the last major battle Sherman's troops fought. On April 26, 1865, two weeks after Grant accepted Lee's surrender of the Army of Northern Virginia, Sherman accepted Johnston's at Durham Station.

Participants and contemporary observers almost immediately began debating the efficacy and novelty of Sherman's raids through Georgia and the Carolinas. Recollecting the march through Georgia, Capt. George Pepper from Ohio wrote, "Considered as a spectacle, the march of General Sherman's Army surpassed, in some respects, all marches in history."

> The flames of a city lighted its beginning; desolation, which in one sense is
> sublime, marked its progress to the sea. Its end was a beautiful possession—a
> city spared from doom. Underneath smiling skies, cooled by airs balmy as the
> breath of a Northern summer, the Army of the West, slowly transforming into
> an Army of the East, moved from sunset to sunrise, through a territory rich
> in all things wherein the themes of Statesmen have declared it poor. Food in
> gardens, food in cellars, stock in fields, stock in barns, poultry everywhere, ap-

peared in the distance, disappeared in the presence, and was borne away upon the knapsacks and bayonets of thousands of soldiers.[127]

David Conyngham, the *New York Herald* correspondent, suggested that the Carolinas portion must not "be judged by hitherto recognized military rules of precedents," because Sherman "proved himself not only a great fighter and flanker, but also a great strategist. He inaugurated a new code of tactics, which completely bewildered and defeated the enemy. He discarded the old, effete style of sitting down before natural barriers and fortified places, to take them by assault, or tire them out by siege. Had he done so, owing to the nature of the country over which he had to operate, his march would have been slow indeed."[128]

In contrast, Confederate colonel Charles Jones called the campaign through his native Georgia "a sad chapter" in that state's history, "which has been written chiefly by those who made light of her afflictions, laughed at her calamities, gloated over her losses, and lauded her spoilers." He characterized the march not as a military innovation or victory but as "an invasion inaugurated with a full knowledge of [Georgia's] weakness, conceived largely in a spirit of wanton destruction, conducted in many respects in manifest violation of the rules of civilized warfare, and compassed in the face of feeble resistance."[129] Mary Anna Randolph Lee believed "nothing can ever *palliate* Sherman's conduct during his campaign thru' Georgia and the Carolinas & instead of being lauded for it, it should cover him with shame & ignominy."[130] The attack against the agroecological foundations transcended the bounds of acceptable behavior, even in time of war. Destroying improvements—the symbols of power to manage nature—was savagery.

Regardless of whether one saw the campaign as a brilliant military success or as a brutal attack against defenseless civilians, one common element flows through all accounts: Sherman's army devastated the landscapes through which it passed. Indeed, Sherman's campaigns through Georgia and the Carolinas left behind an awesome spectacle of destruction, though perhaps none more so than the burning of turpentine stores in North Carolina. Moses Gage recalled one such conflagration:

The flames roared fearfully as they broke forth—like the fitful glare of lightning—from the impenetrable volume of smoke, which rose in awful grandeur toward the heavens. The vast mass of rosin, melted by the intense heat, had run down the hillside, on which the store-house stood, into a ravine through which a narrow swamp stretched away toward the east. Upon the surface of the water a crust, of emerald hue, had formed. The fire had not yet reached this point, and a handful of lighted grass was thrown upon the surface, igniting the combustible mass, and producing a flame that leaped to the highest tree-tops, melting the branches like threads of wax, and sending a column of smoke aloft that was awful to behold. Mingled with the roar and crackling of the flames was the hissing produced by the commingling of the burning mass with the water beneath.

For Gage, the spectacle "recalled the vivid pictures of Dante's Inferno, Milton's Paradise Lost, and the Scriptures of Divine truth, illustrative of the punishment prepared for the devil and his angels."[131]

For some of Sherman's men, like Daniel Oakey, scenes of burning forests verged on the sublime. Describing the army's advance into "the wild regions of North Carolina," he wrote,

> The scene before us was very striking; the resin pits were on fire, and great columns of black smoke rose high into the air, spreading and mingling together in gray clouds, and suggesting the roof and pillars of a vast temple. All traces of habitation were left behind, as we marched into that grand forest with its beautiful carpet of pine-needles. The straight trunks of the pine-tree shot up to a great height, and then spread out into a green roof, which kept us in perpetual shade. As night came on, we found that the resinous sap in the cavities cut in the trees to receive it, had been lighted by "bummers" in our advance. The effect of these peculiar watch-fires on every side, several feet above the ground, with flames licking their way up the tall trunks, was peculiarly striking and beautiful.

Despite the scene's allure, however, Oakey concluded that the "wanton" destruction was "sad to see," all the more so because the "country was necessarily left to take care of itself, and became a 'howling waste.'"[132]

Rural or urban, wild or "improved"—no landscape was immune from Sherman's devastation. The war damage to both the built and natural landscapes of the South was obvious, and sources describing the destructiveness of Sherman's *chevauchées* abound. Trees, in particular, suffered at the hands of the Union army. Sherman himself recalled one house near Pocotaligo, South Carolina, that had "a majestic avenue of live-oaks, whose limbs had been cut away by the troops for firewood, and desolation marked one of those splendid South Carolina estates where the proprietors formerly had dispensed a hospitality that distinguished the old *régime* of that proud State."[133] Observing a similar scene, Henry Hitchcock sardonically remarked, "It is bad for the live oaks and cedars that so many soldiers are camped round here in cold weather."[134]

Used for other purposes as well, trees were frequent targets of the soldier's axe. Confederate soldiers felled trees across the sodden roads in South Carolina to slow Union progress, and Union troops cut them down to speed their marches through the swamps. In one particular instance, trees "quickly became logs" to rebuild a bridge over a flooded river. "No matter if logs disappeared in the floating mud; thousands more were coming from all sides," placed "layer by layer" to build a "wooden causeway" over the aptly named Lumber River.[135] Destruction also came in the form of battle. Henry Marcy, a surgeon with the Thirty-Fifth Connecticut, wrote in his diary on January 17, 1865, from near Grahamsville, South Carolina, "With saddened hearts we looked over the field where our brave boys fell and saw the pits in which they were burried. The forest trees gave the most marked evidence of suffering—their amputated limbs and scarred trunks pointed out where the fiery storm had raged with the greatest violence."[136]

The primary target, however, of the March to the Sea and the campaigns through the Carolinas was the root of Confederate power—the rich agricultural lands of the Deep South. To attack this resource, Sherman refined the *chevauchée* and implemented it on a grander scale. His foragers carried out sections 4 through 7 of Special Field Orders No. 120 with awesome zeal, leaving local citizens with a diminished ability to feed themselves and with bleak prospects ahead. Late in the war Sherman articulated as much in a letter to his adopted brother Philemon Ewing. Describing his progress through North Carolina in April 1865, Sherman wrote, "I necessarily make such havoc that the farmers & People are getting very tired. They expected we would confine ourselves to public stores, but I take all food, sometimes leaving with a family a small supply enough to last them till the male part can come home & procure more. This gives the men an occupation different from fighting us at a distant point."[137] In destroying the agricultural products of individuals, Sherman's army inevitably forced Confederate soldiers to desert the battlefield in order to return home to feed and protect their families.

The campaigns successfully destroyed the last sources of supplies available to the dwindling rebel armies and sent a powerful message to the Confederate populace about the reach of Federal power. Historian Mark Grimsley concluded, "Ultimately these marches, more than anything else, destroyed the Confederacy. They smashed the remainder of the Confederate rail network, eliminated foodstuffs and war resources, completed the ruin of southern morale, and caused the desertion of thousands of Confederate soldiers who had resisted valiantly for years."[138] Carving a path sixty miles wide in Georgia and nearly as wide in the Carolinas, Sherman's final campaigns were instrumental in the drive to defeat the Confederacy. The swath of devastation was to the war as a back burn is to a wildfire: isolating the valuable resources of Georgia and the Carolinas from the rest of the Confederacy prevented these states from feeding the fire of rebellion.

The nature of Sherman's strategy—to "forage liberally off the land"—targeted the South's agricultural landscape, its most important resource and the basis of its economy, society, and identity. Union troops destroyed or confiscated cotton, food, forage, crops, livestock, and farming implements. Ironically, some drew on images or the very tools and processes of agriculture to describe the devastation of the Confederacy's agroecological system. Chaplain George Bradley wrote the following from Savannah on December 28: "Sherman has been SKINNING and *carving* and taking out the vitals in Georgia, and soon you will hear of his plowing up South Carolina. And he will not do it with a one-horse affair either, but setting his coulter deep, he will cut their secession roots and turn up a better soil."[139] From Fayetteville, North Carolina, he wrote, "Sherman has been swinging his big scythe right and left, and South Carolina has tasted some of the legitimate fruits of nullification and secession."[140]

Others made analogies to natural disasters, like David Conyngham, the army correspondent with the *New York Herald*, who reported that Sherman's foragers "spread like locusts over the country," and John H. Kennaway, an English traveler, who described Sherman as a "tornado [sweeping] through the heart of the Confederacy, [. . .] leaving nothing but destruction and desolation in his rear."[141] George Pepper equated Sherman's army to "a roaring wave"; Eliza Andrews of Washington, Georgia, called it a "pent-up torrent" and a "destroying flood" of "angry waters"; and a Fayetteville woman wrote, "Sherman has gone and terrible has been the storm that has swept over us with his coming and going."[142]

Regardless of the metaphors used to describe them, the immediate effects of the campaigns were obvious to all who witnessed them. George Pepper wrote, "From Atlanta to Savannah there was presented to the eye one vast sheet of misery. The fugitives from ruined villages or desolated fields, seek shelter in caves and dens," reduced to primitive, uncivilized conditions.[143] Alexander Lawson, a major in Kentucky's famous Orphan Brigade, was held prisoner for part of the march through Georgia. He vividly recalled "the davastations that [Sherman's] army committed" and that Sherman "made brags that he would make a black mark to the sea. He certainly did." Lawson escaped just outside of Savannah and turned back along Sherman's path. "I found nothing, no hogs, cattle, sheep chicken or anything else to eat. I saw a number of the very finest ladies in Georgia in the camps picking up grains of corn for the purpose of sustaining life, who a week before that did not know what it was to want for anything. I finally crossed the Savannah River into South Carolina, where his army hadn't been, and it was the first food that I had for about eighteen days." For these depredations, Lawson believed that Sherman had earned a "warm spot in Hell."[144]

Civilians, too, recorded their reactions to the ruin left in Sherman's wake. Georgian Eliza Andrews "almost felt as though [she] should like to hang a Yankee" after witnessing the damage done to her native state. Near Sparta, Georgia, twenty-five miles northeast of Milledgeville, she came upon what she called the "burnt country." "There was hardly a fence left standing all the way from Sparta to Gordon. The fields were trampled down and the road was lined with carcasses of horses, hogs, and cattle that the invaders, unable either to consume or to carry away with them, had wantonly shot down, to starve out the people and prevent them from making their crops." Calling the passing troops "savages," Andrews excoriated them for leaving no grain "except [the] little patches they had spilled when feeding their horses." Remarking that "there was not even a chicken left in the country to eat," she claimed that a "bag of oats might have lain anywhere along the road without danger from the beasts of the field, though I cannot say it would have been safe from the assaults of a hungry man." Farther into her journey, Andrews observed a field near Milledgeville used as a camp by thirty thousand Union soldiers, "strewn with the debris they had left behind." She expressed sadness that "the poor people of the neighborhood were wandering over it, seeking for anything they could find to eat, even picking up grains of corn that were scattered around where the Yankees had fed their horses." In the midst of the wreckage, however, Andrews noticed some men "plowing in one part of the field, making ready for next year's crop."[145]

As Andrews's account reveals, for most of the South, the destruction of crops elicited only temporary consequences. Sherman did not literally destroy the land. He did not salt the earth, as Halleck suggested he do. Nor did his men poison wells, as they were accused of doing. What was laid waste, however, was the agroecological foundation of the Confederacy, ensuing in what might be called an emancipation of the land.[146] Edmund L. Drago has argued that Sherman's march to Savannah "shattered" the "last remnants of slave control" and as a result, "the breakdown of the plantation system became irreversible."[147] With the departure of the slaves, farmers and planters could no longer maintain either the agroecological system or the physical landscape that symbolized the Confederacy. The mortar that had held them in place—an insecure system of control grounded in the oppression of black Americans and constant and delicate negotiations with nature—could not hold in the face of a direct attack. Sherman's *chevauchées* through Georgia and the Carolinas capitalized on the tenuous character of the southern agricultural system, shifting the balance of power just enough to cause the Confederacy to topple upon itself.

CONCLUSION

Making a Desert and Calling It Peace

IN AD 84 THE ROMAN MILITARY COMMANDER and governor of Britain Gnaeus Julius Agricola determined to solidify Rome's control over the island's northern frontier. That year he engaged the last holdouts against Roman rule, the Scottish forces united under the chieftain Calgacus, at Mons Graupius. On the eve of battle Calgacus spoke to his warriors, rousing their courage by decrying Roman tyranny: "To plunder, butcher, steal, these things they misname empire." Calling them "robbers of the world," Calgacus accused the Romans of making "a desolation and [calling] it peace." Agricola crushed the Caledonian resistance, but though he lost, Calgacus's words were immortalized.[1]

Nearly eighteen centuries later, echoes of Calgacus's speech could be heard ringing across the American South. The metaphors "desert," "wasteland," and "wilderness" punctuate the written records of those who witnessed the war's destruction, especially in those areas where the Union *chevauchées* occurred. Observers often associated the war-torn landscapes across the South with the imposition of absolute Federal power. Some saw it as deserved retribution for treasonous acts, others as sheer rapaciousness—unjust, unwarranted, and uncivilized. Critics of the "hard hand of war" connected the abuse of power to the subjugation of people not only by military means but also by denying them the ability to gain sustenance from the land. The immediate material effects of such policies and military strategies were devastating and resulted in malnutrition, vulnerability to disease, and economic hardship. Equally important were the war's longer-term implications for Americans' relationships with those transformed environments.

Antebellum Americans were well aware that their actions affected the natural environment. Though most believed that human efforts to "improve" nature were both proper and good, some began to question that assumption. Romantics like Henry David Thoreau, Ralph Waldo Emerson, and Thomas Cole criticized Americans' seeming drive to eradicate nature, fearing that if such "progress" went unchecked, America would lose its spiritual and moral center. Edmund Ruffin knew that agriculture, improperly practiced, undermined soil fertility and contributed to erosion. An avid agricultural reformer, Ruffin understood that not all "improvements" actually improved the land. George Perkins Marsh, concerned about deforestation, agricultural expansion, and industrial development, concluded in 1864 that "man is everywhere a disturbing agent."[2] But the developments condemned by Thoreau, Ruffin, Marsh, and others took time, sometimes centuries, to manifest. In contrast, the devastation wrought by the Civil War was immediately visible on the landscape.

In four years of war, the Union and the Confederacy clashed militarily over ten thousand times. These engagements ranged from battles involving over 150,000 troops to skirmishes between a few dozen men. The war combined massive military forces and industrial technologies with modern ideologies, resulting in widespread, large-scale damage not just where battles occurred but anywhere armies encamped or gathered resources. In addition, armies carried with them diseases that affected nearby human and animal populations: measles, smallpox, dysentery, and glanders, to name but a few.[3] Civil War armies were essentially mobile cities that affected the landscape everywhere they went and that could not help but consume everything in their path. The arrival of an army, sometimes reaching over one hundred thousand men, put stress on a neighborhood's available resources, including water, fences, woodlands, livestock, game, and of course, fruit, vegetable, and grain stores.[4]

Whether stationary or on the move, the soldiers required food, water, firewood, and shelter, some of which they requisitioned from nearby farms and plantations, taking or destroying the improvements locals had made to their environments. A Confederate soldier camped near Cumberland Gap remarked, "You can not well imagine how destructive the march of an army through a country is [. . .]. Hungry men seize stock. Cold men burn fences."[5] A resident of Pontotoc, Mississippi, wrote to a friend in the Confederate army, "We have had some stirring and trying times in Mississippi since you left and have fully and truly realized the troubles and horrors of war." He complained that "our own army has eaten up the larger portion of the subsistence of the county."[6] Another soldier wrote from Jackson, Tennessee, "You can't think what a destruction of farms there is here[,] fences burnt and houses torn down."[7] Charles Wills of the 103rd Illinois Infantry, also camped near Jackson, wrote, "One gentleman living between our camp and town has 10,000 pines, hollies, cedars, etc., in the grounds surrounding his house. [. . .] I mean he had 10,000 trees, but the Yankees burned the fences around his paradise, and have in various ways managed to destroy a few thousand evergreens. A kind of parody, you understand, on that Bible story of the devil in Eden."[8] As these examples suggest, armies living off—and on—the land produced serious consequences not only for local residents but for the landscape as well.

With no prior human event to compare it to, witnesses to the Civil War turned to the imagery of nature and natural disasters for words to describe their experiences. Shenandoah Valley farmer Randolph Barton remarked that after Sheridan's army had passed, "the spirit of the people had begun to break. So many had been killed, so many widows and orphans peopled the land. Food was so hard to get. The locusts of Egypt seemed small in number compared to the ever-enlarging Yankee army, and I think I can now trace the fatal despondency of our people step by step."[9] On learning of Sherman's approach a South Carolina woman wrote, "We were not threatened with a mere raiding party, it was Sherman—Sherman on his 'march to the sea,' and we lay in the course of his march. We were indeed paralyzed. Had we not all heard of him? Like a huge octopus, he stretched out his long arms and gathered everything in, leaving only ruin and desolation behind him."[10]

Maj. Henry Hitchcock, a staff officer under Sherman, declared, "When a thunderstorm clears the air some trees are apt to be blown down and some houses struck by lightning; but after all we must have thunderstorms." Hitchcock believed that the "outrages of war" were "as much a part of the inscrutable and all-wise providence of God, and as necessary and ultimately as beneficial, as the terror which His wisdom has made part of the visible phenomena of Nature."[11] Tina Johnson, a slave in Georgia during Sherman's March, recalled that though she never saw a "Yankee," she heard their "guns roarin' an' felt de earth shakin' lak a earthquake was hittin' it."[12] Such references speak volumes that even the massive lists in the official reports enumerating the livestock, provisions, cotton stores, barns, mills, and farming implements taken or destroyed could not convey.

Some southerners believed that such a fate was preferable to being subjected to northern rule. In February 1862 James Campbell of Mississippi exhorted, "Let men, women, and children of the South determine to be exterminated and bats, owls, and rats inhabit our lovéd soil before we will submit."[13] In March that same year George Anderson Mercer, a Confederate soldier from Georgia, wrote in his diary, "[O]ur cause is the cause of truth and religion, against the tyranny of the mob, and the infidelity of the fanatic; under these circumstances I am convinced of our final success! We will never be subdued; I do not believe a just God will allow our extirpation! Our sufferings may long continue, our beloved land may be made a desert, our best and bravest may fall, but our noble and holy cause will not perish; in the end we shall triumph gloriously!"[14] Most southerners, however, deeply mourned the devastation war brought to their homes.

Sherman's March as chaos: This 1868 engraving by Alexander Hay Ritchie (based on a drawing by F. O. C. Darley) captures a popular image of Sherman's March through Georgia: through his destruction of the elements of civilization, Sherman left Georgia a chaotic wilderness. Prints and Photographs Division, Library of Congress, LC-DIG-ppmsca-09326.

Perhaps the most powerful metaphors were those that invoked barren or unimproved landscapes, "desert," "waste" land, and "wilderness." David Gavin from Colleton County, South Carolina, noted early in the war that the "enemy who should be our friends are devastating our country and laying waste our land."[15] General Sherman, describing Union operations in northern Georgia, wrote that "the country is high, mountainous, with splendid water & considerable forage in the nature of fields of growing wheat, oats & corn, but we sweep across it leaving it as bare as a desert."[16] Alva Sinks of Ohio wrote home during the battle for Atlanta, "[T]he whole country is laid a perfect waste & desolate."[17] Immediately after the war, one observer called Columbia, South Carolina, "a wilderness of ruins."[18]

Tellingly, sources evoking that "terrifying symbol of chaos," wilderness, frequently ascribed it to the landscapes created by the Union *chevauchées*.[19] Shenandoah Valley resident Thomas Ashby recalled, "The close of the war found our country almost a desert." He declared, "Little was left but the land and the buildings on it, many of which had been so neglected during the four years of war that they were almost uninhabitable. Fences, barns, granaries, and the outbuildings on many of the farms were completely destroyed." Even the mills, of which only two or three remained, "were in a dilapidated condition." Furthermore, the farms "had grown up in weeds and bushes and were scarcely fit for pasturage. [. . .] With everything in this condition, and with little or no money to buy the necessary articles for industrial work, the problem of rebuilding the waste places was a serious one."[20] Margaretta Barton Colt, who edited her ancestors' letters and memoirs about the war, echoed Ashby's sentiment. "The Valley soldiers came home to a wasteland—no trees, no fences, no barns, no mills. One Scottish visitor compared it to a moor."[21]

Rosa Witte of South Carolina wrote, "1865 dawned for us with the deepest gloom. Sherman was marching through the Southern country to the coast and making war upon women and children, driving them from their homes, setting fire to their houses even before they were well out of them, destroying crops, devastating and laying waste everything that came in his way."[22] In February 1865 diarist Mary Chesnut reported hearing that Sherman had marched on from Columbia, "leaving not so much as a blade of grass behind, but howling wilderness, the land laid waste, all dust and ashes." In June she wrote, "We are shut in here, with our faces turned to a dead wall; no mails except that a letter is sometimes brought by a man on horseback travelling through the wilderness made by Sherman."[23] A postwar observer of Sherman's campaigns remarked, "Truly might it have been said, 'The land is as the garden of Eden before him, and behind him a desolate wilderness.' The spirit of the South fairly broke down under the infliction, and her soldiers in many cases refused any longer to fight for a Government which had proved itself powerless to protect their families and their homes."[24] In targeting southern improvements, the *chevauchées* undermined southerners' abilities to manage and manipulate their environments as they wanted. By destroying barns, tools, crops, and fences, the Union army effectively obliterated the evidence of southern attempts to control and improve the natural environment, returning the South to a state of (imagined) wilderness.

According to Steven Stoll, *wilderness* in the nineteenth century "defined places and times when humans did not yet control their environment or where they had lost that control."[25] One of the most visible signs that southerners had lost such power was the proliferation of weeds. Henry Deedes, a British traveler who visited the South immediately after the war, recalled the extent to which weeds had overtaken the untended fields across the region. "Every one who knows anything of a southern climate is aware of the rapid growth of weeds of every description," Deedes wrote, "and how much more difficult they are to eradicate than is the artificial growth of the cultivated plants." He described the area between Jackson and Vicksburg, Mississippi, as "given on to sedge-grass and cotton-wood, the most difficult of all weeds to eradicate."

Likewise, Deedes noted that the country between Montgomery, Alabama, and Atlanta, Georgia, "had evidently lain uncultivated for some time, and was overgrown with weeds." As he neared Atlanta, Deedes remarked on the absence of any sign of civilized existence and noted, "[R]uin and destruction were all around—trees cut down, fences gone, nothing but chimneys to mark where had stood the homesteads. Perhaps a cotton-press was still standing in a wild waste of sedge-grass and all sorts of weeds."[26]

J. T. Trowbridge, a northern visitor to the war-torn South, wrote that on their way to Charlestown, Virginia, he and his companion traveled through "a region of country stamped all over by the devastating heel of war. For miles not a fence or cultivated field was visible." At Charlestown they "alighted from the train on the edge of boundless unfenced fields, into whose melancholy solitudes the desolate streets emptied themselves—rivers to that ocean of weeds." While there, Trowbridge wanted to visit the site of John Brown's hanging. A young woman guided him and his companion to the approximate location, leading them "into the wilderness of weeds, waist-high to her as she tramped on, parting them with her hands. The country all around us lay utterly desolate, without enclosures, and without cultivation." The landscape struck him as akin to "the rolling prairies of the West, except that these fields of ripening and fading weeds had not the summer freshness of the prairie-grass." Groves of trees occasionally broke the monotony of the tall vegetation, and "here and there a fenceless road drew its winding, dusty line away over the arid hills."[27]

Trowbridge also described Virginia's "oldfields," once devoted to tobacco, as covered with briars and broomsedge. Trowbridge noted that "a thick growth of infant pines" frequently came up "like grass" in such fields as well. "Much of the land devastated in the war lies in this condition," he reported. "In two or three years, these young pines [will] shoot up their green plumes five or six feet high" and soon become "a young forest."[28] If left to its own devices, in other words, the landscape soon would return to nature's control. This, of course, was not news to any southerner. "When the scrub and brush of southern 'oldfield' fallow turned to woods," Steven Stoll noted, "planters said that the wilderness had returned."[29] What was different this time was that the transformation from cultivated fields to old fields was not of the southern farmers' making.

The decline from a civilized landscape into a wild one would have caused concern for most Americans at the time. Because of this, some predicted a dark future for the South, marked by barren fields and abandoned farms. In February 1865, after campaigning through Georgia with Sherman, Thomas Osborn remarked that unless the war ended soon "the people of Georgia, South Carolina and North Carolina will do no producing this year, positively from an inability to do it, and partially from actual discouragement." Osborn understood that people across the globe "raise crops for their support and making money, but if it yields them neither, they will not do much at it. This certainly has been the case in these three states, as well as in a considerable portion of Mississippi the last year."[30] He also anticipated that the devastation to agricultural regions would unhinge southern society and prompt its citizens to desert their homes. "Our Army has travelled over thousands of miles of territory which will be abandoned by the inhabitants who will never return, and these sections will grow up to a wilderness."[31] Similarly, the area between Fredericksburg and Richmond, Virginia, seemed to J. T. Trowbridge "uninhabited" and "always to have been so—at least to the eye familiar with New-England farms and villages." He remarked, "Where Southern State pride sees prosperous settlements, the travelling Yankee discovers little more than uncultivated wastes."[32]

As early as April and May of 1865, however, some southern farmers had begun the slow process of reclaiming the land. Historians Thomas Clark and Albert Kirwan argued that in "an agrarian society like that of the ante-bellum South, ravages of war are erased from the land more quickly than in urban, industrialized countries." However, they noted, "[I]t would be long years before physical reminders of the devastation disappeared from the southern countryside."[33] At least one farmer hoped to speed the process. A few days after Lee's surrender at Appomattox Court House, Randolph Barton was home at Springdale in the Shenandoah Valley, where his "sword was turned into a pruning hook," a transformation he hoped would be "perpetual."[34]

On his postwar tour of the defenses of Vicksburg in 1865, Whitelaw Reid stated that "one could trace for miles along the tops of the hills the successive lines of intrenchment, and mark the spots where assault after assault illustrated the various skill of the Generals, and the unvaried gallantry of the soldiers they more than once led to needless slaughter." For Reid, the most notable aspect of these fields of death was that cotton "already dotted every little spot of arable land within the [former] Rebel lines, and beyond them many a broad field, enriched by Northern blood, was promising a rich harvest to Northern lessees." He noted that "[e]verybody was planting cotton; every little valley bloomed with it, and up hill-sides, that further south would have been called waste land, were everywhere to be traced the long undulations of the cotton ridges. [. . .] A quarter of a million acres, more or less, were waiting to sprout fortunes under every stroke of the hoe."[35] Seventeen years later T. J. Charlton noted, "The ravages of war have been repaired. Cotton and corn now grow on fields once drenched with human gore, and the discharged soldier has long since worn out his last suit of army uniform."[36] Sanford Kellogg wrote in 1903, "Much as it suffered then," the Shenandoah Valley "is to-day once more the garden spot of Virginia; its wounds of forty years ago were rapidly healed as soon as peace was allowed to stand vigil over the thousands of dead, in gray and blue, that dotted the banks of its rivers."[37]

The relatively quick reinstitution of agriculture to the southern environment should not be mistaken for a return to the antebellum status quo. Even if farmers continued to grow cotton after the war as they had before it, they did so under new social, political, and economic systems that would have important environmental consequences for the South. Mart Stewart has argued that emancipation destroyed "the equilibrium of social relations that allowed planters to maintain the illusion of control over both nature and humans."[38] Landowners had to renegotiate their terms with both the environment and the newly freed labor force. Though freedmen and freedwomen had hoped to gain their share of prosperity and civic belonging through land-ownership, many were forced instead into tenancy or to uproot themselves and their families and move to urban areas.[39] The white yeoman farmer also became entrenched in the sharecropping system, as did the land itself.

To a certain degree, the reimposition of "civilization" onto the postwar southern "wilderness" was not the work of southerners but of "outsiders, who cut its forests, bought up its land, and financed its railroads and many of its nascent industries." According to Albert Cowdrey, the postwar period brought "exploitation unlimited" to the region.[40] Mart Stewart assigned at least part of the blame for that increased exploitation to the southerners themselves. Regardless of who perpetrated it, the ramping up of resource extraction after the war left the region impoverished and subjugated.[41] Deforestation and the decline of the open range ensued as more people sought land on which to grow crops. Jack Temple Kirby argued that the postwar landscape, "relentlessly reorganized, deforested, and cotton-spread, gradually closed out remnants of the open range and opportunity for poor people of any color."[42] The war brought new ways, grafted at times on to the old, of negotiating with the southern environment.

Though a great many witnesses to the war focused on the destruction of the South's agroecological system, others bore witness to nature's agency. Many elements in nature showed remarkable resiliency, a fact not lost on those engaged in the war. Minnesotan Thomas Christie, writing home from camp near Corinth, Mississippi, surmised, "I should think there would be a great deal more game up your way this Summer than usual, owing to the absence of the most of the hunting population and the consequent application of the rest to the work of the Community. The game is plenty enough down here, if we only had permission to hunt the Camp would never be out of meat of some kind. I have seen Possum, turkey, and any quantity of Squirrel and woodcock, quail and partridge, there are also plenty of deer and Raccoon in the neighborhood."[43] In June 1864 Henry Solomon of Augusta, Georgia, wrote to his brother in Vancouver, Canada, about the effects of war on the local wildlife. "I will tell you a strange turn in some affairs. The country people complain of ravages committed by the abundance of wild rabbits since the war. The quantity of small birds have increased beyond description. This war among mankind has been peace to game. Ammunition has been too scarce to be wasted upon those luxuries."[44] Another Georgian remarked that buzzards enjoyed a feast after Sherman's troops had passed.[45] From outside Savannah, Union soldier John Geary wrote, "Almost every breeze bears the hostile blast of the trumpet, and the thunder of the enemy's guns answers loudly to the thunder of our own," but the weather was warm "and every insect is creeping about. Butterflies are dallying in the sunshine and even snakes of every kind are creeping about."[46]

That nature retained its beauty in the face of an ugly war seemed to bring solace to some. From near Wilmington, North Carolina, Lt. Samuel Lowry of South Carolina took time to record a description of his surroundings in his diary. On April 21, 1864, he wrote, "We are now located in splendid quarters" located near "one of the most beautiful little rivers that I ever beheld. The dark blue canopy above, studded with stars, unutterably bright, illuminated by a fair luna[']s beams, was one that would compare with the brightest skies that ever blessed a tropical June. California celebrated for its illumined skies, Cuba blessed with the rays of a tropical clime, could not surpass it." He disparaged his ability to provide a just description of the East River, where his camp lay, but tried nonetheless:

> This lovely stream, pearls along its transparent waters amid the towering forest like a silvery beam athwart the darken clouds, bounded by the most luxuriant of lowland vegetation on its banks; crystal waves of most astounding transparency, all combined to render it one of nature's brightest gems. No one with a love for the works of nature could have failed to admire it. How could he pass it unobserved. Sailing over its still waters by moonlight, inhaling the delicious fragrance of its flower covered banks listening to the gentle murmurs of the waves, the musical whistle of the still night breeze, varied by the hoarse growl of the native crocodile, and the answering call of the shrill throated whippoorwill, all point out the favoring hand of nature.[47]

Perhaps the beauty of the river helped him to forget the war that raged around him.

Others saw in nature a sympathy that mirrored the political and military developments of the time. Elizabeth Aldridge of Mississippi awoke one August morning cheered by the return of sunshine, noting that "hearts oppressed with sorrow are gloomier and sadder when the earth seems to sympathize with its clouds and rain." She "felt that every drop that fell was a tear for the woes of a ruined nation."[48] Her husband, Francis, also saw a reflection of human strife in the weather. Before a heated skirmish in the mountains of Tennessee, he wrote, "We had not progressed more than a mile on our route before the rain commenced falling, and just as we reached the ford of the Cumberland river, the clouds dashed about with all the fury of fanaticism, and as we waded the river, the heavens seemed to have opened and Heaven's vast artillery played around the mountain tops."[49] Willis Perry Burt of Cusseta, Georgia, recorded in his diary on December 31, 1863, "But a few hours of 1863 remain to pass away; like 61 and 62 it has rolled down the tide of time upon a flood of blood. It is fast sinking into that interminable abyss, from which nothing has ever returned, stained with the blood of the slain. The winds are sighing around the corners of our humble cabin, as if singing the requiem of the illustrious dead."[50] Mary Chesnut praised the elements in January 1865: "It rains a flood, freshet after freshet. The forces of nature are befriending us, for our enemies have to make their way through swamps." Just a month later, the rain instead reflected her misery. "Heaven is helping us weep," she wrote, "rain, rain, rain."[51]

Still others criticized humanity's propensity for conflict when nature seemed at peace. In March 1863 Henry Kircher wrote, "[S]pring seems to be coming on strong, as the sun is burning according to form, the birds are pleasantly chatty, the forest seems to be curtained with a magnificent green veil with a colorful pattern. Everything, everything seems friendly, lively and happy to have the cold, nasty winter behind it. But not the people, the pitiable creatures—they scuffle, quarrel, murder and plunder in winter and in summer, in autumn and in spring." Kircher wondered that the "beautification in nature seems not to arouse really good thoughts in mankind; continual hate, strife, envy and dissatisfaction are what man always find in it. How can it be otherwise? How else would people who live in such a great, spacious and rich land get involved in such a terrible conflict as the one that has been raging for almost two full years among us[?]"[52] Georgian Willis Perry Burt also noted the juxtaposition. In his diary entry for April 11, 1864, he wrote, "What a contrast between the apparent face of nature and the people's conduct. The budding trees and blossoming flowers seem to smile in cheerful mood on all around us, while man is seeking to destroy man with all the implements of modern warfare."[53]

Perhaps it was that very paradox—that nature seemed to find ways to prosper even as human communities fought and suffered in its midst—that led one postwar traveler to take deeper meaning from nature's resiliency. On his walk across the South in 1867, John Muir wrote,

> The traces of war are not only apparent on the broken fields, burnt fences,
> mills, and woods ruthlessly slaughtered, but also on the countenances of the

people. A few years after a forest has been burned another generation of bright and happy trees arises, in purest, freshest vigor; only the old trees, wholly or half dead, bear marks of the calamity. So with the people of the war-field. Happy, unscarred, and unclouded youth is growing up around the aged, half-consumed, and fallen parents, who bear in sad measure the ineffaceable marks of the farthest-reaching and most infernal of all civilized calamities.[54]

A devastated landscape produced a devastated people, but as nature regenerated and produced new life, so, too, could society, if it would only take nature's example. Muir, who fled to Canada in 1864 to escape conscription and participation in a war of which he did not approve, determined after the conflict to "see as much of wild nature as he could before it passed him by forever."[55] His ultimate goal was South America, but after his arduous trek through the South and a nearly fatal bout with malaria in the Florida keys, he diverted to California, where he would go on to play a critical role in the reevaluation of American notions of wilderness and help to create a preservation movement that firmly planted that new conception into the cultural and environmental fabric of the nation.

Muir's first destination when he arrived in California was the famed Yosemite Valley. Incidentally, it was that other famous traveler to the South, Frederick Law Olmsted, who two years prior had helped to preserve the area for visitors like Muir. After two years heading the U.S. Sanitary Commission, during which he saw the destructive effects of war, Olmsted accepted the position of superintendent of Mariposa Estate in California in September 1863. The following summer he spent time in Yosemite, where he was captivated by its park-like beauty. In August 1865 he submitted his "Preliminary Report upon the Yosemite and Big Tree Grove" to the state of California, recommending a plan for preserving the valley for future recreational use by all Americans.

The opening paragraphs of Olmsted's report tapped into emotions regarding the recent war and praised Americans for their ingenuity and dedication to art and beauty in the face of national trauma. Olmstead stated, "It is a fact of much significance with reference to the temper and spirit which ruled the loyal people of the United States during the war of the great rebellion, that a livelier susceptibility to the influence of art was apparent, and greater progress in the manifestations of artistic talent was made, than in any similar period before in the history of the country." Olmsted noted several important wartime accomplishments, including completion of the dome on the nation's Capitol, the opening of Central Park in New York, and the organization of the California Art Union. Moreover, Olmsted noted,

It was during one of the darkest hours, before Sherman had begun the march upon Atlanta or Grant his terrible movement through the Wilderness, when the paintings of Bierstadt and the photographs of Watkins, both productions of the War time, had given to the people on the Atlantic some idea of the sublimity of the Yo Semite, and of the stateliness of the neighboring Sequoia grove, that consideration was first given to the danger that such scenes might become private property and through the false taste, the caprice or the requirements of some industrial speculation of their holders; their value to posterity be injured.[56]

Despite the war, Olmsted implied, Americans had the good sense to look to their future.

Olmsted feared the degenerative social effects of limiting access to nature's healthful properties to the wealthy elite. Preventing that decline was government's responsibility, "the grounds of which rest on the same eternal base, of equity and benevolence with all other duties of a republican government." Indeed, Olmsted argued, "It is the main duty of government, if not the sole duty of government, to provide means of protection for all its citizens in the pursuit of happiness against the obstacles, otherwise insurmountable, which the selfishness of individuals or combinations of individuals is liable to interpose to that pursuit."[57] Olmsted linked access to sublime nature to the mental and physical health of the individual, which in turn supported the health of the republic.

Though both Muir and Olmsted developed their passion for nature long before the Civil War commenced, at least one scholar has linked the trauma of the war to their postwar nature preservation activity. Jack Temple Kirby believed "it more than coincidental" that both men, who witnessed such destruction during the war, would become involved in such efforts. He argued "[T]he Civil War is connected, causatively (within a larger context, to be sure) with the emergence of modern nature-protection."[58] There is some evidence to support this contention, even beyond Muir's and Olmsted's involvement. Harvey Meyerson revealed in *Nature's Army* that ironically, though perhaps fittingly, it was the U.S. Army, mostly Civil War veterans, that ensured the first parks' protection. Furthermore, he noted that it was Gen. Philip H. Sheridan—known for his ruthlessness in the Shenandoah Valley—who played a "central role in creating Yellowstone National Park and preventing its early collapse."[59] In a tangential way, perhaps, these soldiers' experiences during the war provided them with the skills and training to support America's first efforts to preserve its natural heritage.

Other scholars have made the connection between the war and nature preservation less explicitly but nonetheless their work reveals the war to be a turning point in Americans' approaches to nature. Angela Miller suggested that by midcentury "the [Romantic] taste for wilderness had largely given way to a preference for the pastoral landscape." After the war, however, "the nation's relationship to its wilderness had changed directions once again, producing the first official acknowledgement that wilderness was an embattled condition that required federal protection." According to Miller, "[T]he postwar American ideal of wilderness now fully embraced the concept of the powerful nation-state. The wilderness preservation movement and the national park system offered a resolution of sorts to the prewar dilemma of nature's nation by setting aside areas of nature as national shrines protected from development."[60]

Perhaps the postwar wilderness movement was an effort on the part of Americans to create a new social narrative in the face of the war's massive destruction and bloodshed. Or perhaps these areas served as a requiem for what was lost, not just in terms of the Romantic critique of "progress" and "manifest destiny" but as a monument to the loss of life in four years of bloody, ideological conflict. The connections between the Civil War and late-nineteenth-century actions to preserve the nation's wilderness are suggestive but not conclusive and deserve further exploration. Another form of preservation, however, that did have direct links to the Civil War and, indirectly, to nature conservation in America was the creation of national battlefield memorial parks.

Efforts to commemorate battlefield sacrifices and acts of heroism began just months after the war erupted. One of the first monuments was dedicated in September 1861 to honor Confederate colonel Francis Bartow, who died July 21, 1861, at the first battle of Bull Run. In the summer of 1863 the Union brigade led by then-colonel William B. Hazen erected a stone monument on the Stones River battle site near Murfreesboro, Tennessee, to mark the burial site of their fellow soldiers. It still stands today.[61] The most famous wartime dedication occurred in November 1863, when Abraham Lincoln, among others, honored the Union dead at Gettysburg. Historian Timothy Smith has suggested that the "monuments and cemeteries established by and for soldiers during the Civil War reveal much about what the men thought of their actions. The dual emphasis on memorialization and preservation is evident. The early monuments were primarily places to honor fallen comrades, with a secondary purpose of marking specific and important sites of battle. Likewise, national cemeteries, grander and more impressive than single monuments, performed the same functions."[62] What these men wanted preserved were the sites of battle and of their sacrifice, but in so doing they helped protect elements of nature as well.

The establishment of national cemeteries beginning in the 1860s and of national military parks in the 1890s has had a lasting impact on the way Americans interpret, remember, and (through reenactment) experience the Civil War.[63] There are currently over twenty such parks across the nation, ranging from Pennsylvania to Georgia, Virginia to Louisiana, and as far afield as New Mexico and Colorado, managed by the National Park Service (NPS) and encompassing over sixty thousand acres. Additional sites are maintained by states and private citizens, but over seventy "of the nation's most significant Civil War battlefields have been lost" and fifty more "require urgent preservation."[64] The battlefield parks have inadvertently helped protect valuable ecological systems from agricultural, industrial, and urban development.

One park in particular serves as an excellent model. "Since the late nineteenth century," Brian Black has suggested, "the [Gettysburg] battlefield had inadvertently become a participant in one of the greatest ecological recoveries in history."[65] Deer in particular benefited from the de facto nature preserve. Ecological recovery presented a problem for the NPS, however, in that trees, shrubs, and other growth impeded the agency's efforts to preserve the park's cultural landscape and provide visitors with an accurate representation of the battle's history. To rectify this situation, the NPS made the controversial decision to restore the battlefield to its 1863 condition. This has entailed culling over eleven hundred white-tailed deer, the removal of "non-historic trees," the "eradication of non-native, pioneer species and the planting of thousands of native plants and shrubs, and the re-arrangement of orchards and farms." While some improvement in watershed quality may have resulted, attempting to preserve the landscape as it was at a certain moment of time is troubling. Black argued that attempting to "shape the natural landscape to conform to such ideals is folly and opens up an era of preservation likely to bring unfulfilled expectations."[66]

As the NPS's work at Gettysburg attests, the drive to "improve" on nature to suit cultural needs and desires continues to exist, even as the lasting legacy of the postwar wilderness movement has helped to limit the effects of that impetus. Though the war did not reconcile the competing visions Americans held with regard to nature, it did put in place the mechanisms by which those who sought to preserve or protect the nation's natural heritage could mitigate the ongoing push to make nature conform. The Civil War established a strong central government that expanded its powers during and after the military conflict to an unprecedented degree.[67] In expanding the federal government's powers and authority, the Civil War created the circumstances in which that government could set aside land from economic development, create agencies to oversee and manage those lands, and establish in perpetuity a system of parks and wilderness areas for the benefit of all Americans. This, perhaps, is the Civil War's greatest environmental legacy.

NOTES

INTRODUCTION

1. George Squire to Ellen Squire, September 8, 1864, in Squire, *This Wilderness of War*, 81, 83. All quotations from primary source materials follow the spelling and grammar of the original. The upas tree, *Antiaris toxicaria*, is native in several parts of Africa, Asia, and the South Pacific. Some cultures use its poisonous sap on arrow and dart tips.

2. Schantz, *Awaiting the Heavenly Country*, 2.

3. Faust, *This Republic of Suffering*, xii.

4. Ibid., xv.

5. Thaddeus Minshall to Friend, November 26, 1862, and March 26, 1863, Papers of Judge Thaddeus A. Minshall, FHS.

6. Upson, *With Sherman to the Sea*, 114–15.

7. Nichols, *Story of the Great March*, 16.

8. Theodore Allen diary, January 12, [1865], FHS.

9. John H. Tilford diary, May 16, 1864, FHS.

10. *Natchez Weekly Courier*, November 15, 1864, LCNPR. Originally published in the *Indianapolis Journal*.

11. Nichols, *Story of the Great March*, 16.

12. Hahn, *Nation under Our Feet*; Silver, *New Face on the Countryside*; Stewart, *"What Nature Suffers to Groe"*; and Glave and Stoll, *"To Love the Wind."*

13. Linda Nash, "Agency of Nature," 69.

14. Hess, "Nature of Battle," 47.

15. Winters et al., *Battling the Elements*, 1.

16. Weigley, *Great Civil War*, 268, 418.

17. Grabau, *Ninety-Eight Days*. See also McElfresh, *Maps and Mapmakers*.

18. Linda Nash, "Agency of Nature," 68.

19. Kirby, "American Civil War," pt. 5.

20. Steinberg, *Down to Earth*, 89–98.

21. Fiege, "Gettysburg," 93–95.

22. Meier, "'No Place for the Sick,'" dissertation; Meier, "'No Place for the Sick,'" *Journal of the Civil War Era*; and Meier, "Fighting in 'Dante's Inferno.'"

23. Humphreys, *Intensely Human*; Bell, *Mosquito Soldiers*.

24. Stroud, "Does Nature Always Matter?" 80.

25. Spirn, *Language of Landscape*, 24.

26. Worster, "Transformations of the Earth," 1093.

27. Stoll, *Larding the Lean Earth*, 8.

28. Cowdrey, *This Land, This South*; Lynn Nelson, *Pharsalia*; Saikku, *This Delta, This Land*; Silver, *New Face on the Countryside*; and Stewart, *"What Nature Suffers to Groe."*

29. Kirby, "American Civil War," pt. 6.

30. Howe, *What Hath God Wrought*, 244.

31. Stoll, *Larding the Lean Earth*, 20.

32. Ibid., 9, 20–21.

33. Nye, *America as Second Creation*, 19.

34. Bell, *Mosquito Soldiers*; Humphreys, *Intensely Human*; Langston, *Toxic Bodies*; Linda Nash, *Inescapable Ecologies*; and Valenčius, *Health of the Country*.

35. LeCain, *Mass Destruction*, 9.

36. Stilgoe, *Common Landscape of America*, 3.

37. Meinig, *Interpretation of Ordinary Landscapes*, 2.

38. Michael Lewis, "American Wilderness," 5.

39. This idea comes from one of this book's anonymous prepublication reviewers, whom I would like to thank for helping me to clarify my argument along these lines.

40. Perreault, "American Wilderness and First Contact," 20. Bradford quotation from Bradford, *Of Plimouth Plantation*, 62.

41. Roderick Nash, *Wilderness and the American Mind*, 7, 24.

42. Cronon, "Trouble with Wilderness."

43. Spirn, *Language of Landscape*, 18.

44. Merchant, *Death of Nature*, 2.

45. Shiman, "Engineering Sherman's March," 7.

46. Rae and Volti, *Engineer in History*, 85. See also Reynolds, "Engineer in 19th-Century America"; Seelye, *Beautiful Machine*; and Shallat, *Structures in the Stream*.

47. Raymond Merritt, *Engineering in American Society*, 133, 135, 132, respectively.

48. Raymond Merritt, *Engineering in American Society*, 7, citing *Proceedings of the American Society for Civil Engineering* 1 (1874): 175.

49. Crackel, *West Point*, 81.

50. Tillman, "Academic History," 232.

51. Morrison, "Educating the Civil War Generals," 108.

52. Ibid.

53. Fryman, "Fortifying the Landscape," 45.

54. Shallat, "The West Point Connection," in *Structures in the Stream*, 79–116.

55. Reill, *Vitalizing Nature*, 38.

56. Worster, *Nature's Economy*, x.

57. Ibid., 421.

58. Ibid., 2.

59. Angela Miller, "Fate of Wilderness," 95, 96.

60. Worster, *Nature's Economy*, 29.

61. Ibid., 36.

62. Nye, *America as Second Creation*, 10.

63. See Bagley, *Soil Exhaustion*; Cowdrey, *This Land, This South*; Knobloch, *Culture of Wilderness*; Majewski, *Modernizing a Slave Economy*; Silver, *New Face on the Countryside*; and Stewart, *"What Nature Suffers to Groe."*

64. Majewski, *Modernizing a Slave Economy*, 35. For an overview of soil types in the United States, see Natural Resources Conservation Service, *Soil Taxonomy*.

65. Majewski, *Modernizing a Slave Economy*, 16. See also Bagley, *Soil Exhaustion*, 3, 4, 8.

66. Paludan, *People's Contest*, 152.

67. Ibid., 154.

68. Ibid., 156.

69. Clark and Kirwan, *South since Appomattox*; Cowdrey, *This Land, This South*; Gates, *Agriculture and the Civil War*; Kirby, *Poquosin*; Lynn Nelson, *Pharsalia*; Otto, *Southern Agriculture*; Saikku, *This Delta, This Land*; Stewart, *"What Nature Suffers to Groe"*; and Stoll, *Larding the Lean Earth*.

70. Cowdrey, *This Land, This South*, 83.

71. Majewski and Tchakerian, "Environmental Origins," 523.

72. DeJohn Anderson, "Animals into the Wilderness," 26.

73. Stoll, *Larding the Lean Earth*, 31–37. See also Cashin, "Landscape and Memory."

74. Stewart, "If John Muir," 143.

75. Ibid., 144–45. See also Blum, "Power, Danger, and Control"; Camp, *Closer to Freedom*; Carney, "Landscapes of Technology Transfer"; Cowdrey, *This Land, This South*; Edelson, "Clearing Swamps, Harvesting Forests"; Giltner, "Slave Hunting and Fishing"; Kirby, *Poquosin*; Lynn Nelson, *Pharsalia*; Silver, *New Face on the Countryside*; Stewart, "Slavery and the Origins"; Stewart, *"What Nature Suffers to Groe"*; and Stoll, *Larding the Lean Earth*.

76. Majewski and Tchakerian, "Environmental Origins," 544.

77. Olmsted, *Cotton Kingdom*. Quotations on pp. 11, 8, 12, and 86, respectively.

78. See Hyde, "Plain Folk Yeomanry"; Kirby, *Poquosin*, 105–11; Majewski and Tchakerian, "Environmental Origins," 541; and Winders, "Imperfectly Imperial."

79. Cashin, "Landscape and Memory," 480–81.

80. Ruffin, "An Address on the Opposite Results of Exhausting and Fertilizing Systems of Agriculture," in *Nature's Management*, 324.

81. Kirby, *Poquosin*, 64. See also Stoll, *Larding the Lean Earth*.

82. Stewart, "If John Muir," 141.

83. Stewart, *"What Nature Suffers to Groe,"* 90.

84. Worster, "Transformations of the Earth," 1093. Clearly, Worster was referring not to the South specifically but to the purpose of agroecological systems generally.

85. Weigley, "Strategy of Annihilation," 145.

86. David Dixon Porter to David Glasgow Farragut, July 13, 1862, in *War of the Rebellion* (hereafter *OR*), ser. 1, vol. 15, p. 532.

87. Kircher to Parents, April 15, 1863, in Kircher, *German in the Yankee Fatherland*, 89.

88. Grimsley, *Hard Hand of War*, 190–91.

89. Ibid., 215.

90. Cashin, "Landscape and Memory"; Kirby, *Poquosin*; Lawrence, "Historic Change in Natural Landscape"; Schama, *Landscape and Memory*; Spirn, *Language of Landscape*; and Stilgoe, "Landschaft and Linearity."

CHAPTER 1. Hostile Territory

1. Barry, *Rising Tide*, 40–42; Kelman, *River and Its City*, 161–63; and Shallat, *Structures in the Stream*, 79–116.

2. Barry, *Rising Tide*, 21.

3. See Gudmestad, "The Nature of Improvements," in *Steamboats*, 117–39; and Reuss, "Clearing the Streams," in *Designing the Bayous*, 26–36.

4. Pabis, "Delaying the Deluge," 422.

5. See Barry, *Rising Tide*, 21–54. See also Shallat, *Structures in the Stream*.

6. Grabau, *Ninety-Eight Days*, 4.

7. Hubbard, "Civil War Papers," 572.

8. William Tecumseh Sherman to David F. Boyd, May 13, 1861, in Sherman, *Sherman's Civil War*, 84.

9. Sherman to John Sherman, October 5, 1861, in ibid., 142. He wrote the same sentiment to Salmon P. Chase, secretary of the treasury, nine days later (ibid., 149–50).

10. See Weigley, *Great Civil War*, 45–49; and Shea and Winschel, *Vicksburg Is the Key*, 1–8.

11. Shea and Winschel, *Vicksburg Is the Key*, 1.

12. Grimsley, *Hard Hand of War*, 26–30; McPherson, *Battle Cry of Freedom*, 333–34; and Shea and Winschel, *Vicksburg Is the Key*, 1–2.

13. Quoted in Shea and Winschel, *Vicksburg Is the Key*, 1.

14. Grillis, *Vicksburg and Warren County*, 19–33; Christopher Morris, *Becoming Southern*, 3–41; and Saikku, *This Delta, This Land*, 52–86.

15. Kircher to Mother, March 10, 1863, in Kircher, *German in the Yankee Fatherland*, 74.

16. Lycurgus Remley to Pa, April 1, 1863, in Holcomb, *Southern Sons, Northern Soldiers*, 52 (emphasis in original).

17. Lycurgus Remley to Pa, April 11, 1863, in ibid., 55.

18. George Remley to Pa, April 18, 1863, in ibid., 58–59.

19. Campbell diary, March 4, 1863, in John Campbell, *Union Must Stand*, 82 (emphasis in original).

20. Wills, *Army Life of an Illinois Soldier*, 8, 31, 73.

21. Ague and other types of fever were also transmitted by mosquitoes. Bell, *Mosquito Soldiers*, 18–19.

22. Humphreys, *Yellow Fever and the South*, 5.

23. See Bell, *Mosquito Soldiers*; Carrigan, "Yankees versus Yellow Jack"; Humphreys, *Yellow Fever and the South*; Megan Nelson, "Landscape of Disease"; and Valenčius, *Health of the Country*, esp. "Airs" and "Waters," 109–58.

24. Edward Bacon, *Among the Cotton Thieves*, 32–33.

25. Winfield Scott to George B. McClellan, May 3, 1861, *OR*, ser. 1, vol. 51, pt. 1, p. 370.

26. *Weekly Vicksburg Whig*, August 14, 1861, 1, LCNPR.

27. Catherine Anderson McWillie to William McWillie, April 28, 1862, McWillie and Compton Family Papers (z 953.001 F), MDAH.

28. Sheriff, *Artificial River*. See also Seelye, *Beautiful Machine*.

29. J. P. McCown to G. A. Henry, August 18, 1861, *OR*, ser. 1, vol. 3, p. 661.

30. Jno. Pope to J. W. Bissel, March 19, 1862, *OR*, ser. 1, vol. 8, p. 625.

31. H. W. Halleck to Pope, March 21, 1862, ibid., 629.

32. Bissel, "Sawing Out the Channel," 461.

33. Pope to Halleck, April 2, 1862, *OR*, ser. 1, vol. 8, p. 657.

34. Pope, Report to Halleck, March 28, 1862, ibid., 646.

35. Pope to Halleck, May 2, 1862, ibid., 87.

36. See Shea and Winschel, *Vicksburg Is the Key*, 1–16.

37. Gage, *From Vicksburg to Raleigh*, 79.

38. Ibid., 80–81.

39. Shea and Winschel, *Vicksburg Is the Key*, 78–79.

40. McPherson, *Battle Cry of Freedom*, 620–25; Steinberg, *Down to Earth*, 96–97; and Weigley, *Great Civil War*, 70.

41. Barton, *Autobiography*, 89.

42. Bastian, *Grant's Canal*.

43. Edward Fontaine to Governor Moore, December 18, 1861, *OR*, ser. 1, vol. 6, p. 784.

44. G. T. Beauregard to D. B. Harris, April 21, 1862, *OR*, ser. 1, vol. 10, pt. 2, p. 430.

45. Benj. F. Butler to Thomas Williams, June 6, 1862, *OR*, ser. 1, vol. 15, pp. 25–26.

46. Thomas Williams to Mary Neosho Williams, June 28, 1862, in Williams, "Letters," 322.

47. For maps and descriptions of soils in the United States, see Natural Resources Conservation Service, *Soil Taxonomy*, http://soils.usda.gov/technical/classification /taxonomy/.

48. Williams to R. S. Davis, July 4, 1862, *OR*, ser. 1, vol. 15, p. 27.

49. Williams to Davis, July 17, 1862, ibid., 32.

50. David D. Porter to D. G. Farragut, July 13, 1862, ibid., 531.

51. Porter, *Naval History of the Civil War*, 250.

52. Edward Bacon, *Among the Cotton Thieves*, 5–6.

53. Ibid., 15.

54. Guernsey and Alden, *Harper's Illustrated*, 2:441.

55. Williams to Mary Williams, July 20, 1862, in Williams, "Letters," 324–25.

56. Bell, *Mosquito Soldiers*, 60.

57. *New Orleans Daily Times Picayune*, August 28, 1862, LCNPR.

58. Grant, *Memoirs*, 291 (emphasis in original).

59. Quoted in Morgan, "Assault on Chickasaw Bluffs," 463.

60. Sherman, *Memoirs*, 313.

61. Porter, *Naval History of the Civil War*, 286.

62. Morgan, "Assault on Chickasaw Bluffs," 463.

63. Grimsley, *Hard Hand of War*, 101.

64. Gabriel M. Killgore diary, March 22, 1863, in Maynard, "Vicksburg Diary," 38.

65. Kircher to Father, January 26, 1863, in Kircher, *German in the Yankee Fatherland*, 58.

66. Hubbard, "Civil War Papers," 560.

67. Sherman, *Memoirs*, 329.

68. J. H. Wilson to Jos. G. Totten, April 9, 1863, Item W 2639, Record Group (RG) 77, Textual Records of the Offices of the Chief of Engineers, Letters Received, 1826–66, NARA.

69. Ibid.

70. Grant, *Memoirs*, 300.

71. W. L. B. Jenney to Frederick Prime, May 1, 1863, Item P1385, RG 77, NARA.

72. Quoted in Bearss, *Campaign for Vicksburg*, 49.

73. Jenney to Prime, May 1, 1863, NARA.

74. Hubbard, "Civil War Papers," 560.

75. Ibid., 561.

76. Sherman, *Memoirs*, 329.

77. Kircher to Father, January 26, 1863, in Kircher, *German in the Yankee Fatherland*, 59–60.

78. Grant, *Memoirs*, 304.

79. James Gardiner Crozer to Lucy Ann Oatman, February 1, 1863, James Gardiner Crozer Papers, USMAL/SCAD.

80. Crozer to Oatman, February 16, 1863, Crozer Papers, USMAL/SCAD.

81. Barton, *Autobiography*, 96.

82. Grant, *Memoirs*, 304.

83. Mitman, "In Search of Health," 193.

84. Crozer to Oatman, February 19, 1863, Crozer Papers, USMAL/SCAD (emphasis in original).

85. Crozer to Oatman, March 11, 1863, Crozer Papers, USMAL/SCAD (emphasis in original).

86. Sherman, *Memoirs*, 338.

87. Porter, *Naval History of the Civil War*, 286.

88. Lossing, *Pictorial Field Book*, 244.

89. Edward Bacon, *Among the Cotton Thieves*, 15.

CHAPTER 2. Broken Country

1. Sherman to John Sherman, April 3, 1863, in Sherman, *Sherman's Civil War*, 437.

2. Taylor Peirce to Catharine Peirce, March 28, 1863, in Kiper, *Dear Catharine, Dear Taylor*, 90.

3. Lycurgus Remley to Pa, April 1, 1863, in Holcomb, *Southern Sons, Northern Soldiers*, 54.

4. Grant, *Memoirs*, 317.

5. Taylor Peirce to Catharine Peirce, March 28, 1863, in Kiper, *Dear Catharine, Dear Taylor*, 89.

6. Taylor Peirce to Catharine Peirce, undated [April 4, 1863?], in ibid., 92.

7. Force, *Personal Recollections*, 6.

8. Sherman to Ellen Sherman, April 17, 1863, in Sherman, *Sherman's Civil War*, 453.

9. Sherman to Ellen Sherman, April 23, 1863, in ibid., 455.

10. S. C. Jones, *Reminiscences*, 27.

11. Sherman to John Sherman, April 3, 1863, in Sherman, *Sherman's Civil War*, 437.

12. Kircher to Parents, April 15, 1863, in Kircher, *German in the Yankee Fatherland*, 88.

13. Force, *Personal Recollections*, 4–5.

14. Sherman to John Sherman, April 23, 1863, in Sherman, *Sherman's Civil War*, 459.

15. Wilcox, "Onward to Vicksburg," 651–52 (emphasis in original).

16. Ibid., 654.

17. Grant, *Memoirs*, 321.

18. Ibid., 322–23.

19. Grant to Sherman, May 9, 1863, *OR*, ser. 1, vol. 24, pt. 3, p. 285.

20. Sherman to John Sherman, April 3, 1863, in Sherman, *Sherman's Civil War*, 439.

21. Greene, *Mississippi*, 144.

22. Grant, *Memoirs*, 328.

23. Sherman to Frederick Steele, April 19, 1863, *OR*, ser. 1, vol. 24, pt. 3, p. 209.

24. Grant to Sherman, May 9, 1863, ibid., 285.

25. Grant to Stephen A. Hurlbut, May 5, 1863, ibid., 274–75.

26. Greene, *Mississippi*, 120.

27. Grierson, "Colonel Grierson Discovers," quotations from 657 and 658, respectively.

28. Greene, *Mississippi*, 121.

29. Grabau, *Ninety-Eight Days*, 148.

30. Grant to Henry Wager Halleck, May 3, 1863, *OR*, ser. 1, vol. 24, pt. 1, p. 32.

31. Taylor Peirce to Catharine Peirce, May 4, 1863, in Kiper, *Dear Catharine, Dear Taylor*, 107.

32. McPherson, *Battle Cry*, 629.

33. Grant, *Memoirs*, 328–29.

34. Grant to Sherman, May 9, 1863, *OR*, ser. 1, vol. 24, pt. 3, pp. 285–86.

35. Greene, *Mississippi*, 147.

36. Grant, *Memoirs*, 334.

37. J. A. McClernand to Grant, May 14, 1863, *OR*, ser. 1, vol. 24, pt. 3, p. 311.

38. Force, *Personal Recollections*, 9.

39. Greene, *Mississippi*, 154.

40. Grant, *Memoirs*, 342.

41. Grant, *Memoirs*, 349–50, quotations from 350.

42. E. Paul Reichhelm diary transcript, 21, Thomas Ewing Family Papers, container 183, LCMD.

43. Greene, *Mississippi*, 136.

44. Lockett, "Defense of Vicksburg," 483. See also Grant, *Memoirs*, 359–60; and Abrams, *Full and Detailed History*, 14.

45. Lockett, "Defense of Vicksburg," 484.

46. Grant, *Memoirs*, 359–60.

47. Hubbard, "Civil War Papers," 566.

48. William Henry Harrison Clayton to Father and Mother, June 18, 1863, in Clayton, *Damned Iowa Greyhound*, 74–75.

49. Hubbard, "Civil War Papers," 567.

50. Sherman to Ellen Sherman, May 25, 1863, in Sherman, *Sherman's Civil War*, 472.

51. Grant to Halleck, May 22, 1863, *OR*, ser. 1, vol. 24, pt. 1, p. 37.

52. Grant to Hurlbut, May 31, 1863, *OR*, ser. 1, vol. 24, pt. 3, p. 368.

53. Grant, *Memoirs*, 360.

54. Martin, "Vicksburg Mine," 155.

55. Hickenlooper, "Vicksburg Mine," 542.

56. Martin, "Vicksburg Mine," 163. The most famous of such mines was detonated at Petersburg, Virginia, about a month after the one at Vicksburg. That mine's "explosion obliterated nine companies of Confederate troops and created a crater 170 feet long, 80 feet wide and 30 feet deep, several times larger than the Vicksburg mine" (ibid., 163–64).

57. Grant, *Memoirs*, 365.

58. Grant to Jos. A. Mower, June 2, 1863, *OR*, ser. 1, vol. 24, pt. 3, p. 375.

59. Grant to Nathan Kimball, June 3, 1863, ibid., 379.

60. Grant to Halleck, June 8, 1863, *OR*, ser. 1, vol. 24, pt. 1, p. 41.

61. Abrams, *Full and Detailed History*, 14.

62. Virginia Gordon to Susan Miller, June 4, 1863, Hugh Reid and Susan (Grey) Walton Miller Family Papers (z 2215.000 s), box 9, MDAH.

63. Clayton to Father and Mother, June 18, 1863, in Clayton, *Damned Iowa Greyhound*, 75. See also Clayton to Father and Mother, July 15, 1863, and Clayton to Brothers, July 22, 1863, in ibid., 84–86.

64. Sherman to Ellen Sherman, June 27, 1863, in Sherman, *Sherman's Civil War*, 493.

65. Killgore diary, April 6 and 30, in Maynard, "Vicksburg Diary," 42, 44.

66. *Natchez Weekly Courier*, December 25, 1863, LCNPR.

67. *Vicksburg Daily Citizen*, July 2, 1863. Courtesy the Kansas Collection, Spencer Research Library, University of Kansas Libraries, Lawrence, Kans.

68. George to Family, July 16, 1863, in Holcomb, *Southern Sons, Northern Soldiers*, 86.

69. Taylor Peirce to Catharine Peirce, June 20, 1863, in Kiper, *Dear Catharine, Dear Taylor*, 117–18.

70. J. W. Greenman diary, June 10, 1863 (z1180m), MDAH.

71. George Remley to Pa, June 23, 1863, in Holcomb, *Southern Sons, Northern Soldiers*, 76 (emphasis in original).

72. Grillis, *Vicksburg and Warren County*, 66–67.

73. Ibid., 73.

74. Sherman to David Dixon Porter, June 14, 1863, in Sherman, *Sherman's Civil War*, 484.

75. Guernsey and Alder, *Harper's Illustrated*, 474.

76. Ibid., 475.

77. Anonymous, "Union Woman Suffers," 665, 667.

78. *Vicksburg Daily Citizen*, July 2, 1863. Courtesy the Kansas Collection, Spencer Research Library, University of Kansas Libraries, Lawrence, Kans.

79. *Natchez Weekly Courier*, December 25, 1863, LCNPR.

80. Grant, *Memoirs*, 375.

81. Taylor Peirce to Catharine Peirce, July 4, 1863, in Kiper, *Dear Catharine, Dear Taylor*, 125.

82. Sherman, *Memoirs*, 345.

83. Grant, *Memoirs*, 373.

84. Taylor Peirce to Catharine Peirce, April 18, 1863, in Kiper, *Dear Catharine, Dear Taylor*, 99.

85. Force, *Personal Recollections*, 8.

86. Grant, *Memoirs*, 375.

87. Sherman to Ellen Sherman, April 10, 1863, in Sherman, *Sherman's Civil War*, 448.

88. Nehemiah Davis Starr to Ettie, February 7 [17th?], 1865, 21st Missouri Volunteer Infantry Regiment Letters, Leslie Anders Collection, MHI.

89. Anonymous, "Union Woman Suffers," 666.

90. Sherman to Grant, July 4, 1863, *OR*, ser. 1, vol. 24, pt. 3, p. 474.

91. Sherman to Grant, telegraph, July 18, 1863, Papers of Ulysses S. Grant, series 10, box 2, Personal and Professional Correspondence, July 1863, LCMD.

92. Taylor Peirce to Catharine Peirce, March 28, 1863, in Kiper, *Dear Catharine, Dear Taylor*, 89.

93. George Remley to Pa, April 18, 1863, in Holcomb, *Southern Sons, Northern Soldiers*, 57.

94. William Nugent to wife, July 28, 1863, and September 7, 1863, in Tapert, *Brothers' War*, 167, 176.

95. Halleck to Grant, March 31, 1863, *OR*, ser. 1, vol. 24, pt. 3, pp. 156–57. *Hors de combat*, loosely translated, means disabled or rendered unfit for combat duty.

96. Halleck to Grant, March 31, 1863, *OR*, ser. 1, vol. 24, pt. 3, 157.

97. Grant to F. Steele, April 11, 1863, ibid., 187.

98. Grant to Samuel J. Nasmith, June 25, 1863, ibid., 437.

99. Sherman to Judge John T. Swayne, June 11, 1863, in Sherman, *Sherman's Civil War*, 480.

100. Sherman to Ellen Sherman, July 5, 1863, in ibid., 500.

CHAPTER 3. Ravaged Ground

1. Jefferson, "Notes on the State of Virginia," 192–93. See also Silver, *New Face on the Countryside*, 23–24.

2. Silver, *New Face on the Countryside*.

3. Michael Mahon, *Shenandoah Valley*, 6; William Thomas, "Nothing Ought to Astonish Us," 226; and Heatwole, *The Burning*, 3.

4. Kercheval, *History of the Valley of Virginia*, 305.

5. Phillips, *Shenandoah Valley in 1864*, 23; Michael Mahon, *Shenandoah Valley*, 4–5.

6. Richard Taylor, *Destruction and Reconstruction*, 45.

7. Wilbur Fisk to *Green Mountain Freeman* (Montpelier, Vt.), September 4, 1864, in Fisk, *Hard Marching Every Day*, 253.

8. Taylor Peirce to Sister, September 2, 1864, in Kiper, *Dear Catharine, Dear Taylor*, 260–61.

9. Taylor Peirce to Sister, September 10, 1864 [continuation of September 2 letter], in ibid., 265.

10. Michael Mahon, *Shenandoah Valley*, 6.

11. Pond, *Shenandoah Valley in 1864*, 1.

12. Gallagher, "Shenandoah Valley in 1864," 3.

13. Stephen Ramseur to Wife, September 11, 1864, in Ramseur, "General Ramseur Fights and Dies," 1045.

14. Gallagher, "Shenandoah Valley in 1864," 2–3.

15. Thomas Lewis, *Guns of Cedar Creek*, 5.

16. Flinn, *Campaigning*, 163.

17. See Ayers, *In the Presence of Mine Enemies*; Cozzens, *Shenandoah in 1862*; Ecelbarger, *Three Days in the Shenandoah*; Gallagher, *Shenandoah Valley Campaign of 1862*; Krick, *Conquering the Valley*; Royster, *Destructive War*; Sutherland, "Abraham Lincoln, John Pope"; and Tanner, *Stonewall in the Valley*.

18. Pond, *Shenandoah Valley in 1864*, 4.

19. Wert, *From Winchester to Cedar Creek*, 27, citing George T. Stevens, *Three Years in the Sixth Corps: A Concise Narrative of Events in the Army of the Potomac, from 1861 to the Close of the Rebellion, April, 1865* (Albany, N.Y.: S. R. Gray, 1866), 390.

20. Wesley Merritt, "Sheridan in the Shenandoah Valley," 500.

21. Wise, "Boys in Battle." See also Gallagher, "Shenandoah Valley in 1864," 5–6; Pond, *Shenandoah Valley in 1864*, 9–22; Sheehan-Dean, "Success Is So Blended with Defeat," 265–66; and Weigley, *Great Civil War*, 344–47.

22. Wesley Merritt, "Sheridan in the Shenandoah Valley," 500.

23. Grant, *Memoirs*, 568.

24. Heatwole, *The Burning*; Kleese, *Shenandoah County in the Civil War*.

25. Imboden, "General Hunter Devastates the Valley," 1040.

26. Grant to Halleck, July 14, 1864, *OR*, ser. 1, vol. 37, pt. 2, p. 301. Halleck relayed this directly to Hunter in a July 17 communication: Halleck to Hunter, July 17, 1864, ibid., 366. This order is often mistakenly associated with Sheridan's later raids.

27. Gallagher, "Shenandoah Valley in 1864," 5–13.

28. Thomas Lewis, *Guns of Cedar Creek*, vii.

29. Sheridan, *Personal Memoirs*, 266–67.

30. Grant to Sheridan, August 26, 1864, in Grant, *Memoirs*, 1067.

31. Sheridan, *Personal Memoirs*, 258.

32. John Hartwell diary, July 30, 1864, in Hartwell, *To My Beloved Wife*, 262–63 (emphasis in original).

33. Hartwell to Wife, August 14, 1864, in ibid., 270.

34. Wesley Merritt, "Sheridan in the Shenandoah Valley," 503.

35. I. Norval Baker, diary fragment (transcript), 7, I. Norval Baker Papers (MS #357), VMI, http://www.vmi.edu/uploadedFiles/Archives/Manuscripts/00357 Baker/Baker%20Full%20text.pdf, accessed December 18, 2009.

36. *New York Herald*, September 15, 1864, LCNPR.

37. George Remley to Pa, August 20, 1864, in Holcomb, *Southern Sons, Northern Soldiers*, 153.

38. Ramseur, "General Ramseur Fights and Dies," 1045.

39. Robert Barton memoir excerpt, in Colt, *Defend the Valley*, 339.

40. George Remley to Ma, September 9, 1864, in Holcomb, *Southern Sons, Northern Soldiers*, 157.

41. Robert Barton memoir excerpt, in Colt, *Defend the Valley*, 340.

42. Hazard Stevens to Margaret Hazard Stevens, September 16, 1864, Hazard Stevens Papers (4909-1), box 1/39, UWL, digital ID number cwv040, http://content .lib.washington.edu/cdm4/document.php?CISOROOT=/civilwar&CISOPTR=633& REC=6, accessed September 8, 2009.

43. Gordon, *Reminiscences*, 327.

44. Ibid., 326.

45. Ibid., 330.

46. Grant, *Memoirs*, 622.

47. Jedediah Hotchkiss to Sara A. Hotchkiss, October 8, 1864, Hotchkiss Family Letters, VS, http://valley.lib.virginia.edu/papers/A4098; and Jedediah Hotchkiss to Nelson H. Hotchkiss, October 3, 1864, ibid., http://valley.lib.virginia .edu/papers/A2593, accessed September 8, 2009.

48. Weddel, "Tough Tussle with Sheridan," 506.

49. Taylor Peirce to Catharine Peirce, September 26, 1864 [?], in Kiper, *Dear Catharine, Dear Taylor*, 275.

50. Wilbur Fisk to *Green Mountain Freeman*, November 8, 1864, in Fisk, *Hard Marching Every Day*, 275.

51. James H. Kidd to Father, December 5, 1864, in Kidd, *One of Custer's Wolverines*, 120–21.

52. J. H. Wilson to Grant, October 4, 1864, Philip Henry Sheridan Papers (microfilm ed.), LCMD.

53. Sheridan to Grant, October 7, 1864, 9 p.m., ibid.

54. Gordon, *Reminiscences*, 334–35, 336, 341.

55. Ibid., 373.

56. *New York Herald*, October 5, 1864, LCNPR.

57. *New York Herald*, March 13, 1865, LCNPR.

58. Sheridan to Halleck, November 24, 1864, "Report of property captured and destroyed (from the enemy) by the Middle Military Division during the campaign commencing August 10, 1864, and ending November 16, 1864," in *OR*, ser. 1, vol. 43, pt. 1, p. 37.

59. Michael Mahon, *Shenandoah Valley*, 59.

60. Winslow Semmes Hoxton to Sarah (Hoxton) Randolph, September 4, 1864, Randolph Family Papers (Mss1 R1586 b 137-161), section 8, folder 137, VHS.

61. Mary Bruckner Thurston (Magill) Randolph to Sarah Griffith (Hoxton) Randolph, September 9, 1864, Randolph Family Papers (Mss1 R1586 b 103-119), section 5, folder 117, VHS (emphasis in original).

62. Gallagher, "Shenandoah Valley in 1864," 16.

63. On Mosby's role in the Valley, see Frye, "'I Resolved to Play.'"

64. Ashby, *Valley Campaigns*, 278.

65. Henrietta (Bedinger) Lee to [General] David Hunter, July 20, 1864, Pegram Johnson McIntosh Family Papers (Mss1 P3496a 291-296), section 16, VHS.

66. Catherine Mary Powell Noland Cochran, entry dated September [1864], "Recollections," vol. 2 (Mss5:1 C6433: 1-2), VHS.

67. Daniel K. Schreckhise to James M. Schreckhise, October 17, 1864, Letters of James M. Schreckhise, VS, http://valley.lib.virginia.edu/papers/A9507, accessed September 8, 2009.

68. George Michael Neese, *Three Years in the Confederate Horse Artillery* (New York and Washington: Neale, 1911), 355–61, quoted in Phillips, *Lower Shenandoah Valley*, 169.

69. Ashby, *Valley Campaigns*, 298–302.

70. Gordon, *Reminiscences*, 374–75.

71. Ramseur, "General Ramseur Fights and Dies," 1048 (emphasis in original).

72. Wesley Merritt, "Sheridan in the Shenandoah Valley," 512.

73. George Remley to Brother Milton, August 30, 1864, in Holcomb, *Southern Sons, Northern Soldiers*, 155.

74. Sheridan, *Personal Memoirs*, 267.

75. Gallagher, *Struggle for the Shenandoah*; Gallagher, *Shenandoah Valley Campaign of 1864*; Thomas Lewis, *Guns of Cedar Creek*; Thomas Lewis, *Shenandoah in Flames*; and Wert, *From Winchester to Cedar Creek*.

76. Pond, *Shenandoah Valley in 1864*, 3.

77. R. G. Horton, *A Youth's History of the Great Civil War* (New York: Van Evrie Horton, 1866), 338–39, quoted in Heatwole, *The Burning*, 231.

78. Hale, *Four Valiant Years*, 434.

79. Gallagher, "Shenandoah Valley in 1864," 18.

80. Michael Mahon, *Shenandoah Valley*, xii.

81. Ibid., 60.

82. Neely, *Civil War and the Limits of Destruction*, 113.

83. Ibid., 115.

84. William Thomas, "Nothing Ought to Astonish Us," 240–41.

85. Phillips, *Shenandoah Valley in 1864*, 29.

86. Phillips, *Lower Shenandoah Valley*, 169.

CHAPTER 4. Devoured Land

1. William T. Sherman to Ellen Ewing Sherman, June 26, 1864, in Sherman, *Sherman's Civil War*, 657.

2. Caudill and Ashdown, *Sherman's March*. See also Blight, *Race and Reunion*; Grow, "Shadow of the Civil War"; Kennett, *Marching through Georgia*, 321–24; and Trudeau, *Southern Storm*, 525–48.

3. Jacqueline Glass Campbell, *When Sherman Marched North*, 4.

4. The anonymous surgeon's letter was published in the *Natchez Weekly Courier*, December 2, 1864, LCNPR.

5. W. T. Sherman to Henry Wager Halleck, December 24, 1864, in Sherman, *Memoirs*, 705.

6. Grimsley, *Hard Hand of War*, 190–91. For discussion of other means of bringing war to civilians during the Civil War, see Fellman, "At the Nihilist Edge"; Grimsley, "'Rebels' and 'Redskins'"; and Neely, *Civil War and the Limits of Destruction*.

7. See Foster, *Sherman's Mississippi Campaign*.

8. W. T. Sherman to Ulysses S. Grant, November 6, 1864, in Sherman, *Sherman's Civil War*, 751.

9. Sherman, *Memoirs*, 651–53.

10. Ibid.

11. Most scholars now prefer the term "hard war," a concept laid out in Mark Grimsley's excellent book *The Hard Hand of War*. Grimsley defines "hard war" operations as having a common element: "the erosion of the enemy's will to resist by deliberately or concomitantly subjecting the civilian population to the pressures of war" (*Hard Hand of War*, 4–5, quotation from 5). The phrase itself is taken from Sherman's description of the type of war he waged during these campaigns (Sherman, *Memoirs*, 705). The following sources represent a mere fraction of the literature available on Sherman's marches but provide a variety of analytical perspectives: Bailey, *War and Ruin*; Davis, *Sherman's March*; Jacqueline Glass Campbell, *When Sherman Marched North*; Glatthaar, *March to the Sea*; Hanson, "Army of the West"; Janda, "Shutting the Gates of Mercy"; Kennett, *Marching through Georgia*; Miers, *General Who Marched to Hell*; Neely, "Was the Civil War a Total War?"; Royster, *Destructive War*; Sutherland, "Abraham Lincoln, John Pope"; Trudeau, *Southern Storm*; and Walters, "General William T. Sherman."

12. Nichols diary, November 13, 1864, in Nichols, *Story of the Great March*, 37.

13. This discussion is derived from Trudeau, *Southern Storm*, 26–27. Sherman's quotation on the principles of war originated in his article "The Grand Strategy of the War of the Rebellion," *Century Magazine* 35, no. 4 (February 1888): 582. Sherman's assessment of his abilities is quoted in Kennett, *Sherman*, 240.

14. Sherman, *Memoirs*, 29–30.

15. *New York Herald*, November 28, 1864, reprinted in *Natchez Weekly Courier*, December 9, 1864, LCNPR.

16. Sherman to Halleck, October 19, 1864, in Sherman, *Sherman's Civil War*, 736.

17. The majority of this description is derived from several of Maj. Henry Hitchcock's diary entries. See Hitchcock, *Marching with Sherman*, 60, 65, 76, 90.

18. Thomas Ward Osborn to Abraham C. Osborn, December 26, 1864, in Osborn, *Fiery Trail*, 63.

19. Bull, *Soldiering*, 179–80.

20. Hitchcock diary, November 29, 1864, in Hitchcock, *Marching with Sherman*, 110–11 (emphasis in original). What Hitchcock describes as "pine barrens" was more likely old-field woodland—cropland abandoned to natural vegetation. The pine barrens are an ecosystem specific to the southern and coastal regions of Georgia, which Hitchcock would not yet have reached by late November.

21. Cox, *March to the Sea*, 42.

22. Gustavus Smith, "Georgia Militia during Sherman's March," 667.

23. Cox, *March to the Sea*, 25–26. Sherman's line mainly stayed in the area between the Ocmulgee and the Oconee.

24. Shiman, "Engineering Sherman's March," 264.

25. Sherman, *Memoirs*, 653.

26. Trudeau, *Southern Storm*, 55.

27. Ibid., 538.

28. Thomas Osborn to Abraham Osborn, December 26, 1864, in Osborn, *Fiery Trail*, 54.

29. George S. Bradley, diary entry, December 6, 1864, in Bradley, *Star Corps*, 207.

30. Cox, *March to the Sea*, 39–40.

31. Hitchcock diary, November 18, 1864, in Hitchcock, *Marching with Sherman*, 69.

32. Belknap, *Recollections of a Bummer*, 3, 6.

33. It should be noted that Gen. Joseph Wheeler's Confederate cavalry, charged with harassing Sherman's lines, was also involved in foraging in Georgia. One Georgia woman, attempting after the war to receive compensation from the federal government for lost goods, was disappointed when the investigators attributed her losses to Wheeler. See "List of Items of Claim of Mrs. Sarah Ogden Delannoy," Letters to Mrs. Sarah Ogden Delannoy from Sanborn & King, Attorneys, March 24, 1874, and February 3, 1875, items 6, 7, and 8, John D. Delannoy Papers (MS 208), GHS.

34. Bull, *Soldiering*, 180.

35. Sherman, *Memoirs*, 658.

36. Hitchcock diary, November 28, 1864, in Hitchcock, *Marching with Sherman*, 108 (emphasis in original).

37. Burge, November 19, 1864, in Burge, *Diary*, 159–60.

38. Hitchcock diary, December 4, 1864, in Hitchcock, *Marching with Sherman*, 137.

39. Nichols diary, November 27, 1864, in Nichols, *Story of the Great March*, 65–66.

40. Cox, *March to the Sea*, 22.

41. George Cram to Mother, December 18, 1864, in Cram, *Soldiering with Sherman*, 151.

42. Upson diary, December 11, 1864, in Upson, *With Sherman to the Sea*, 139.

43. Bull, *Soldiering*, 196.

44. Sherman, *Memoirs*, 669.

45. George Cram to Mother, December 18, 1864, in Cram, *Soldiering with Sherman*, 151.

46. Bull, *Soldiering*, 196–98.

47. Sherman to Ellen Sherman, December 16, 1864, in Sherman, *Sherman's Civil War*, 768.

48. Cox, *March to the Sea*, 43–44.

49. Ibid., 44.

50. See Stewart, *"What Nature Suffers to Groe."*

51. Bradley, *Star Corps*, 215.

52. Cox, *March to the Sea*, 44.

53. Sherman to Grant, December 16, 1864, in Sherman, *Sherman's Civil War*, 766.

54. Cox, *March to the Sea*, 41–42.

55. Ibid., 56.

56. Sherman to Abraham Lincoln, December 22, 1864, in Sherman, *Memoirs*, 711.

57. Hitchcock diary, December 10, 1864, in Hitchcock, *Marching with Sherman*, 167.

58. Thomas Osborn to S. C. Osborn, December 31, 1864, in Osborn, *Fiery Trail*, 80.

59. Sherman to Philemon B. Ewing, January 29, 1865, in Sherman, *Sherman's Civil War*, 811.

60. Thomas Ward Osborn to S. C. Osborn, December 17, 1864, in Osborn, *Fiery Trail*, 47.

61. Nichols diary, December 3, 1864, in Nichols, *Story of the Great March*, 81.

62. Sherman to Halleck, December 24, 1864, in Sherman, *Memoirs*, 704.

63. Sherman to Halleck, January 1, 1865, in *OR*, ser. 1, vol. 44, pp. 7–14, quotations from p. 13.

64. Oakey, "Marching through Georgia," 674.

65. Emma LeConte diary, December 31, 1863, in Emma LeConte, *When the World Ended*, 3–4.

66. Sherman to Grant, December 22, 1864, in Sherman, *Sherman's Civil War*, 772.

67. Grant, *Memoirs*, 671–72.

68. Pepper, *Personal Recollections*, 300.

69. Hitchcock to Mary C. Hitchcock, January 22, 1865, in Hitchcock, *Marching with Sherman*, 214 (emphasis in original).

70. Connolly, *Three Years*, 380.

71. Oakey, "Marching through Georgia," 764–65.

72. Pepper, *Personal Recollections*, 336.

73. For an excellent examination of both the subtle and obvious differences in Union soldiers' implementation of Special Field Orders No. 120 as they applied to Georgia and South and North Carolina, see Grimsley, *Hard Hand of War*, 190–204.

74. Pepper, *Personal Recollections*, 329.

75. Halleck to Sherman, December 18, 1864, in Sherman, *Memoirs*, 700 (emphasis in original).

76. Sherman to Halleck, December 24, 1864, in Sherman, *Sherman's Civil War*, 776.

77. Hitchcock diary, January 30, 1865, in Hitchcock, *Marching with Sherman*, 229.

78. Conyngham, *Sherman's March through the South*, 300–301.

79. Simms, *City Laid Waste*, 49–50.

80. Thomas Osborn to S. C. Osborn, January 25, 1865, in Osborn, *Fiery Trail*, 83.

81. Cox, *March to the Sea*, 168.

82. Sherman to Grant, January 29, 1865, in Sherman, *Sherman's Civil War*, 817.

83. Cox, *March to the Sea*, 165.

84. Hitchcock diary, February 6, 1865, in Hitchcock, *Marching with Sherman*, 259.

85. Thomas Osborn journal, February 1, 1865, in Osborn, *Fiery Trail*, 92.

86. Cox, *March to the Sea*, 171–72.

87. Osborn journal, February 1, 1865, in Osborn, *Fiery Trail*, 92.

88. "Extracts from Colonel Poe's Report," in Nichols, *Story of the Great March*, 387.

89. Cox, *March to the Sea*, 171.

90. The rules of war were not hard and fast and were based on prior military experience and evolving political theory. Swiss jurist Emmerich de Vattel's *The Law of Nations*, published in 1758, was the standard reference for such questions. Vattel proscribed making war against enemy civilians who make no resistance. For a brief discussion of Vattel and the more general rules of war Civil War combatants believed they operated under, see Grimsley, *Hard Hand of War*, 11–22, esp. 14.

91. Sherman to Lt. Genl. Wade Hampton (CSA), February 24, 1865, in Sherman, *Sherman's Civil War*, 820.

92. Sherman to Halleck, December 24, 1864, in Sherman, *Memoirs*, 705.

93. Oakey, "Marching through Georgia," 674.

94. Nichols diary, February 4, 1865, in Nichols, *Story of the Great March*, 136.

95. Cox, *March to the Sea*, 172.

96. Ibid., 171.

97. Oakey, "Marching through Georgia," 675.

98. Osborn journal, February 20, 1865, in Osborn, *Fiery Trail*, 139.

99. Weigley, *Great Civil War*, 418.

100. Glatthaar, *March to the Sea and Beyond*, 108.

101. Harmon, "Military Experiences of James A. Peifer," 563.

102. Weigley, *Great Civil War*, 419.

103. Jacqueline Glass Campbell, *When Sherman Marched North*, 41–42. See also p. 32.

104. Miller diary, December 5, 1864, in William Miller, *Fighting for Liberty and Right*, 286.

105. Hitchcock, *Marching with Sherman*, 240–41 (emphasis in original).

106. E. D. Fennell to wife, November 12, 1863, E. D. Fennell Letters (MS 251), GHS.

107. Nichols diary, February 1, 1865, in Nichols, *Story of the Great March*, 132.

108. Jacqueline Glass Campbell, *When Sherman Marched North*, 42.

109. See Bagley, *Soil Exhaustion*, and Majewski, *Modernizing a Slave Economy*.

110. Thomas Taylor, *Tom Taylor's Civil War*, 195–97.

111. Gage, *From Vicksburg to Raleigh*, 274–75.

112. Wills, *Army Life of an Illinois Soldier*, 376.

113. Gage, *From Vicksburg to Raleigh*, 275.

114. Bull, *Soldiering*, 181.

115. Nichols, *Story of the Great March*, 115.

116. Joseph LeConte journal, February 8–15, [1865], in Joseph LeConte, *'Ware Sherman*, 81.

117. Simms, *City Laid Waste*.

118. Sherman to [Secretary of War] Edwin M. Stanton, January 2, 1865, in Sherman, *Sherman's Civil War*, 789.

119. Thomas Osborn journal, February 20, 1865, in Osborn, *Fiery Trail*, 139.

120. Oakey, "Marching through Georgia," 675.

121. Connolly to Wife, March 12, 1865, in Connolly, *Three Years*, 384.

122. Charles Jackson Paine to Charles Cushing Paine, April 15, 1865, Charles Jackson Paine Papers (Mss1 P1615a 47–50), section 4, folder 4, VHS.

123. Thomas Osborn to Abraham Osborn, March 12, 1865, in Osborn, *Fiery Trail*, 177.

124. Weigley, *Great Civil War*, 422.

125. John Mahon, "Civil War Letters," 260.

126. Cox, *March to the Sea*, 184.

127. Pepper, *Personal Recollections*, 259–60.

128. Conyngham, *Sherman's March through the South*, 300.

129. Charles Jones, *General Sherman's March*, 5–6.

130. Mary Anna Randolph (Custis) Lee to Carolina (Steenbergen) Blackford, January 28, 1866, Bemis Family Papers, 1779–1921 (Mss1 B4255d 189), section 20, VHS (emphasis in original).

131. Gage, *From Vicksburg to Raleigh*, 280–81.

132. Oakey, "Marching through Georgia," 677–78.

133. Sherman, *Memoirs*, 736.

134. Hitchcock to Mary C. Hitchcock, January 29, 1865, in Hitchcock, *Marching with Sherman*, 219.

135. Oakey, "Marching through Georgia," 677.

136. Marcy, "Diary of a Surgeon in U.S. Army (35th USCT)" (Collection #34/496), SCHS.

137. W. T. Sherman to Philemon B. Ewing, April 9, 1865, in Sherman, *Sherman's Civil War*, 852.

138. Grimsley, *Hard Hand of War*, 169–70.

139. Bradley, "Savannah, Ga., Dec. 28, 1864 (Letter XI)," in Bradley, *Star Corps*, 224–25 (emphasis in original).

140. Bradley, "Fayetteville, N.C., March 12, 1865 (Letter XV)," in Bradley, *Star Corps*, 263.

141. Conyngham, *Sherman's March through the South*, 243; Kennaway, *On Sherman's Track*, 7.

142. Pepper, *Personal Recollections*, 260; Eliza Andrews, *War-Time Journal*, 19–20; and Anonymous, "Terrible Has Been the Storm," 285.

143. Pepper, *Personal Recollections*, 279.

144. Alex Lawson to Mr. S. A. Cunningham, December 12, 1910, courtesy FHS.

145. Eliza Andrews, "Eliza Andrews Comes Home." See also the full diary in Eliza Andrews, *War-Time Journal*. Tamara Elaine Bruch provides an excellent analysis of Andrews's diary in terms of what it reveals about the links between nature and southern identity during and after the war. See Bruch, "Evolution of the South."

146. This idea, which deserves greater attention elsewhere, was suggested to me by one of the book manuscript's anonymous reviewers. Mart Stewart addresses a similar notion with regard to coastal Georgia in *"What Nature Suffers to Groe,"* 193ff.

147. Drago, "How Sherman's March Affected the Slaves," 363.

1. In Latin: "auferre trucidare rapere falsis nominibus imperium, atque ubi solitudinem faciunt, pacem appellant." *Solitudinem* is translated variously as "solitude," "desolation," "desert," and "wilderness." Quotation from Tacitus, *Agricola*, 30.6, in *Tacitus in Five Volumes*, vol. 1, trans. M. Hutton, rev. R. M. Ogilvie (1914; reprint, Cambridge: Harvard University Press, 1970), 80–81.

2. Marsh, *Man and Nature*, 36.

3. See Bell, "'Gallinippers' & Glory"; Bell, *Mosquito Soldiers*; Cropley, "Dermatology and Skin Disease"; Sharrer, "Great Glanders Epizootic"; and Steiner, *Disease in the Civil War*.

4. For a good compendium of the various resources soldiers used, see Ouchley, *Flora and Fauna*.

5. Francis Marion Aldridge to Lizzie Aldridge, October 30, 1861, Aldridge Family Papers (z 1755.000 f), box 1, folder 6, MDAH.

6. R. W. Edmondson to Col. Hugh R. Miller, August 16, 1862, Miller Family Papers (z 2215.000 s), Series 1: Correspondence, box 9, MDAH.

7. Richard Prowse to Wife, November 7, 1862, Prowse Family Papers (z 2192.000 s), box 1, MDAH.

8. Wills, *Army Life of an Illinois Soldier*, 158.

9. Randolph Barton memoir in Colt, *Defend the Valley*, 362.

10. Cooper, "Where Shall We Flee?," 26.

11. Henry Hitchcock to Mary Collier Hitchcock, January 29, 1865, in Hitchcock, *Marching with Sherman*, 217.

12. Tina Johnson, "Narrative," 21.

13. James Campbell to Sister, February 3, 1862, Nash-Campbell Family Papers (z 2050.000 s), box 1, folder 3, MDAH.

14. G. A. Mercer diary, March 24, 1862, transcription, vol. 2, pp. 102–3, Mercer Family Papers (MS 553), GHS.

15. Entry for May 6, 1862, David Gavin Diary, 1855–1874 (34/645), SCHS.

16. William T. Sherman to Ellen Sherman, July 9, 1864, in Sherman, *Sherman's Civil War*, 664.

17. Alva Sinks to Father, September 20, 1864, typed transcript, Alva Sinks Letter (MS 732), GHS.

18. Sidney Andrews, *South since the War*, 33.

19. Spirn, *Language of Landscape*, 18.

20. Ashby, *Valley Campaigns*, 314.

21. Colt, *Defend the Valley*, 19.

22. Rosa Glen Reeves Witte, "Reminiscences of the Sixties, ca. 1920," typed transcript, p. 4 (43/2189), SCHS.

23. Chesnut, *Diary from Dixie*, 489, 542.

24. Kennaway, *On Sherman's Track*, 7.

25. Stoll, "Farm against Forest," 57.

26. Deedes, *Sketches of the South and West*, 96, 100, 148.

27. Trowbridge, "Trip to Charlestown," in *The South*, 69–74. Quotations from pp. 69, 70, 73.

28. Trowbridge, *The South*, 225.

29. Stoll, "Farm against Forest," 57.

30. Osborn diary, February 27, 1865, in Osborn, *Fiery Trail*, 154.

31. Osborn diary, March 22, 1865, in ibid., 201.

32. Trowbridge, *The South*, 143.

33. Clark and Kirwan, *South since Appomattox*, 23. See also Otto, *Southern Agriculture*, 44–45.

34. Randolph Barton memoir, in Colt, *Defend the Valley*, 373.

35. Whitelaw Reid, *After the War*, 290.

36. T. J. Charlton, "Through the Carolinas," *Indianapolis Journal*, December 9, 1882, James J. Garver Papers, MHI.

37. Kellogg, *Shenandoah Valley and Virginia*, 8.

38. Stewart, *"What Nature Suffers to Groe,"* 193.

39. For a discussion of land issues regarding freedmen and freedwomen, see Edward Magdol, "Shall We Have Land?"

40. Cowdrey, *This Land, This South*, 103. See also Saikku, *This Delta, This Land*, 173ff.

41. Stewart, "If John Muir," 142.

42. Kirby, "American Civil War," pt. 5.

43. Thomas D. Christie to Father, July 4, 1862, MNHS, http://www.mnhs .org/library/Christie/letters/transcripts/td620704.html, accessed August 10, 2009.

44. Henry Solomon to N. E. Solomon, June 8, 1864, Henry Solomon Papers (MS 745), GHS.

45. John Stevens, "Personal Narrative of Sherman's Raid in Liberty County," typed transcript, p. 7, John Stevens Papers (MS 758), GHS.

46. John W. Geary to Mary Geary, December 18, 1864, John W. Geary Papers (MS 2030), GHS.

47. Samuel C. Lowry diary, April 21, 1864, transcription by Sumter L. Lowry, pp. 24–5, Samuel Catawba Lowry Papers (43/0056), SCHS.

48. Elizabeth (Lizzie) Aldridge to Francis Marion Aldridge, August 31, 1861, Aldridge Family Papers (Z 1755.000 F), box 1, folder 5, MDAH.

49. Francis Marion Aldridge to Sister Sue, October 5, 1861, Aldridge Family Papers (Z 1755.000 F), box 1, folder 6, MDAH.

50. Willis Perry Burt diary, December 31, 1863, transcript, p. 17, Laura Burt Brantley Collection (MS 85), GHS.

51. Chesnut, *Diary from Dixie*, 472, 486.

52. Kircher to Everybody, March 18, 1863, in Kircher, *German in the Yankee Fatherland*, 81–82.

53. Burt diary, p. 49, Laura Burt Brantley Collection, GHS.

54. Muir, *Thousand-Mile Walk to the Gulf*, 84.

55. Worster, *Passion for Nature*, 114.

56. Olmsted, "Preliminary Report," 488–89.

57. Ibid., 502.

58. Kirby, "American Civil War," pt. 4.

59. Meyerson, *Nature's Army*, 77. See also Barker, *Scorched Earth*.

60. Angela Miller, "Fate of Wilderness," 104, 105–6.

61. Timothy Smith, *Golden Age of Battlefield Preservation*, 14–15.

62. Ibid., 19.

63. See ibid.

64. The National Parks Service website lists over seventy Civil War–related sites that include monuments to various individuals and groups: http://www.nps.gov /features/waso/cw150th/civwarparks.html. Of those, twenty-two are actual battlefield sites. The military parks came under NPS jurisdiction by an executive order in 1933. http://www.nps.gov/cwindepth/battlefieldprot.htm, accessed May 29, 2011.

65. Black, "Addressing the Nature of Gettysburg," 38. This is not true of all NPS battlefield parks, especially those in urban areas like Richmond and Petersburg. Additionally, some sites were heavily industrial at the time, like Harpers Ferry, and postwar development continued, rather than interrupted, those trends. See Shackel, "Memorializing Landscapes."

66. Black, "Gallery," 309. See also Black, "Addressing the Nature of Gettysburg."

67. McPherson, *Battle Cry of Freedom*, 859.

BIBLIOGRAPHY

PRIMARY SOURCES

Archival and Manuscript Collections

FHS	Filson Historical Society, Louisville, Ky.
GHS	Georgia Historical Society, Savannah, Ga.
LCMD	Library of Congress Manuscripts Division, Washington, D.C.
LCNPR	Library of Congress Newspapers and Periodicals Room, Washington, D.C.
MDAH	Mississippi Department of Archives and History, Jackson, Miss.
MHI	Military History Institute, Carlisle, Pa.
MNHS	Minnesota Historical Society (http://www.mnhs. org/collections/museum/civilwar/civilwar.htm)
NARA	National Archives and Records Administration, Washington, D.C.
SCHS	South Carolina Historical Society, Charleston, S.C.
USMAL/SCAD	United States Military Academy Library, Special Collections and Archives Division, West Point, N.Y.
UWL	University of Washington Libraries Digital Special Collections: Civil War Letters (http://content.lib.washington.edu/civilwarweb/index.html)
VHS	Virginia Historical Society, Richmond, Va.
VMI	Virginia Military Institute Archives (http://www.vmi.edu/archives/)
VS	The Valley of the Shadow: Two Communities in the American Civil War, Virginia Center for Digital History, University of Virginia (http://valley.lib.virginia.edu)

Published Diaries, Letters, Memoirs, Reminiscences, and Document Collections

Abrams, A. S. *A Full and Detailed History of the Siege of Vicksburg*. Atlanta: Intelligencer Steam Power Presses, 1863.

Adams, Rachel. "Narrative." In Rawick, *American Slave*, ser. 2, vol. 12, pt. 1, *Georgia Narratives*, 1–8.

Andrews, Eliza. "Eliza Andrews Comes Home through the Burnt Country." In Commager, *Blue and the Gray*, 2:958–59.

———. *The War-Time Journal of a Georgia Girl, 1864–1865*. Lincoln: University of Nebraska Press, 1997.

Andrews, Sidney. *The South since the War*. Boston: Ticknor and Fields, 1866.

Anonymous. "Terrible Has Been the Storm." In K. Jones, *When Sherman Came*, 284–86.

Anonymous. "A Union Woman Suffers through the Siege of Vicksburg." In Commager, *Blue and the Gray*, 2:662–68.

Ashby, Thomas A. *The Valley Campaigns: Being the Reminiscences of a Non-combatant while between the Lines in the Shenandoah Valley during the War of the States.* New York: Neale, 1914.

Bacon, Edward. *Among the Cotton Thieves.* Detroit: Free Press Steam Book and Job Printing House, 1867.

Barton, Thomas H. *Autobiography of Dr. Thomas H. Barton, the Self-Made Physician.* Charleston: West Virginia Publishing, 1890.

Belknap, Charles E. *Recollections of a Bummer.* War Papers, no. 28. Washington, D.C.: The Commandery of the Military Order of the Loyal Legion of the United States, 1898.

Bissel, J. W. "Sawing Out the Channel above Island Number Ten." In Johnson and Buel, *Battles and Leaders*, vol. 1, *From Sumter to Shiloh*, 460–62.

Bradford, William. *Of Plimouth Plantation.* Edited by Samuel Eliot Morrison. New York: Modern Library, 1952.

Bradley, G. S. *The Star Corps; or, Notes of an Army Chaplain, during Sherman's Famous "March to the Sea."* Milwaukee: Jermain and Brightman, 1865.

Buffum, Francis Henry. *Sheridan's Veterans: A Souvenir of Their Two Campaigns in the Shenandoah Valley.* Boston: W. F. Brown, 1883.

Bull, Rice C. *Soldiering: The Civil War Diary of Rice C. Bull, 123rd New York Volunteer Infantry.* Edited by K. Jack Bauer. San Rafael, Calif.: Presidio Press, 1977.

Burge, Dolly Lunt. *The Diary of Dolly Lunt Burge, 1848–1879.* Edited by Christine Jacobson Carter. Athens: University of Georgia Press, 1997.

Calkin, Homer L., ed. "'Elk Horn to Vicksburg': The Diary of James Henry Fauntleroy, 1862." *Civil War History* 2, no. 1 (1956): 7–43.

Campbell, John Quincy Adams. *The Union Must Stand: The Civil War Diary of John Quincy Adams Campbell, Fifth Iowa Volunteer Infantry.* Edited by Mark Grimsley and Todd D. Miller. Knoxville: University of Tennessee Press, 2000.

Chesnut, Mary Boykin. *A Diary from Dixie.* Edited by Ben Ames Williams. 1905. Reprint, Boston: Houghton Mifflin, 1961.

Clayton, William Henry Harrison. *A Damned Iowa Greyhound: The Civil War Letters of William Henry Harrison Clayton.* Edited by Donald C. Elder III. Iowa City: University of Iowa Press, 1998.

Colt, Margaretta Barton, ed. *Defend the Valley: A Shenandoah Family in the Civil War.* New York: Orion Books, 1994.

Commager, Henry Steele, ed. *The Blue and the Gray: The Story of the Civil War as Told by Participants.* 2 vols. Indianapolis: Bobbs-Merrill, 1950.

Connolly, James A. *Three Years in the Army of the Cumberland: The Letters and Diary of Major James A. Connolly.* Edited by Paul M. Angle. Bloomington: Indiana University Press, 1959. Reprint, New York: Kraus Reprint, 1969.

Conyngham, David P. *Sherman's March through the South with Sketches and Incidents of the Campaign.* New York: Sheldon, 1865.

Cooper, A. C. "Where Shall We Flee?" In K. Jones, *When Sherman Came*, 24–27.

Cozzens, Peter, ed. *Battles and Leaders of the Civil War.* Vols. 5 and 6. Urbana: University of Illinois Press, 2002, 2004.

Cram, George F. *Soldiering with Sherman: Civil War Letters of George F. Cram.* Edited by Jennifer Cain Bohrnstedt. Dekalb: Northern Illinois University Press, 2000.

Deedes, Henry. *Sketches of the South and West.* Edinburgh: William Blackwood and Sons, 1869.

Dennett, John Richard. *The South as It Is: 1865–1866.* Edited by Henry M. Christman. New York: Viking, 1965.

Fisk, Wilbur. *Hard Marching Every Day: The Civil War Letters of Private Wilbur Fisk, 1861–1865.* Edited by Emil and Ruth Rosenblatt. Lawrence: University Press of Kansas, 1992.

Flinn, Frank M. *Campaigning with Banks in Louisiana, '63 and '64 and with Sheridan in the Shenandoah Valley in '64 and '65.* Boston: W. B. Clarke, 1889.

Force, Manning F. *Personal Recollections of the Vicksburg Campaign, A Paper Read before the Ohio Commandery of the Military Order of the Loyal Legion of the United States, January 7, 1885.* Cincinnati: Henry C. Sherick, 1885.

French, Samuel F. *Two Wars: An Autobiography.* Nashville, Tenn.: Confederate Veteran, 1901.

Gage, M. D. *From Vicksburg to Raleigh; or, a Complete History of the Twelfth Regiment Indiana Volunteer Infantry, and the Campaigns of Grant and Sherman, with an Outline of the Great Rebellion.* Chicago: Clarke, 1865.

Gardiner, William. "Operations of the Cavalry Corps, Middle Military Division, Armies of the United States, from February 27 to March 8, 1865, Participated in by the First Rhode Island Cavalry." In *Personal Narratives of Events in the War of the Rebellion*, Fifth Series, no. 5. Providence: Rhode Island Soldiers and Sailors Historical Society, 1896.

Gordon, John B. *Reminiscences of the Civil War.* New York: Charles Scribner's Sons, 1903.

Grant, Ulysses S. *Memoirs and Selected Letters.* Edited by Mary Drake McFeely and William S. McFeely. New York: Library of America, 1990.

Grierson, B. H. "Colonel Grierson Discovers that the Confederacy Is a Hollow Shell." In Commager, *Blue and the Gray*, 2:656–62.

Guernsey, Alfred H., and Henry M. Alden, eds. *Harper's Illustrated History of the Great Rebellion.* 2 vols. New York: Harper and Bros., 1866, 1868.

Hartwell, John F. L. *To My Beloved Wife and Boy at Home: The Letters and Diaries of Orderly Sergeant John F. L. Hartwell.* Edited by Ann Hartwell Britton and Thomas J. Reed. Madison, N.J.: Fairley Dickinson University Press, 1997.

Hickenlooper, Andrew. "The Vicksburg Mine." In Johnson and Buel, *Battles and Leaders*, vol. 3, *Retreat from Gettysburg*, 539–42.

Hitchcock, Henry. *Marching with Sherman: Passages from the Letters and Campaign Diaries of Henry Hitchcock.* Edited by M. A. DeWolfe Howe. New Haven, Conn.: Yale University Press, 1927.

Holcomb, Julie, ed. *Southern Sons, Northern Soldiers: The Civil War Letters of the Remley Brothers, 22nd Iowa Infantry.* DeKalb: Northern Illinois University Press, 2004.

Hotchkiss, Jedediah. *Make Me a Map of the Valley: The Civil War Journal of Stonewall Jackson's Topographer.* Edited by Archie P. McDonald. Dallas: Southern Methodist University Press, 1973.

Hubbard, Lucius F. "Civil War Papers." *Minnesota Historical Society Collections* 12 (December 1908): 531–638.

Imboden, John. "General Hunter Devastates the Valley." In Commager, *Blue and the Gray,* 2:1039–42.

Jefferson, Thomas. "Notes on the State of Virginia." In *The Life and Selected Writings of Thomas Jefferson.* Edited by Adrienne Koch and William Peden. New York: Modern Library, 1944.

Johnson, Robert Underwood, and Clarence Clough Buel, eds. *Battles and Leaders of the Civil War.* 4 vols. 1887. Reprint, New York: Castle Books, 1956.

Johnson, Tina. "Narrative." In Rawick, *American Slave,* ser. 2, vol. 15, pt. 2, *North Carolina Narratives,* 20–22.

Jones, Charles C. *General Sherman's March from Atlanta to the Coast: An Address Delivered before the Confederate Survivors' Association.* Augusta, Ga.: Chronicle, 1884.

Jones, Katharine M., ed. *When Sherman Came: Southern Women and the "Great March."* Indianapolis: Bobbs-Merrill, 1964.

Jones, S. C. *Reminiscences of the Twenty-Second Iowa Volunteer Infantry.* Iowa City, Iowa, 1907.

Kennaway, John H. *On Sherman's Track; or, The South after the War.* London: Seeley, Jackson and Halliday, 1867.

Kidd, James H. *One of Custer's Wolverines: The Civil War Letters of Brevet Brigadier General James H. Kidd, 6th Michigan Cavalry.* Edited by Eric J. Wittenberg. Kent, Ohio: Kent State University Press, 2000.

Kiper, Richard L., ed. *Dear Catharine, Dear Taylor: The Civil War Letters of a Union Soldier and His Wife.* Lawrence: University Press of Kansas, 2002.

Kircher, Henry A. *A German in the Yankee Fatherland: The Civil War Letters of Henry A. Kircher.* Edited by Earl J. Hess. Kent, Ohio: Kent State University Press, 1983.

LeConte, Emma. *When the World Ended: The Diary of Emma LeConte.* Edited by Earl Schenck Miers. New York: Oxford University Press, 1957.

LeConte, Joseph. *'Ware Sherman: A Journal of Three Months' Personal Experience in the Last Days of the Confederacy.* Berkeley: University of California Press, 1937.

Lockett, S. H. "The Defense of Vicksburg." In Johnson and Buel, *Battles and Leaders,* vol. 3, *Retreat from Gettysburg,* 482–92.

Lossing, Benson J. *Pictorial Field Book of the Civil War: Journeys through the Battlefields in the Wake of Conflict.* Vol. 2. Baltimore: Johns Hopkins University Press, 1868.

Mahon, John K., ed. "The Civil War Letters of Samuel Mahon, Seventh Iowa Infantry." *Iowa Journal of History* 51 (July 1953): 233–66.

Marsh, George Perkins. *Man and Nature; or, Physical Geography as Modified by Human Action.* New York: Charles Scribner, 1864.

Maynard, Douglas, ed. "Vicksburg Diary: The Journal of Gabriel M. Killgore." *Civil War History* 10, no. 1 (March 1964): 33–53.

Merritt, Wesley. "Sheridan in the Shenandoah Valley." In Johnson and Buel, *Battles and Leaders,* vol. 4, *The Way to Appomattox,* 500–521.

Miller, William Bluffton. *Fighting for Liberty and Right: The Civil War Diary of William Bluffton Miller, First Sergeant, Company K, Seventy-Fifth Indiana Volunteer*

Infantry. Edited by Jeffrey L. Patrick and Robert J. Willey. Knoxville: University of Tennessee Press, 2005.

Morgan, George W. "The Assault on Chickasaw Bluffs." In Johnson and Buel, *Battles and Leaders*, vol. 3, *Retreat from Gettysburg*, 462–70.

Morrison, James L., ed. "Getting through West Point: The Cadet Memoirs of John C. Tidball, Class of 1848." *Civil War History* 26 (December 1980): 304–25.

Muir, John. *A Thousand-Mile Walk to the Gulf*. Boston: Houghton Mifflin, 1998.

Nichols, George Ward. *The Story of the Great March from the Diary of a Staff Officer*. New York: Harper and Brothers, 1865.

Oakey, Daniel. "Marching through Georgia and the Carolinas." In Johnson and Buel, *Battles and Leaders*, vol. 4, *The Way to Appomattox*, 671–79.

Official Atlas of the Civil War. Washington, D.C.: General Printing Office, 1891–95. Reprint, New York: Thomas Yoseloff, 1958.

Olmsted, Frederick Law. *The Cotton Kingdom: A Traveller's Observations on Cotton and Slavery in the American Slave States*. Edited by Arthur M. Schlesinger. 1861. Reprint, New York: Alfred A. Knopf, 1953.

———. "Preliminary Report upon the Yosemite and Big Tree Grove." In *The Papers of Frederick Law Olmsted*, vol. 5, *The California Frontier, 1863–1865*, edited by Victoria Post Ranney, 488–516. Baltimore: Johns Hopkins University Press, 1990.

Osborn, Thomas Ward. *The Fiery Trail: A Union Officer's Account of Sherman's Last Campaigns*. Edited by Richard Harwell and Philip N. Racine. Knoxville: University of Tennessee Press, 1986.

Pepper, George W. *Personal Recollections of Sherman's Campaigns in Georgia and the Carolinas*. Zanesville, Ohio: Hugh Dunne, 1866.

Photographic History of the Civil War in Ten Volumes. New York: Review of Reviews, 1911.

Ramseur, Stephen Dodson. "General Ramseur Fights and Dies for His Country." In Commager, *Blue and the Gray*, 2:1042–49.

Rawick, George P., ed. *The American Slave: A Composite Autobiography*. 19 vols. Westport, Conn.: Greenwood, 1972.

Reid, Whitelaw. *After the War: A Southern Tour*. Cincinnati: Moore, Wilstach and Baldwin, 1866.

Ruffin, Edmund. *Nature's Management: Writings on Landscape and Reform, 1822–1859*. Edited by Jack Temple Kirby. Athens: University of Georgia Press, 2006.

Sheridan, Philip H. *Personal Memoirs of P. H. Sheridan*. 2 vols. in 1. New York: C. L. Webster, 1888. Reprint, New York: Da Capo, 1992.

Sherman, William T. *Memoirs of William T. Sherman*. Edited by Charles Royster. New York: Library of America, 1990.

———. *Sherman's Civil War: Selected Correspondence of William T. Sherman, 1860–1865*. Edited by Brooks D. Simpson and Jean V. Berlin. Chapel Hill: University of North Carolina Press, 1999.

Simms, William Gilmore. *A City Laid Waste: The Capture, Sack, and Destruction of the City of Columbia*. Edited by David Aiken. Columbia: University of South Carolina Press, 2005.

Smith, Gustavus W. "The Georgia Militia during Sherman's March to the Sea." In Johnson and Buel, *Battles and Leaders*, vol. 4, *The Way to Appomattox*, 667–71.

Somers, Robert. *The Southern States since the War*. London: Macmillan, 1871.

Squire, George W. *This Wilderness of War: The Civil War Letters of George W. Squire, Hoosier Volunteer.* Edited by Julie A. Doyle, John David Smith, and Richard M. McMurry. Knoxville: University of Tennessee Press, 1998.

Tapert, Annette, ed. *The Brothers' War: Civil War Letters to Their Loved Ones from the Blue and Gray.* New York: Times Books, 1988.

Taylor, Richard. *Destruction and Reconstruction: Personal Experiences of the Late War.* Edited by Richard Harwell. New York: Longmans, Green, 1955.

Taylor, Thomas T. *Tom Taylor's Civil War.* Compiled by Albert Castel. Lawrence: University Press of Kansas, 2000.

Trowbridge, J. T. *The South: A Tour of Its Battle-Fields and Ruined Cities, A Journey through the Desolated States, and Talks with the People.* Hartford, Conn.: Stebbins, 1866.

Upson, Theodore F. *With Sherman to the Sea: The Civil War Letters, Diaries, and Reminiscences of Theodore F. Upson.* Edited by Oscar Osburn Winther. Bloomington: Indiana University Press, 1958.

War of the Rebellion: A Compilation of the Official Records of the Union and Confederate Armies. 70 vols. in 128 parts. Washington, D.C.: Government Printing Office, 1880–91.

Weddel, Jacob. "A Tough Tussle with Sheridan." In Cozzens, *Battles and Leaders,* 5:506–10.

Wilcox, Charles. "Onward to Vicksburg." In Commager, *Blue and the Gray,* 2:649–56.

Williams, Thomas. "Letters of General Thomas Williams, 1862." *American Historical Review* 14, no. 2 (January 1909): 304–28.

Wills, Charles W. *Army Life of an Illinois Soldier: Including a Day by Day Record of Sherman's March to the Sea, Letters and Diary of the Late Charles W. Wills.* Compiled by Mary E. Kellogg. Washington, D.C.: Globe Printing, 1906.

Wise, John. "Boys in Battle at New Market." In Cozzens, *Battles and Leaders,* 5:510–25.

Newspapers and Periodicals
Daily Citizen, Vicksburg, Miss., 1863
Daily Times Picayune, New Orleans, La., 1862
Harper's Weekly, 1862–65
New York Herald, 1862–65
Weekly Courier, Natchez, Miss., 1863–64
Weekly Vicksburg Whig, Vicksburg, Miss., 1861

SECONDARY SOURCES

Arnold, James R. *Grant Wins the War: Decision at Vicksburg.* New York: John Wiley and Sons, 1997.

Ayers, Edward L. *In the Presence of Mine Enemies: The Civil War in the Heart of America, 1859–1863.* New York: W. W. Norton, 2003.

Bacon, Benjamin. *Sinews of War: How Technology, Industry, and Transportation Won the Civil War.* Novato, Calif.: Presidio, 1997.

Bagley, William Chandler, Jr. *Soil Exhaustion and the Civil War.* Washington, D.C.: American Council on Public Affairs, 1942.

Bailey, Anne J. *The Chessboard of War: Sherman and Hood in the Autumn Campaigns of 1864.* Lincoln: University of Nebraska Press, 2000.

———. *War and Ruin: William T. Sherman and the Savannah Campaign.* Wilmington, Del.: Scholarly Resources Books, 2003.

Ballard, Michael B. *Vicksburg: The Campaign That Opened the Mississippi.* Chapel Hill: University of North Carolina Press, 2004.

Barker, Rocky. *Scorched Earth: How the Fires of Yellowstone Changed America.* Washington, D.C.: Island Press, 2005.

Barry, John M. *Rising Tide: The Great Mississippi Flood of 1927 and How It Changed America.* New York: Simon and Schuster, 1997.

Bastian, David F. *Grant's Canal: The Union's Attempt to Bypass Vicksburg.* Shippensburg, Pa.: Burd Street Press, 1995.

Bearss, Edwin Cole. *The Campaign for Vicksburg.* Vol. 2, *Grant Strikes a Fatal Blow.* Dayton, Ohio: Morningside, 1986.

Bell, Andrew McIlwaine. "'Gallinippers' and Glory: The Links between Mosquito-Borne Disease and U.S. Civil War Operations and Strategy, 1862." *Journal of Military History* 74 (April 2010): 379–405.

———. *Mosquito Soldiers: Malaria, Yellow Fever, and the Course of the American Civil War.* Baton Rouge: Louisiana State University Press, 2010.

Beringer, Richard E., Herman Hattaway, Archer Jones, and William N. Still Jr. *Why the South Lost the Civil War.* Athens: University of Georgia Press, 1986.

Black, Brian. "Addressing the Nature of Gettysburg: 'Addition and Detraction' in Preserving an American Shrine." *Reconstruction: Studies in American Culture* 7, no. 2 (2007). http://reconstruction.eserver.org/072/black.shtml. Also in Pearson, Coates, and Cole, *Militarized Landscapes,* 171–88.

———. "Civil War." In *Nature and the Environment in 19th-Century American Life,* edited by Brian Black, 95–114. Westport, Conn.: Greenwood, 2006.

———. "Gallery: The Copse at Gettysburg." *Environmental History* 9, no. 2 (April 2004): 306–10.

Blight, David W. *Race and Reunion: The Civil War in American Memory.* Cambridge, Mass.: Belknap Press of Harvard University Press, 2001.

Blum, Elizabeth D. "Power, Danger, and Control: Slave Women's Perceptions of Wilderness in the Nineteenth Century." *Women's Studies* 31, no. 2 (March 2002): 247–65.

Brady, Lisa M. "Devouring the Land: Sherman's 1864–1865 Campaigns." In *War and the Environment,* edited by Charles E. Closmann, 49–67. College Station: Texas A&M University Press, 2009.

———, ed. "'This Terrible Conflict of the American People': The Civil War Letters of Thaddeus Minshall." *Ohio Valley History* 4, no. 1 (Spring 2004): 3–20.

———. "The Wilderness of War: Nature and Strategy in the American Civil War." *Environmental History* 10, no. 3 (July 2005): 421–47.

Brinkley, Garland L. "The Decline in Southern Agricultural Output, 1860–1880." *Journal of Economic History* 57, no. 1 (March 1997): 116–38.

Bruch, Tamara Elaine. "The Evolution of the South: Eliza Frances Andrews, General William T. Sherman, and Green Interpretations of the Civil War." MA thesis, Auburn University, 2009.

Burne, Alfred H. *Lee, Grant, and Sherman: A Study in Leadership in the 1864–1865 Campaign*. 1938. Reprint, Lawrence: University Press of Kansas, 2000.

Calore, Paul. "The Vicksburg Campaign." In *Land Campaigns of the Civil War*, 90–106. Jefferson, N.C.: McFarland, 2000.

Camp, Stephanie M. H. *Closer to Freedom: Enslaved Women and Everyday Resistance in the Plantation South*. Chapel Hill: University of North Carolina Press, 2004.

Campbell, Jacqueline Glass. *When Sherman Marched North from the Sea: Resistance on the Confederate Home Front*. Chapel Hill: University of North Carolina Press, 2003.

Carney, Judith. "Landscapes of Technology Transfer: Rice Cultivation and African Continuities." In Sutter and Manganiello, *Environmental History and the American South*, 80–105.

Carrigan, Jo Ann. "Yankees versus Yellow Jack in New Orleans, 1862–1866." *Civil War History* 9, no. 3 (September 1963): 248–60.

Carter, Samuel. *The Final Fortress: The Campaign for Vicksburg, 1862–1863*. New York: St. Martin's, 1980.

Cashin, Joan E. "Landscape and Memory in Antebellum Virginia." *Virginia Magazine of History and Biography* 102, no. 4 (October 1994): 477–500.

Catton, Bruce. *The Centennial History of the Civil War*. 3 vols. Garden City, N.Y.: Doubleday, 1961–65.

Caudill, Edward, and Paul Ashdown. *Sherman's March in Myth and Memory*. Lanham, Md.: Rowman and Littlefield, 2008.

Clark, Thomas D., and Albert D. Kirwan. *The South since Appomattox: A Century of Regional Change*. New York: Oxford University Press, 1967.

Clinton, Catherine, and Nina Silber, eds. *Divided Houses: Gender and the Civil War*. New York: Oxford University Press, 1992.

Cobb, James C. *Away Down South: A History of Southern Identity*. New York: Oxford University Press, 2005.

Cowdrey, Albert E. "Environments of War." *Environmental Review* 7, no. 2 (Summer 1983): 155–64.

———. *This Land, This South: An Environmental History*. Rev. ed. Lexington: University Press of Kentucky, 1996.

Cox, Jacob D. *March to the Sea*. Vol. 12, *Campaigns of the Civil War*. 1882. Reprint, New York: The Blue and the Gray Press, n.d.

Cozzens, Peter. *Shenandoah 1862: Stonewall Jackson's Valley Campaign*. Chapel Hill: University of North Carolina Press, 2008.

Crackel, Theodore J. *West Point: A Bicentennial History*. Lawrence: University Press of Kansas, 2002.

Cronon, William. "A Place for Stories: Nature, History, and Narrative." *Journal of American History* 78, no. 4 (March 1992): 1347–76.

———. "The Trouble with Wilderness; or, Getting Back to the Wrong Nature." In *Uncommon Ground: Toward Reinventing Nature*, edited by William Cronon, 69–90. New York: Norton, 1995.

Cropley, Thomas G. "Dermatology and Skin Disease in the American Civil War." *Dermatology Nursing* 20, no. 1 (February 2008): 29–33.

Crowley, Robert, ed. *With My Face to the Enemy: Perspectives on the Civil War*. New York: Putnam, 2001.

Daniel, Larry J., and Lynn N. Bock. *Island No. 10: Struggle for the Mississippi Valley.* Tuscaloosa: University of Alabama Press, 1996.

Davis, Burke. *Sherman's March.* New York: Vintage Books, 1980.

DeJohn Anderson, Virginia. "Animals into the Wilderness: The Development of Livestock Husbandry in the Seventeenth-Century Chesapeake." In Sutter and Manganiello, *Environmental History and the American South*, 25–60.

Donnelly, Ralph W. "Scientists of the Confederate Nitre and Mining Bureau." *Civil War History* 2, no. 4 (December 1956): 69–92.

Drago, Edmund L. "How Sherman's March through Georgia Affected the Slaves." *Georgia Historical Quarterly* 57, no. 3 (1973): 361–75.

Ecelbarger, Gary. *Three Days in the Shenandoah: Stonewall Jackson at Front Royal and Winchester.* Norman: University of Oklahoma Press, 2008.

Edelson, S. Max. "Clearing Swamps, Harvesting Forests: Trees and the Making of a Plantation Landscape in the Colonial South Carolina Lowcountry." In Sutter and Manganiello, *Environmental History and the American South*, 106–30.

Elam, Mark. "The Road to Atlanta: The Role of Geography in Command and Decision Making during the Atlanta Campaign." PhD diss., Florida State University, 1996.

Faust, Drew Gilpin. *This Republic of Suffering: Death and the American Civil War.* New York: Alfred A. Knopf, 2008.

Fellman, Michael. "At the Nihilist Edge: Reflections on Guerrilla Warfare during the American Civil War." In Förster and Nagler, *On the Road to Total War*, 519–40.

Ferguson, R. Brian, ed. *Warfare, Culture, and Environment.* New York: Academic, 1984.

Fiege, Mark. "Gettysburg and the Organic Nature of the American Civil War." In Tucker and Russell, *Natural Enemy, Natural Ally*, 93–109.

Fite, Emerson David. *Social and Industrial Conditions in the North during the Civil War.* 1910. Reprint, New York: Frederick Ungar, 1963.

Florman, Samuel C. *The Civilized Engineer.* New York: St. Martin's Griffin, 1987.

Foner, Eric. *Free Soil, Free Labor, Free Men: The Ideology of the Republican Party before the Civil War.* New York: Oxford University Press, 1970.

Foote, Shelby. *The Civil War: A Narrative.* 3 vols. 1958–74. Reprint, New York: Vintage, 1986.

Förster, Stig, and Jörg Nagler, eds. *On the Road to Total War: The American Civil War and the German Wars of Unification, 1861–1871.* Washington, D.C.: German Historical Institute; New York: Cambridge University Press, 1997.

Foster, Buck T. *Sherman's Mississippi Campaign.* Tuscaloosa: University of Alabama Press, 2006.

Frye, Dennis E. "'I Resolved to Play a Bold Game': John S. Mosby as a Factor in the 1864 Valley Campaign." In Gallagher, *Struggle for the Shenandoah*, 107–26.

Fryman, Robert J. "Fortifying the Landscape: An Archaeological Study of Military Engineering and the Atlanta Campaign." In Geier and Potter, *Archaeological Perspectives*, 43–55.

Fullenkamp, Leonard, Stephen Bowman, and Jay Luvaas, eds. *Guide to the Vicksburg Campaign.* Lawrence: University Press of Kansas, 1998.

Gallagher, Gary W. "Blueprint for Victory: Northern Strategy and Military Policy." In McPherson and Cooper, *Writing the Civil War*, 8–35.

———, ed. *The Shenandoah Valley Campaign of 1862*. Chapel Hill: University of North Carolina Press, 2003.

———, ed. *The Shenandoah Valley Campaign of 1864*. Chapel Hill: University of North Carolina Press, 2006.

———, ed. *Struggle for the Shenandoah: Essays on the 1864 Valley Campaign*. Kent, Ohio: Kent State University Press, 1991.

———. "The Shenandoah Valley in 1864." In Gallagher, *Struggle for the Shenandoah*, 1–18.

Gates, Paul. *Agriculture and the Civil War*. New York: Knopf, 1965.

Geier, Clarence, Jr. and Stephen R. Potter, eds. *Archaeological Perspectives on the American Civil War*. Gainesville: University Press of Florida, 2000.

Geier, Clarence, Jr. and Susan E. Winter, eds. *Look to the Earth: Historical Archaeology and the American Civil War*. Knoxville: University of Tennessee Press, 1994.

Giltner, Scott. "Slave Hunting and Fishing in the Antebellum South," In Glave and Stoll, *"To Love the Wind,"* 21–36.

Glatthaar, Joseph T. "Battlefield Tactics." In McPherson and Cooper, *Writing the Civil War*, 60–80.

———. *The March to the Sea and Beyond: Sherman's Troops in the Savannah and Carolinas Campaigns*. Baton Rouge: Louisiana State University Press, 1985.

Glave, Dianne D., and Mark Stoll, eds. *"To Love the Wind and the Rain": African Americans and Environmental History*. Pittsburgh, Pa.: University of Pittsburgh Press, 2006.

Grabau, Warren E. *Ninety-Eight Days: A Geographer's View of the Vicksburg Campaign*. Knoxville: University of Tennessee Press, 2000.

Greene, Francis Vinton. *The Mississippi*. Vol. 9, *Campaigns of the Civil War*. New York: Charles Scribner and Sons, 1883. Reprint, New York: Blue and Gray Press, n.d.

Grillis, Pamela Lea. *Vicksburg and Warren County: A History of People and Place*. Vicksburg, Miss.: Dancing Rabbit Books, 1992.

Grimsley, Mark. *The Hard Hand of War: Union Military Policy toward Southern Civilians, 1861–1865*. New York: Cambridge University Press, 1995.

———. "'Rebels' and 'Redskins': U.S. Military Conduct toward White Southerners and Native Americans in Comparative Perspective." In *Civilians in the Path of War*, edited by Mark Grimsley and Clifford J. Rogers, 137–61. Lincoln: University of Nebraska Press, 2002.

Grow, Matthew J. "The Shadow of the Civil War: A Historiography of Civil War Memory." *American Nineteenth Century History* 4, no. 2 (Summer 2003): 77–103.

Gudmestad, Robert H. *Steamboats and the Rise of the Cotton Kingdom*. Baton Rouge: Louisiana State University Press, 2011.

Hagerman, Edward. *The American Civil War and the Origins of Modern Warfare: Ideas, Organization, and Field Command*. Bloomington: Indiana University Press, 1988.

———. "From Jomini to Dennis Hart Mahan: The Evolution of Trench Warfare and the American Civil War." *Civil War History* 13 (September 1967): 197–220.

Hahn, Steven. *A Nation under Our Feet: Black Political Struggles in the Rural South from Slavery to the Great Migration*. Cambridge, Mass.: Belknap Press of Harvard University Press, 2003.

Hale, Laura Virginia. *Four Valiant Years in the Lower Shenandoah Valley, 1861–1865.* Strasburg, Va.: Shenandoah Publishing House, 1968.

Hanson, Victor Davis. "The Army of the West: Sherman's March to the Sea." In *The Soul of Battle: From Ancient Times to the Present Day, How Three Great Liberators Vanquished Tyranny*, 121–260. New York: Anchor Books, 1999.

———. *Ripples of Battle: How Wars of the Past Still Determine How We Fight, How We Live, and How We Think.* New York: Doubleday, 2003.

Harmon, George D., ed. "The Military Experiences of James A. Peifer, 1861–1865." *North Carolina Historical Review* 32, no. 3 (July 1955): 385–409; 32, no. 4 (October 1955): 544–72.

Harrell, Virginia Calohan. *Vicksburg and the River.* Jackson: University Press of Mississippi, 1982.

Harsh, Joseph. "Battlesword and Rapier: Clausewitz, Jomini, and the American Civil War." *Military Affairs* 38 (December 1974): 133–38.

Hattaway, Herman. *Shades of Blue and Gray: An Introductory Military History of the Civil War.* Columbia: University of Missouri Press, 1997.

Hattaway, Herman, and Archer Jones. *How the North Won: A Military History of the Civil War.* Urbana: University of Illinois Press, 1983.

Hays, Samuel P. *Conservation and the Gospel of Efficiency: The Progressive Conservation Movement, 1890–1920.* Cambridge: Harvard University Press, 1959.

Heatwole, John L. *The Burning: Sheridan in the Shenandoah Valley.* Charlottesville, Va.: Rockbridge, 1998.

Hess, Earl J. "The Nature of Battle." In *The Union Soldier in Battle: Enduring the Ordeal of Combat*, 45–72. Lawrence: University Press of Kansas, 1997.

Holden, Edward S., and W. L. Ostrander. "Tentative List of the Text-Books Used at the U.S. Military Academy at West Point, 1802–1902." In *The Centennial of the United States Military Academy at West Point, New York, 1802–1902*, vol. 1, *Addresses and Histories*, 439–66. Westport, Conn.: Greenwood, 1903.

Hong, Sok Chul. "Burden of Early Exposure to Malaria in the United States, 1850–1860." *Journal of Economic History* 67, no. 4 (December 2007): 1001–35.

Howe, Daniel Walker. *What Hath God Wrought: The Transformation of America, 1815–1848.* New York: Oxford University Press, 2007.

Humphreys, Margaret. *Intensely Human: The Health of the Black Soldier in the American Civil War.* Baltimore: Johns Hopkins University Press, 2008.

———. *Yellow Fever and the South.* New Brunswick, N.J.: Rutgers University Press, 1992.

Hyde, Samuel C., Jr. "Plain Folk Yeomanry in the Antebellum South." In *A Companion to the American South*, edited by John B. Boles, 139–55. Malden, Mass.: Blackwell, 2002.

Janda, Lance. "Shutting the Gates of Mercy: The American Origins of Total War, 1860–1880." *Journal of Military History* 59 (January 1995): 7–26.

Jones, Archer. "Jomini and the Strategy of the American Civil War: A Reinterpretation." *Military Affairs* 34 (December 1970): 127–31.

Kellogg, Sanford C. *The Shenandoah Valley and Virginia, 1861–1865.* New York: Neale, 1903.

Kelman, Ari. *A River and Its City: The Nature of Landscape in New Orleans.* Berkeley: University of California Press, 2003.

Kennett, Lee. *Marching through Georgia: The Story of Soldiers and Civilians during Sherman's Campaign.* New York: HarperCollins, 1995.

———. *Sherman: A Soldier's Life.* New York: HarperCollins, 2001.

Kercheval, Samuel. *A History of the Valley of Virginia.* 4th ed. 1833. Reprint, Strasburg, Va.: Shenandoah Publishing House, 1925.

Kirby, Jack Temple. "The American Civil War: An Environmental View." National Humanities Center, *Nature Transformed: The Environment in American History.* Revised July 2001; accessed July 6, 2006. http://nationalhumanitiescenter.org /tserve/nattrans/ntuseland/essays/amcwar.htm.

———. *Poquosin: A Study of Rural Landscape and Society.* Chapel Hill: University of North Carolina Press, 1995.

Kleese, Richard B. *Shenandoah County in the Civil War: The Turbulent Years.* 2nd ed. Lynchburg, Va.: H. E. Howard, 1992.

Knobloch, Frieda. *The Culture of Wilderness: Agriculture as Colonization in the American West.* Chapel Hill: University of North Carolina Press, 1996.

Krick, Robert K. *Civil War Weather in Virginia.* Tuscaloosa: University of Alabama Press, 2007.

———. *Conquering the Valley: Stonewall Jackson at Port Republic.* New York: Morrow, 1996.

Langston, Nancy. *Toxic Bodies: Hormone Disruptors and the Legacy of DES.* New Haven, Conn.: Yale University Press, 2010.

Lawrence, Henry W. "Historic Change in Natural Landscape: The Experimental View." *Environmental Review* 6, no. 1 (Spring 1982): 14–37.

LeCain, Timothy J. *Mass Destruction: The Men and Giant Mines that Wired America and Scarred the Planet.* New Brunswick, N.J.: Rutgers University Press, 2009.

Lewis, Michael, ed. *American Wilderness: A New History.* New York: Oxford University Press, 2007.

———. "American Wilderness: An Introduction." In Lewis, *American Wilderness*, 3–13.

Lewis, Thomas A. *The Guns of Cedar Creek.* New York: Harper and Row, 1988.

———. *The Shenandoah in Flames: The Valley Campaign of 1864.* Alexandria, Va.: Time-Life Books, 1987.

Lynn, John. "The Embattled Future of Academic Military History." *Journal of Military History* 61 (October 1997): 777–89.

Magdol, Edward. "Shall We Have Land?" In *A Right to the Land: Essays on the Freedmen's Community*, 139–73. Westport, Conn.: Greenwood, 1977.

Mahon, Michael G. *The Shenandoah Valley, 1861–1865: The Destruction of the Granary of the Confederacy.* Mechanicsburg, Pa.: Stackpole Books, 1999.

Majewski, John. *Modernizing a Slave Economy: The Economic Vision of the Confederate Nation.* Chapel Hill: University of North Carolina Press, 2009.

Majewski, John, and Viken Tchakerian. "The Environmental Origins of Shifting Cultivation: Climate, Soils, and Disease in the Nineteenth-Century U.S. South." *Agricultural History* 81, no. 4 (Fall 2007): 522–49.

Martin, David G. "The Vicksburg Mine." In *The Vicksburg Campaign: April 1862– July 1863*, 155–64. Rev. ed. Pennsylvania: Combined Books, 1994.

McElfresh, Earl B. *Maps and Mapmakers of the Civil War.* New York: Harry N. Abrams, 1999.

McPhee, John. *The Control of Nature.* New York: Farrar, Straus and Giroux, 1989.

McPherson, James M. *Battle Cry of Freedom: The Civil War Era*. New York: Oxford University Press, 1988.

McPherson, James M., and William J. Cooper Jr., eds. *Writing the Civil War: The Quest to Understand*. Columbia: University of South Carolina Press, 1998.

Meier, Kathryn S. "Fighting in 'Dante's Inferno': Changing Perceptions of Civil War Combat in the Spotsylvania Wilderness from 1863 to 1864." In Pearson, Coates, and Cole, *Militarized Landscapes: From Gettysburg to Salisbury Plain*, 39–58.

———. "'No Place for the Sick': Nature's War on Civil War Soldier Health in 1862 Virginia." PhD diss., University of Virginia, 2010.

———. "'No Place for the Sick': Nature's War on Civil War Soldier Mental and Physical Health in the 1862 Peninsula and Shenandoah Valley Campaigns." *Journal of the Civil War Era* 1, no. 2 (June 2011): 176–206.

Meinig, D. W., ed. *Interpretation of Ordinary Landscapes: Geographical Essays*. New York: Oxford University Press, 1979.

Merchant, Carolyn. *The Death of Nature: Women, Ecology and the Scientific Revolution*. 1980. Reprint, New York: HarperSanFrancisco, 1990.

Merritt, Raymond H. *Engineering in American Society, 1850–1875*. Lexington: University Press of Kentucky, 1969.

Meyerson, Harvey. *Nature's Army: When Soldiers Fought for Yosemite*. Lawrence: University Press of Kansas, 2001.

Miers, Earl Schenck. *The General Who Marched to Hell: William Tecumseh Sherman and His March to Fame and Infamy*. New York: Alfred A. Knopf, 1951.

Miller, Angela. "The Fate of Wilderness in American Landscape Art." In Lewis, *American Wilderness*, 91–112.

Mitman, Gregg. "In Search of Health: Landscape and Disease in American Environmental History." *Environmental History* 10, no. 2 (April 2005): 184–210.

Morris, Christopher. *Becoming Southern: The Evolution of a Way of Life, Warren County and Vicksburg, Mississippi, 1770–1860*. New York: Oxford University Press, 1995.

———. "A More Southern Environmental History." *Journal of Southern History* 75, no. 3 (August 2009): 581–98.

Morris, Roy, Jr. *Sheridan: The Life and Wars of General Phil Sheridan*. New York: Crown, 1992.

Morrison, James L., Jr. *The Best School in the World: West Point, the Pre–Civil War Years, 1833–1866*. Kent, Ohio: Kent State University Press, 1986.

———. "Educating the Civil War Generals: West Point, 1833–1861." *Military Affairs* 38, no. 3 (October 1974): 108–11.

Moten, Matthew. *The Delafield Commission and the American Military Profession*. College Station, Tex.: Texas A&M University Press, 2000.

Nash, Linda. "The Agency of Nature or the Nature of Agency?" *Environmental History* 10, no. 1 (January 2005): 67–69.

———. *Inescapable Ecologies: A History of Environment, Disease, and Knowledge*. Berkeley: University of California Press, 2006.

Nash, Roderick. *Wilderness and the American Mind*. 3rd ed. New Haven, Conn.: Yale University Press, 1982.

National Park Service. "The Civil War: 150 Years—National Park Service Sesquicentennial Commemoration." http://www.nps.gov/civilwar150/.

Natural Resources Conservation Service. *Soil Taxonomy: A Basic System of Soil Classification for Making and Interpreting Soil Surveys.* 2nd ed. Washington, D.C.: U.S. Department of Agriculture, 1999. Available online: http://soils.usda .gov/technical/classification/taxonomy/. Accessed May 30, 2011.

Neely, Mark E., Jr. *The Civil War and the Limits of Destruction.* Cambridge, Mass.: Harvard University Press, 2007.

———. "Was the Civil War a Total War?" *Civil War History* 37, no. 1 (March 1991): 5–28.

Nelson, Lynn A. *Pharsalia: An Environmental Biography of a Southern Plantation, 1780–1880.* Athens: University of Georgia Press, 2007.

Nelson, Megan Kate. "The Landscape of Disease: Swamps and Medical Discourse in the American Southeast, 1800–1880." *Mississippi Quarterly* 55, no. 4 (Fall 2002): 535–67.

Nye, David E. *America as Second Creation: Technology and Narratives of New Beginnings.* Cambridge, Mass.: MIT Press, 2003.

Otto, John Solomon. *Southern Agriculture during the Civil War Era, 1860–1880.* Westport, Conn.: Greenwood, 1994.

Ouchley, Kelby. *Flora and Fauna of the Civil War: An Environmental Reference Guide.* Baton Rouge: Louisiana State University Press, 2010.

Pabis, George S. "Delaying the Deluge: The Engineering Debate over Flood Control on the Lower Mississippi River, 1846–1861." *Journal of Southern History* 64, no. 3 (August 1998): 421–54.

Paludan, Phillip Shaw. *A People's Contest: The Union and Civil War, 1861–1865.* 2nd ed. Lawrence: University Press of Kansas, 1996.

Pearson, Chris, Peter Coates, and Tim Cole, eds. *Militarized Landscapes: From Gettysburg to the Salisbury Plain.* London: Continuum Books, 2010.

Perreault, Melanie. "American Wilderness and First Contact." In Lewis, *American Wilderness,* 15–33.

Phillips, Edward Hamilton. *The Lower Shenandoah Valley in the Civil War: The Impact of War upon the Civilian Population and upon Civil Institutions.* Lynchburg, Va.: H. E. Howard, 1993.

———. *The Shenandoah Valley in 1864: An Episode in the History of Warfare.* The Citadel Monograph Series, no. 5. Charleston, S.C.: The Citadel, 1965.

Pond, George E. *The Shenandoah Valley in 1864.* Vol. 11, *Campaigns of the Civil War.* 1883. Reprint, Edison, N.J.: Castle Books, 2002.

Porter, David D. *The Naval History of the Civil War.* New York: Sherman, 1886.

Powell, J. Harrison. "'Seven Year Locusts': The Deforestation of Spotsylvania County during the American Civil War." *Essays in History: Annual Journal of the Corcoran Department of History at the University of Virginia* (2010). Accessed March 15, 2011. http://www.virginia.edu/history/EIH/?p=160.

Rae, John, and Rudi Volti. *The Engineer in History.* New York: Peter Lang, 1993.

Reid, Brian Holden. *America's Civil War: The Operational Battlefield, 1861–1863.* Amherst, N.Y.: Prometheus Books, 2008.

Reill, Peter Hanns. *Vitalizing Nature in the Enlightenment.* Berkeley: University of California Press, 2005.

Reuss, Martin. *Designing the Bayous: The Control of Water in the Atchafalaya Basin, 1800–1995.* Alexandria, Va.: U.S. Army Corps of Engineers Office of History, 1998.

Reynolds, Terry S. "The Engineer in 19th-Century America." In *The Engineer in America: A Historical Anthology from Technology and Culture*, edited by Terry S. Reynolds, 7–26. Chicago: University of Chicago Press, 1991.

Richardson, Lee, Jr. and Thomas D. Godman, eds. *In and about Vicksburg: An Illustrated Guide Book to the City of Vicksburg, Mississippi*. Vicksburg, Miss.: Gibraltar, 1890.

Royster, Charles. *The Destructive War: William Tecumseh Sherman, Stonewall Jackson, and the Americans*. New York: Knopf, 1991.

Saikku, Mikko. *This Delta, This Land: An Environmental History of the Yazoo-Mississippi Floodplain*. Athens: University of Georgia Press, 2005.

Saloutos, Theodore. "Southern Agriculture and the Problems of Readjustment: 1865–1877." *Agricultural History* 30, no. 2 (April 1956): 58–76.

Sartin, Jeffrey S. "Infectious Diseases during the Civil War: The Triumph of the 'Third Army.'" *Clinical Infectious Diseases* 16, no. 4 (April 1993): 580–84.

Schama, Simon. *Landscape and Memory*. New York: Alfred A. Knopf, 1995.

Schantz, Mark S. *Awaiting the Heavenly Country: The Civil War and America's Culture of Death*. Ithaca, N.Y.: Cornell University Press, 2008.

Seelye, John. *Beautiful Machine: Rivers and the Republican Plan, 1755–1825*. New York: Oxford University Press, 1991.

Shackel, Paul A. "Memorializing Landscapes and the Civil War in Harpers Ferry." In Geier and Winter, *Look to the Earth*, 256–70.

Shallat, Todd. *Structures in the Stream: Water, Science, and the Rise of the U.S. Army Corps of Engineers*. Austin: University of Texas Press, 1994.

Sharrer, Terry. "The Great Glanders Epizootic, 1861–1865: A Civil War Legacy." *Agricultural History* 69, no. 1 (Winter 1995): 79–97.

Shea, William L., and Terrence J. Winschel. *Vicksburg Is the Key: The Struggle for the Mississippi River*. Lincoln: University of Nebraska Press, 2003.

Sheehan-Dean, Aaron. "Success Is So Blended with Defeat: Virginia Soldiers in the Shenandoah Valley." In Gallagher, *Shenandoah Valley Campaign of 1864*, 257–98.

Sheriff, Carol. *The Artificial River: The Erie Canal and the Paradox of Progress, 1817–1862*. New York: Hill and Wang, 1996.

Shiman, Philip Lewis. "Engineering Sherman's March: Army Engineers and the Management of Modern War, 1862–1865." PhD diss., Duke University, 1991.

Silver, Timothy. *A New Face on the Countryside: Indians, Colonists, and Slaves in South Atlantic Forests, 1500–1800*. New York: Cambridge University Press, 1990.

Skelton, William. *An American Profession of Arms: The Army Officer Corps, 1784–1861*. Lawrence: University Press of Kansas, 1996.

Smith, Everard H. "Chambersburg: Anatomy of a Confederate Reprisal." *American Historical Review* 96 (April 1991): 432–55.

Smith, Timothy B. *The Golden Age of Battlefield Preservation: The Decade of the 1890s and the Establishment of America's First Five Military Parks*. Knoxville: University of Tennessee Press, 2008.

Spirn, Anne Whiston. *The Language of Landscape*. New Haven, Conn.: Yale University Press, 1998.

Steinberg, Ted. "Down to Earth: Nature, Agency, and Power in History." *American Historical Review* 107 (June 2002): 798–820.

————. *Down to Earth: Nature's Role in American History*. 2nd ed. New York: Oxford University Press, 2009.

Steiner, Paul E. *Disease in the Civil War: Natural Biological Warfare in 1861–1865*. Springfield, Ill.: Charles C. Thomas, 1968.

Stewart, Mart A. "From King Cane to King Cotton: Razing Cane in the Old South." *Environmental History* 12, no. 1 (January 2007): 59–79.

————. "If John Muir Had Been an Agrarian: American Environmental History West and South." *Environment and History* 11 (May 2005): 139–62.

————. "Rice, Water, and Power: Landscapes of Domination and Resistance in the Lowcountry, 1790–1880." *Environmental History Review* 15, no. 3 (Fall 1991): 47–64.

————. "Slavery and the Origins of African American Environmentalism." In Glave and Stoll, *"To Love the Wind,"* 9–20.

————. "Southern Environmental History." In *A Companion to the American South*, edited by John B. Boles, 409–23. Malden, Mass.: Blackwell, 2002.

————. *"What Nature Suffers to Groe": Life, Labor, and Landscape on the Georgia Coast, 1680–1920*. Athens: University of Georgia Press, 1996.

Stilgoe, John R. *Common Landscape of America, 1580–1845*. New Haven, Conn.: Yale University Press, 1982.

————. "Landschaft and Linearity: Two Archetypes of Landscape." *Environmental Review* 4, no. 1 (1980): 2–17.

Stoll, Steven. "Farm against Forest." In Lewis, *American Wilderness*, 55–72.

————. *Larding the Lean Earth: Soil and Society in Nineteenth-Century America*. New York: Hill and Wang, 2002.

Stroud, Ellen. "Does Nature Always Matter? Following Dirt through History." Theme issue, "Environment and History," *History and Theory* 42 (December 2003): 75–81.

Sutherland, Daniel E. "Abraham Lincoln, John Pope, and the Origins of Total War." *Journal of Military History* 56, no. 4 (October 1992): 567–86.

Sutter, Paul S., and Christopher J. Manganiello, eds. *Environmental History and the American South: A Reader*. Athens: University of Georgia Press, 2009.

Tanner, Robert G. *Stonewall in the Valley: Thomas J. "Stonewall" Jackson's Shenandoah Valley Campaign, Spring 1862*. Garden City, N.Y.: Doubleday, 1976.

Thienel, Phillip M. *Seven Story Mountain: The Union Campaigns at Vicksburg*. Jefferson, N.C.: McFarland, 1995.

Thomas, Emory M. "Rebellion and Conventional Warfare: Confederate Strategy and Military Policy." In McPherson and Cooper, *Writing the Civil War*, 36–59.

Thomas, William G. "Nothing Ought to Astonish Us: Confederate Civilians in the 1864 Shenandoah Valley Campaign." In Gallagher, *Shenandoah Valley Campaign of 1864*, 222–56.

Tillman, Samuel E. "The Academic History of the Military Academy, 1802–1902." In *The Centennial of the United States Military Academy at West Point, New York*, vol. 1, *Addresses and Histories*, 223–438. New York: Greenwood, 1903.

Trudeau, Noah Andre. *Southern Storm: Sherman's March to the Sea*. New York: Harper Perennial, 2008.

Tucker, Richard P., and Edmund Russell, eds. *Natural Enemy, Natural Ally: Toward an Environmental History of War*. Corvallis: Oregon State University Press, 2004.

Valenčius, Conevery Bolton. *The Health of the Country: How American Settlers Understood Themselves and Their Land*. New York: Basic Books, 2002.

Walters, John Bennett. "General William T. Sherman and Total War." *Journal of Southern History* 14, no. 4 (November 1948): 447–80.

Wayland, John W. *The German Element of the Shenandoah Valley of Virginia*. 1907. Reprint, Bridgewater, Va.: C. J. Carrier, 1964.

———. *Twenty-Five Chapters on the Shenandoah Valley*. Strasburg, Va.: Shenandoah Publishing House, 1957.

Weigley, Russell F. "American Strategy from Its Beginnings through the First World War." In *Makers of Modern Strategy: From Machiavelli to the Nuclear Age*, edited by Peter Paret, Gordon A. Craig, and Felix Gilbert, 408–43. Princeton: Princeton University Press, 1986.

———. *A Great Civil War: A Military and Political History, 1861–1865*. Bloomington: Indiana University Press, 2000.

———. "A Strategy of Annihilation: U. S. Grant and the Union." In *The American Way of War: A History of United States Military Strategy and Policy*, edited by Russell F. Weigley, 128–52. 1973. Reprint, Bloomington: Indiana University Press; New York: Macmillan, 1977.

Wert, Jeffry D. *From Winchester to Cedar Creek: The Shenandoah Campaign of 1864*. Carlisle, Pa.: South Mountain, 1987.

Wetherington, Mark V. *Plain Folk's Fight: The Civil War and Reconstruction in Piney Woods Georgia*. Chapel Hill: University of North Carolina Press, 2005.

Whites, Lee Ann. *The Civil War as a Crisis in Gender: Augusta, Georgia, 1860–1890*. Athens: University of Georgia Press, 1995.

Wiley, Bell Irvin. *The Life of Billy Yank: The Common Soldier of the Union*. Baton Rouge: Louisiana State University Press, 1952.

———. *The Life of Johnny Reb: The Common Soldier of the Confederacy*. Baton Rouge: Louisiana State University Press, 1943.

Winders, Jamie. "Imperfectly Imperial: Northern Travel Writers in the Postbellum U.S. South, 1865–1880." *Annals of the Association of American Geographers* 95, no. 2 (2005): 391–410.

Winters, Harold A., with Gerald E. Galloway Jr., William J. Reynolds, and David W. Rhyne. *Battling the Elements: Weather and Terrain in the Conduct of War*. Baltimore: Johns Hopkins University Press, 1998.

Worster, Donald. *Nature's Economy: A History of Ecological Ideas*. 2nd ed. New York: Cambridge University Press, 1994.

———. *A Passion for Nature: The Life of John Muir*. New York: Oxford University Press, 2008.

———. "Transformations of the Earth: Toward an Agroecological History." In "Roundtable: Environmental History." *Journal of American History* 76, no. 4 (March 1990): 1087–147.

INDEX

Page numbers in italics refer to figures.

Aedes aegypti mosquito, 29–30
African Americans, 4, 5, 19, 98, 113;
    impressed by Union army as laborers,
    33, 69, 98. *See also* slavery
agriculture: as metaphor for destruction,
    3, 124; northern, 17–18; southern, 18–
    22, 116, 134. *See also* agroecosystems;
    plantation system
agroecosystems: and cultural identity,
    17–19; defined, 9–10; destruction
    of southern, 134; in Georgia and
    Carolinas, 93, 96, 98, 101–3, 107, 111,
    114, 121, 124–26; as hybrid landscape,
    10; and Lower Mississippi Valley, 27–
    28, 42, 70, 71; new southern postwar,
    132–34; northern versus southern,
    17–21; plantations as, 10, 21–22, 28,
    125–26; and Shenandoah Valley,
    73, 78, 87; and Special Field Orders
    No. 120, 96–98, 101, 114; as symbol
    of Confederacy, 125–26; and Union
    strategy, 11–13, 21–23, 42, 55–57, 69–
    71, 72–73, 78–82, 84, 87, 89, 93, 99,
    107, 111, 121; and Vicksburg campaign,
    23, 55–57, 70. See also *chevauchées*;
    plantation system
Aldridge, Elizabeth, 135
Aldridge, Francis, 135–36
Allegheny Mountains, 72, 74, 77, 79, 90
Anderson, Virginia DeJohn, 19
Andrews, Eliza, 124, 125, 156n145
Anopheles mosquito, 29–30, 46–47
Appomattox Court House, 133
"arcadian" tradition (ecological view of
    nature), 16–17

Army of Northern Virginia
    (Confederate), 71, 78, 79, 120
Army of the Potomac (Union), 71, 79,
    83
Army of the Shenandoah (Union), 79,
    85–86, 91
Army of the Tennessee (Union), 51, 52–
    53, 59, 64, 67, 70
Army of the Valley (Confederate), 76–
    77, 79–80, 81, 82–83, *83*, 85, 91
Army of Vicksburg (Confederate), 60
Ashby, Thomas, 87, 88–89, 130–31
Atlanta, 3, 71, 97, 99–101, 107, 111, 124,
    132; destruction of, 99, 120; siege of,
    102, 130, 138
Averasboro, N.C., 120

Bacon, Edward, 30, 40, 48
Baker, Norval, 80–81
Banks, Nathaniel, 71
Barry, John, 24
Barton, Randolph, 129, 133
Barton, Robert, 81, 82
Barton, Thomas, 46
Bartow, Francis, 139
Baton Rouge, La., 26, 34, 41, 56
battlefield parks, 139–40, 159nn64–65
Beaufort, S.C., 112, 115
Beauregard, Pierre G. T., 36
Belknap, Charles, 102
Bell, Andrew McIlwaine, 8, 29
Bentonville, N.C., 120
Big Black River, 35, 58, 59, 63
Bissell, J. W., 31–33
Black, Brian, 140

Blair, Frank P., 63
Blue Ridge Mountains, 72, 74, 77, 82–
    83, 84, 85, 90
Bradford, William, 13
Bradley, George, 102, 124
Breckenridge, John C., 77
Brown, John, 132
Bruch, Tamara Elaine, 156n145
Bruinsburg, Miss., 53, 54, 57, 67
Bull, Rice, 100, 102, 104, 118
Bull Run, 139
Burge, Dolly Lunt, 103
"Burning, The," 78–79, 87. See also
    Sheridan, Philip H.
Burt, Willis Perry, 136
Butler, Benjamin, 35–36, 71

Cairo, Ill., 25, 26, 29
Calgacus, 127
Campbell, Jacqueline Glass, 95, 116
Campbell, James, 129
Campbell, John Quincy Adams, 29
Camp Williams, 30
canals: 11, 18, 74; De Soto Point, 36, 37,
    38, 39–41, 43, 45; Duckport, 44–
    45; and improving nature through
    engineering, 15–16, 31, 36, 48; at Island
    No. 10, 31, 32, 33–34; at Savannah,
    104–5; and slave labor, 38, 39, 40; and
    Union strategy, 31, 36, 43, 48, 78
Carolina campaign. See Georgia and
    Carolina campaigns
Cashin, Joan, 20–21
casualties, Civil War, 1–2
Cedar Creek, 80, 85
Champion's Hill, 58
Charlestown, Va., 132
Chattanooga, Tenn., 71, 95, 99
Chesnut, Mary, 131, 136
chevauchées: as attacks against
    agriculture, 70–71; defined, 22;
    in Georgia and Carolina campaigns,
    96–97, 99, 101–2, 122–26; and
    Grant, 56, 78–79; and metaphors
    of "wilderness," 127, 130–31; in
    Shenandoah Valley campaign, 78; as

uncivilized, 22–23, 121, 124–25; and
    Union strategy, 23, 131
Chickasaw Bluffs, 42
Christie, Thomas, 134
Clark, Thomas, 133
Cochran, Catherine, 88
Cole, Thomas, 16–17, 127–28
colonial era, 13–14; development of
    southern agriculture in, 19, 28
Colt, Margaretta Barton, 131
Columbia, S.C., 108, 110, 112–13, 114, 115,
    118–19, 130–31
Confederacy. See agroecosystems;
    Confederate army; plantation system;
    secession; slavery
Confederate army, 36, 60, 71, 77–78,
    120. See also Early, Jubal A.; Johnston,
    Joe; Lee, Robert E.; Pemberton,
    John C.
Connolly, James, 109, 119
Conyngham, David, 111, 121, 124
Coosa River, 99
Coosawhatchie River, 112
Coosawhatchie Swamp, 116
Corinth, Miss., 41, 134
corps du genie (corps of engineers), 15
Corps of Engineers, 15, 36, 43
Cowdrey, Albert, 18, 134
Cox, Jacob, 100–101, 102, 105, 106, 112,
    113, 114–15, 120
cultural identity, 17–19, 23, 156n145;
    agriculture as, 22; southern, 21; Union
    strategy against southern, 124

Davis, Charles Henry, 35
Davis, Jefferson, 4, 55, 96
Davis, R. S., 39
Davis, Theodore R., 38
death, nineteenth-century ideas on, 1–2
Deedes, Henry, 131–32
deforestation, 11, 128, 134
"desert" as metaphor, 13, 87, 89, 90, 92,
    108, 119, 127, 129, 130, 157n1
De Soto Point, La., 35, 40, 44, 46, 48,
    49, 50–51; canal, 36, 37, 38, 39–41, 43,
    45–46, 48; failure of canal at, 40

disease, 6, 18, 21, 127–28; dysentery, 48, 65, 66, 128; in environmental historiography, 8, 12; in Georgia and Carolina campaigns, 95; in Lower Mississippi Valley, 28–31, 40–41, 45, 46–47, 48, 65–67, 69; measles, 46, 48, 66, 128; and mosquitoes, 8, 28–31, 39, 40, 46–47, 48, 144n21; smallpox, 45, 48, 128; yellow fever, 29–30, 31

Drago, Edmund L., 125

Duckport, La., 44; canal, 44–45

Durham Station, N.C., 120

dysentery, 48, 65, 66, 128

Early, Jubal A., 76, 79–80, 81, 82–83, *83*, 85, 91

East River, 135

ecological view of nature, 16–17

Ellet, Charles, Jr., 25

emancipation, 69, 72–73, 134. *See also* slavery

Emerson, Ralph Waldo, 127–28

engineering: and mechanistic (imperial) view of nature, 14–16; on Mississippi River, 24–25, 27, 31–34, 39–40, 43; and Special Field Orders No. 120, 95, 97–98, 100, 101; and Union strategy, 12, 31. *See also* canals; Vicksburg campaign

Enlightenment, the, 16

environmental historiography, 4–8, 11–14

Ewing, Philemon, 107, 123

Farragut, David Glasgow, 35–36, 39

Fauquier County, Va., 76, 88

Faust, Drew Gilpin, 2

Fayetteville, N.C., 115, 124

Federals. *See* Union army

Fennell, E. D., 116

Fiege, Mark, 7–8

Fisher's Hill, 82, 83, 85

Fisk, Wilbur, 74

Fontaine, Edward, 36

foraging raids. See *chevauchées*

Force, Manning, 50–52, 67

Fort McAllister, 104

Fort Pemberton, 44

Franklin, Tenn., 3

Front Royal, Va., 77, 80, 83

Fryman, Robert, 16

Gage, Moses, 34, 117, *118*, 121–22

Gallagher, Gary, 76, 90

Gavin, David, 130

Geary, John, 135

Georgia: battles in, 99, 111; and destruction, 3, 93; terrain, 99–101. *See also* Georgia and Carolina campaigns

Georgia and Carolina campaigns, 8, 23, 71, *94*, 103, 104, 108; agroecological foundation assault in, 93, 96, 98–99, 101–3, 107, 114, 121, 123–26; approaches to nature in, 95; *chevauchées* in, 96–97, 99–100, 101–3, 117–20, 121, 122–26; engineering in, 95, 97–98, 100–101, 106, 113; and Grant, 108; as "hard war," 98; historiography of, 93–95, 98; and "landscape," 93, 95–96, 102, 106, 115–16, 117, 121, 124, 125; and natural disaster metaphors, 124; nature as obstacle in, 112–13, 114–15, 120; weather in, 100, 112, 114–15; and "wilderness" metaphors for, 108, 117, 122, 130–31. *See also* Sherman, William T.; Special Field Orders No. 120

Gettysburg, Pa., 8, 66, 139, 140

Glatthaar, Joseph T., 115

Goldsboro, N.C., 108, 120

Gordon, John, 82, 85, 89

Grabau, Warren, 7, 25, 57

Grand Gulf, Miss., 26, 53, 56, *59*

Grant, Ulysses S., 11, 96, 138; on challenges of terrain, 53, 56, 57–58, 60–61; *chevauchée* revival by, 23, 42, 53–55, 56, 69–70, 78–79; and control of nature, 23, 48; and De Soto Point canal, 43, 46–47; and Georgia and Carolina campaigns, 108; Lee's surrender to, 120; and Mississippi River engineering operations,

Grant, Ulysses S. (*continued*)
43–45; and raiding strategy, 55; and
Shenandoah Valley campaign, 77–80,
82, 83, 84–85, 87, 89, 91; and strategy
against Mississippi's agroecosystem,
56–68, 63–64, 70; and Vicksburg
campaign, 41–43, 49–50, 53–56, *54*,
57, 62–64, 70; and Vicksburg victory,
66, 68, 70–71
Greene, Francis Vinton, 58, 60
Greenman, J. W., 65
Greenville, Miss., 55
Grierson, B. H., 56–57
Grillis, Pamela Lea, 66
Grimsley, Mark, 22, 23, 123, 152n11

Halleck, Henry Wager, 41, 125; and
canal at Island No. 10, 33–34; Grant's
reports to, 57, 62, 64, 78, 150n26;
Sherman's reports to, 99, 107–8, 111;
and Union slave withdrawal policy,
69–70
Hampton, Wade, 114
Hardee, William, 105–6
"hard war," 98, 152n11
Harmon, George D., 115
Harpers Ferry, Va., 74, *75*, 80, 159n65
*Harper's Illustrated History of the Great
Rebellion*, 40
Harper's Weekly, *38*, 66, *83*, *118*
Hartwell, John, 80
Hazen, William B., 104, 139
Heatwole, John, 73
Hess, Earl J., 6–7
Hickenlooper, Andrew, 62
Hitchcock, Henry: on Carolina
campaign, 108–9, 111, 113; on Georgia
campaign, 100, 102, 103, 106, 153n20;
and South's "inferiority," 116; and
Union *chevauchées*, 122, 129
Holly Springs, Miss., 41, 48, 54
hors de combat, 69, 149n95
Hotchkiss, Jedediah, 83–84
Howe, Daniel Walker, 11
Hoxton, William, 86
Hubbard, Lucius F., 25, 43, 45, 61

Humphreys, Andrew Atkinson, 25
Humphreys, Margaret, 8
Hunter, David, 23, 78–79, 87, 92,
150n26
Hurlbut, Stephen A., 56–57, 62
hybrid landscape: agroecosystem as, 10;
in Georgia, 105; Lower Mississippi as,
27, 48, 56; "second creation" as, 17

imperial view of nature, 17
improvements: Olmsted's description
of southern lack of, 20; Ruffin on
southern need for, 21; Union soldiers'
reactions to southern, 30, 109, 117;
and Union strategy against, 12, 23,
56, 70, 78, 80, 82, 84, 87–88, 99, 108,
121–22, 131
"improving" nature, notion of, 5–6, 11–
12, 73, 74, 127–28, 131, 140; through
agriculture, 6, 13, 17, 128; through
engineering, 14–16, 31, 49, 51
Island No. 10, 31, *32*, 33–34, 36, 44, 48

Jackson, Miss., 41, 53, *54*, 57, 58, *59*, 131
Jackson, Tenn., 128
Jackson, Thomas "Stonewall," 76, 79, 83
James River, 74
Jefferson, Thomas, 72
Jenney, W. L. B., 44–45
Johnson, Tina, 129
Johnston, Joe, 53, 71, 93, 120
Jones, Charles, 121
Jones, S. C., 51

Kellogg, Sanford, 133–34
Kennesaw Mountain, battle of, 2–3, 99
Kidd, James H., 84
Killgore, Gabriel M., 64
Kimball, Nathan, 63–64
Kingston, Ga., 97
Kirby, Jack Temple, 7, 11, 21, 134, 138
Kircher, Henry, 22, 28, 136
Kirwan, Albert, 133

landscape, concept of: in battlefield
restoration, 140; defined, 13, 92;

and engineering, 15–16, 113; in environmental historiography, 7–8, 12; in Georgia and Carolina campaigns, 93, 95–96, 102, 106, 109, 115, 124, 125; in metaphor, 9, 13–14, 87–88, 90, 127, 130–32; in Mississippi River operations, 30, 34–35, 42, 43, 47, 48; postwar, 137–39; in Shenandoah Valley campaign, 72–73, 74–76, 77, 78–80, 86–87, 89; in the South, 19–21; and Union strategy, 12, 18, 23, 71, 78–80, 83, 89, 93, 95–96, 97, 124; in Vicksburg campaign, 53–54, 58, 60, 64, 68–69, 71

landscape, physical: slaves and creation of, 5, 27–28, 68–69, 86–87, 105, 125; transformation of, through war, 3, 6, 7, 23, 56, 86–87, 92, 93, 97, 99, 106–7, 116–17, 121–22, 128–30, 134; Union soldiers' views on southern, 28–29, 115–16, 117. *See also* hybrid landscape

Lawson, Alexander, 124–25

LeCain, Timothy, 12

LeConte, Emma, 108

LeConte, Joseph, 118–19

Lee, Henrietta B., 87

Lee, Mary Anna Randolph, 121

Lee, Robert E., 71, 78, 79–82, 90, 107, 108, 120, 133

Lewis, Michael, 13

Lewis, Thomas, 76

Lexington, Va., 74, *75*, 78

Lincoln, Abraham, 4, 26–27, 69, 106, 139

Little Ogeechee River, 105, 106

Lockett, S. H., 60

Lossing, Benson, 48

Loudoun County, Va., 76, 88

Lower Mississippi Valley: agroecological system of, 27–28; and disease, 29–31, 40–41, 45, 46–47, 48; environment of, 28–31, 40; flood control in, 25; as hybrid landscape, 27, 48, 56; map of, *27*; slavery in, 27–28; Union assault on agroecological foundation of, 42, 71; Union soldiers' reactions to

environment of, 28–29, 30, 34; Union strategy against, 26, 36–39, 41–43, 44, 48. *See also* Mississippi River; Vicksburg campaign

Lowry, Samuel, 135

Luray (Page) Valley, 77, 84

Lynchburg, Va., 78, 79

Mahon, Michael G., 73, 86, 90–91

Mahon, Samuel, 120

Majewski, John, 18–19, 20

malaria, 29, 40, 45, 46–47, 137

March to the Sea. *See* Sherman, William T.

Marcy, Henry, 123

Marsh, George Perkins, 128

Martin, David G., 62

Massanutten Range, 77, 82–83, 85, 88

McAllister, Fort, 104

McClellan, George B., 30

McClernand, John, 58

McPherson, James, 57

McPhersonville, S.C., 117, *118*

Meade, George, 71

measles, 46, 48, 66, 128

mechanistic view of nature, 14–16, 17

Meier, Kathryn Shively, 8

Meinig, D. W., 13

Memphis, Tenn., 26, 30, 34, 41–42

Mercer, George Anderson, 129

Merchant, Carolyn, 14

Merritt, Raymond, 15

Merritt, Wesley, 77–78, 89

Metairie Ridge, 30

metaphor: "desert" as, 13, 21, 87, 89, 90, 92, 108, 119, 127, 129, 130, 157n1; landscape in, 9, 13–14, 87–88, 90, 129, 130–32; "wilderness" as, 1, 9, 12, 13, 73, 82, 87, 90, 104, 108, 127, 130, 131, 157n1. *See also* "waste" or "wasteland" as metaphor

Meyerson, Harvey, 138

Middle Military Division (Army of the Shenandoah), 79, 85–86, 91

Military Division of the Mississippi (Union), 97, 106–7

Milledgeville, Ga., 101, 102–3, 107, 125
Miller, Angela, 16–17, 139
Miller, William Bluffton, 116
Milliken's Bend, La., 28, 44, 47, 49–50, 51, *54*
Minshall, Thaddeus, 2
Mississippi Army (Confederate), 36
Mississippi River: as contested territory, 25–26, 31; and control through engineering, 24–25, 27, 31–34, 36, 39–40, 43, 48; and Duckport canal, 44–45; in Union strategy, 8–9, 26–27, 27, 31–36, *32, 37*, 40, 41–42, 43, 47–48. *See also* De Soto Point, La.: canal; Island No. 10
Missouri River, 26
Mitman, Gregg, 47
Monocacy Creek, 79
Morgan, George W., 42
Morrison, James, 15
Mosby, John, 76–77, 87
Mosby's Rangers, 76–77, 87
mosquitoes, 8, 28–31, 39, 40, 46–47, 48, 144n21. *See also* disease
Mower, Joseph, 61, 63
Muir, John, 136–37, 138

Nash, Linda, 6, 7
Nash, Roderick, 14
Nasmith, Samuel J., 70
Natchez, Miss., 26
Natchez Weekly Courier, 3, 65, 66
national military parks, establishment of, 139–40, 159n64
National Parks Service (NPS), 140, 159nn64–65
Native Americans, 28, 73
nature: "arcadian" tradition (ecological view) of, 16–17; and culture, 18–19, 28, 92, 93, 105; defined, 12–13, 47; and Enlightenment, 16; in environmental historiography, 6–8, 11–13, 14; as historical agent, 3–4, 6–7, 8–9, 45–46, 48, 67, 72; imperial view of, 17; "improvement" of, 6, 11–12, 15–17, 31, 35, 36, 42, 48, 73, 99, 127–28,

140; mechanistic view of, 14–16, 17; as metaphor for destruction, 129; nineteenth-century ideas of, 2–4, 5–6, 8–9, 11, 12, 14, 16–17, 24, 34, 73–75, 88, 92, 127; postwar preservation of, 9, 137–40; power over, 9, 11–12, 16, 19–21, 23, 24, 73, 88–89, 95, 105, 116, 132, 134; as reflection of human experience, 66–67, 135–36; resiliency of, 67–68, 76, 117, 134–37; and Scientific Revolution, 14–15, 16; "second creation" view of, 17; and southern identity, 156n145; Union's interruption of South's relationship with, 11, 23, 68, 73, 78, 88–89, 92, 93, 95, 96, 98, 99, 109, 121, 126, 134; Union strategy thwarted by, 34, 40, 45–46, 48. *See also* agroecosystems; landscape, concept of
Neely, Mark, 91
New Carthage, La., 44, 49–50, 69
New Hope Church, battle of, 99
New Madrid, Mo., 29, 31, *32, 33*
New Market, Va., 77
New Orleans, La., 22, 30, 34, 35–36, 71
New Orleans Daily Times Picayune, 41
New York Herald, 81, 85, 99, 111, 121, 124
New York Times, 30
Nichols, George Ward, 2–3, 98, 103, 107, 114, 116, 118
North Carolina: battles in, 120; destruction in, 121–22, 123, 124, 132
Nye, David, 11, 17

Oakey, Daniel, 108, 109, 115, 119, 122
Ocmulgee River, 101, 153n23
Oconee River, 99, 101, 103, 153n23
Ogeechee River, 101, 105
Ohio River, 26, 31, 34
Olmsted, Frederick Law, 20, 137–38
Osborn, Thomas Ward, 100, 102, 112, 113, 115, 119–20, 132–33

Pabis, George, 25
Paine, Charles Jackson, 119
Paludan, Phillip Shaw, 18

Peach Tree Creek, battle of, 99
Peirce, Taylor, 50, 65, 66–67, 69, 74–76
Pemberton, Fort, 44
Pemberton, John C., 42, 55, 58–59, 60, 64, 66, 67
Pepper, George, 108, 109–11, 120–21, 124
Perreault, Melanie, 13
Petersburg, Va., 71, 147n56, 159n65
Phillips, Edward, 91–92
pioneer battalion: African Americans in, 98, 113; Sherman's, 98, 100, 101, 106, 113
plantation system: as agroecosystem, 10, 21–22, 28, 125–26; breakdown of, 125–26; in Shenandoah Valley, 73. *See also* agroecosystems; slavery
Pocotaligo, S.C., 112, 116, 117, 122
Poe, Orlando M., 101, 113
pontoon bridges and trains, 97, 101, 112, 113
Pope, John, 31, *32*, 33–34. *See also* canals; Island No. 10
Porter, David Dixon, 22, 39–40, 42, 43, 48, 65
Port Gibson, Miss., 57, *59*
Port Hudson, La., 26, 34–35
Port Royal, S.C., 104
Potomac River, 72, 74, 79, 85
preservation movement, wilderness, 137–40
Prime, Frederick E., 44

Raleigh, N.C., 108, 119, 120
Ramseur, Stephen, 76, 81, 89
Randolph, Mary, 86
Randolph, Sallie, 86
Raymond, Miss., 58, 67
Reichhelm, E. Paul, 60
Reid, Whitelaw, 133
Reill, Peter Hanns, 16
Remley, George, 28–29, 65
Remley, Lycurgus, 28
Resaca, battle of, 99
Richmond, La., 50
Richmond, Va., 71, *75*, 76, 77, 85, 90, 108, 133, 159n65

Ritchie, Alexander Hay, *130*
Romantics, 16, 127–28, 139
Ross, Leonard F., 43
Ruffin, Edmund, 21, 128
rules of war, 114, 121, 155n90

Salkahatchie River, 112, 114
Savannah, Ga., 97, 99–100, 103–8, 109, *110*, 111, 112, 124–25, 135. *See also* Sherman, William T.
Savannah River, 99, 100–101, 105–6, 112, 125
Schantz, Mark, 1–2
Schreckhise, Daniel K., 88
Scientific Revolution, 14–15, 16
Scott, Winfield, 26, 30
secession, 1, 4, 17, 25–26, 76, 99, 108–9, 111, 118, 124
Shea, William, 26
Shenandoah River, 72, 85
Shenandoah Valley: as Confederate stronghold, 76–78, 79; destruction of rail links in, 71, 77, 78, 80; and Grant, 77–80, 82, 83, 84–85, 87, 89, 91; landscape described, 73–75; landscape in campaign against, 72–77, 78–80, 86–87, 89; metaphors to describe destruction in, 73, 80, 87–88, 89, 90, 92; slavery in, 73, 75–76, 86; strategic importance of, *75*, 76–79, 81–82, 91; Union strategy to destroy agroecological foundation of, 8, 23, 72–73, 78–82, 84, 87, 89, 92. *See also* Early, Jubal A.; Sheridan, Philip H.
Sheridan, Philip H., 11, 23, 72, 79–88, *83*, 89–92, 129, 138, 150n26
Sherman, Ellen, 51, 61, 93
Sherman, John, 26, 51
Sherman, William T.: attack of, on Confederacy's agroecological foundation, 11, 23, 70, 93, 96, 98, 99, 101–3, 107, 114, 121, 123–26; criticized as savage, 121; descriptions of devastation by, 129, *130*, 130–32, 135; destruction of Confederacy's infrastructure by, 68, 95–96; and

Sherman, William T. (*continued*) "hard war," 98, 152n11; march of, through Georgia and Carolinas, *94*, 96–98, 99–100, 101–2, 106–7, 108–9, *110*, 112, *118*, 119, 120, 122–26, *130*, 153n23; and Mississippi River operations, 43, 45, 47; on nature's resiliency, 67–68; and operations against Atlanta, 71, 99, 102, 130; on power over landscape, 12, 23, 93, 95, 106; and raid through Mississippi, 96; and Savannah, 104–6, 108; and Special Field Orders No. 120, 96–98, 101, 108, 114, 123, 154n73; on Union raids, 55; on Union strategy, 25–26, 55, 119; and Vicksburg campaign, 41–42, 49, 51, 52, 54, 58, 61–62, 64, 66, 67, 68
Shreve, Henry, 25
Shreveport, La., 25
Sigel, Franz, 71, 77–78
Simms, William Gilmore, 111–12
Sinks, Alva, 130
Sister's Ferry, Ga., 112
slavery: and canal building, *38*, 39, 40; as Confederate resource, 69–70; and emancipation, 69, 72–73, 134; in Lower Mississippi Valley, 27–28; in Shenandoah Valley, 73, 75–76, 86–87; Union's dismantling of, 68–70, 86–87, 97–98, 107, 125–26. *See also* plantation system
smallpox, 45, 48, 128
Smith, Gustavus, 100
Smith, Kirby, 50
Smith, Timothy, 139
Solomon, Henry, 134–35
South Carolina: destruction in, *118*, 122–23; terrain in, 7, 109, *110*, 111–13, 114–15, 117, 119; and "wilderness" metaphor, 108–19
Special Field Orders No. 120, 96–98, 101, 108, 114, 123, 154n73. *See also* Sherman, William T.
Spirn, Anne Whiston, 9
Squire, George W., 1
Starr, Nehemiah Davis, 68

Staunton, Va., 74, *75*, 78, 83, 85
Steele, Frederick, 55, 70
Steinberg, Ted, 7
Stewart, Mart, 19, 21, 105, 134
Stilgoe, John, 13
St. John's Bayou, 33
Stoll, Steven, 10, 11, 131, 132
Strasburg, Va., 74, 85
Stroud, Ellen, 8

Tallahatchie-Yazoo River system, 43
Taylor, Richard, 74
Taylor, Tom, 117
Tchakerian, Viken, 18–19, 20
Telford, Thomas, 15
Thayer, Sylvanus, 15
Thomas, William G., 73, 91
Tidball, John, 15
Tilford, John, 3
Trowbridge, J. T., 132, 133
Trudeau, Noah, 101

ultisols (soil), 17
Union army: Army of the Potomac, 71, 79, *83*; Army of the Tennessee, 51, 52–53, 59, 64, 67, 70; destruction of South's agroecological foundation by, 12, 18, 21–23, 42, 55–57, 69–70, 71, 72–73, 78–82, 84, 86–87, 107, 111; and disease, 29–30, 40, 46–47, 48, 64–65; interruption of South's relationship with nature by, 11, 23, 78, 89, 92, 93, 95, 96, 98, 99, 109, 121; Middle Military Division (Army of the Shenandoah), 79, 85–86, 91; Military Division of the Mississippi, 97, 106–7; and slavery, 68–70, 86, 98, 107, 125–26; and South's "inferiority," 115–17; and Special Field Orders No. 120, 96–98, 100, 101, 108, 113, 114, 123; and victory-through-engineering, 9, 15–16, 31, 43, 48, 62, 95, 113
upas tree, 1, 141n1
Upson, Theodore, 2, 104
U.S. Military Academy at West Point, 15–16, 25, 36, 62, 98, 101, 113

U.S. Navy, 26, 30–31, 35–36, 39–40, 41, 42, 43, 104

Van Dorn, Earl, 41
Vattel, Emmerich de, 155n90
Vicksburg, Miss.: geography of, 7, 58, 59, 63, 64; strategic location of, 7, 26, 34–36, 60–62, 67. See also Vicksburg campaign
Vicksburg campaign: aftermath of, 68–69, 133; and Duckport canal, 44–45; engineering in, 35, 62; and final siege, 62–63, 63, 65–67; Grant's strategy in, 41–43, 49–50, 53–56, 54, 57, 62–64, 70; Grant's victory in, 66, 68, 70–71; landscape concept in, 42, 48, 68–69, 71; power over nature in, 8–9, 48; Sherman as western commander in, 41–42, 47, 96; Union assault on agroecological system in, 23, 55–56; and Vicksburg mine, 62, 147n56. See also De Soto Point, La.: canal; Lower Mississippi Valley
Vicksburg Daily Citizen, 65
Vicksburg mine, 62, 147n56
Virginia Military Institute, 77

Wallace, Lew, 79
Walnut Bayou, 44
"waste" or "wasteland" as metaphor, 3, 13, 19, 20, 23, 73, 81, 84, 87, 90, 92, 95, 127, 132; northern soldiers use, 51, 64, 67, 69, 80, 117, 119, 122, 130, 133; southerners use, 130, 131
Waud, Alfred R., 83, 118
weather: in Georgia and Carolina campaigns, 95, 100, 112, 114–15, 119, 120; in Lower Mississippi Valley campaign, 30, 40–41, 45–46, 47; as reflection of human experience, 135–36; in Shenandoah Valley campaign,

80–81, 90–91; in Vicksburg campaign, 49, 50–51, 52, 58, 65, 66, 67
Weddel, Jacob, 84
Weekly Vicksburg Whig, 30–31, 64
Weigley, Russell F., 7, 22, 115, 120
Wert, Jeffry, 77
western theater, 26–27, 35, 41, 96
West Point. See U.S. Military Academy at West Point
Wheeler, Joseph, 153n33
Wilcox, Charles, 52
"wilderness," 4, 5, 10, 11, 19; in colonial America, 13–14; in environmental historiography, 12, 13; in Georgia and Carolina campaigns, 108, 130, 131; as metaphor, 1, 9, 12, 13, 73, 82, 87, 90, 104, 108, 127, 130, 131, 132, 157n1; and perceptions of nature, 10–11, 12–14, 16–17, 18, 137; postwar ideal of, 139–40; in Shenandoah Valley campaign, 80, 82, 87, 90; South perceived as, 19, 29, 116, 133, 134
wilderness preservation movement, 139, 140
Williams, Camp, 30
Williams, Thomas, 36, 39–41, 48
Wills, Charles, 29, 128
Wilson's Bayou, 32, 33
Wilson, J. H., 43–44, 84
Winchester, Va., 74, 75, 77, 80, 81, 82, 85
Winschel, Terrence, 26
Winters, Harold, 7
Witte, Rosa, 131
Worster, Donald, 9–10, 16, 17, 143n84

Yalobusha River, 44
Yazoo Pass, 43–44
Yazoo River, 35, 41–42, 43, 44, 47, 57–58, 63, 64
yellow fever, 29–30, 31
Yosemite Valley, 137–38

ENVIRONMENTAL HISTORY AND THE AMERICAN SOUTH

Pharsalia: An Environmental Biography of a Southern Plantation, 1780–1880
Lynn A. Nelson

An Everglades Providence: Marjory Stoneman Douglas and the American Environmental Century
Jack E. Davis

Spirits of the Air: Birds and American Indians in the South
Shepard Krech III

Environmental History and the American South: A Reader
Paul S. Sutter and Christopher J. Manganiello, eds.

Making Catfish Bait out of Government Boys: The Fight against Cattle Ticks and the Transformation of the Yeoman South
Claire Strom

The Oyster Question: Scientists, Watermen, and the Maryland Chesapeake Bay since 1880
Christine Keiner

My Work Is That of Conservation: An Environmental Biography of George Washington Carver
Mark D. Hersey

Conserving Southern Longleaf: Herbert Stoddard and the Rise of Ecological Land Management
Albert G. Way

Blue Ridge Commons: Environmental Activism and Forest History in Western North Carolina
Kathryn Newfont

War upon the Land: Military Strategy and the Transformation of Southern Landscapes during the American Civil War
Lisa M. Brady

Remaking Wormsloe Plantation: The Environmental History of a Lowcountry Landscape
Drew A. Swanson

CPSIA information can be obtained
at www.ICGtesting.com
Printed in the USA
LVOW12s1953240118
563849LV00002B/158/P